1995

W9-BCE-171

Environmental politics in the

3 0301 00070023 3

ENVIRONMENTAL
POLITICS
IN THE
INTERNATIONAL
ARENA

SUNY Series in Environmental Policy
Lester Milbrath, Editor

Environmental Politics in the International Arena

Movements, Parties, Organizations, and Policy

EDITED BY

SHELDON KAMIENIECKI

State University of New York Press

College of St. Francis Library
Joliet, Illinois

Published by
State University of New York Press, Albany

© 1993 State University of New York

All rights reserved

Printed in the United States of America

No part of this book may be used or reproduced
in any manner whatsoever without written permission
except in the cases of brief quotations embodied in
critical articles and reviews.

For information, address the State University of New York Press,
State University Plaza, Albany, NY 12246

Production by Bernadine Dawes
Marketing by Nancy Farrell

Library of Congress Cataloging-in-Publication Data

Environmental politics in the international arena : movements,
   parties, organizations, and policy / edited by Sheldon Kamieniecki.
        p.   cm.—(SUNY series in environmental public policy)
   Includes bibliographical references and index.
   ISBN 0-7914-1663-1 (alk. paper) —ISBN 0-7914-1664-X
(pbk. : alk. paper)
   1. Environmental policy. 2. Environmental policy—Europe.
3. Green movement. 4. Green movement—Europe. 5. Comparative
government. I. Kamieniecki, Sheldon. II. Series.
HC79.E5E5788 1993
363.7'0526'094—dc20   92-43315
                                                          CIP

1 2 3 4 5 6 7 8 9 10

363.7
K 15

CONTENTS

INTRODUCTION

Emerging Forces in Global Environmental Politics

This book is based on the premise that global environmental issues can be best understood by studying environmental movements, ecological parties, international organizations and regimes, international law, and the problems and policies of specific nations in different regions of the world. The logic underlying this premise is that the activities of citizens, environmental pressure groups, ecological parties, and international organizations, alone and sometimes in concert with one another, help shape politics and policy at the local, national, and international levels. Unfortunately, most researchers tend to study these aspects of global environmental politics in isolation from one another. Those who conduct research on environmental movements, for example, may occasionally analyze ecological parties but will almost never pay attention to international organizations and regimes. Moreover, those who investigate movements and parties primarily incorporate theories from the comparative politics literature, while those who explore international organizations and regimes draw almost entirely on international relations theory (Rosenau 1980). Rarely does a single study include perspectives found in both the comparative politics and international relations literature.

The trend towards increased specialization in the major subfields of political science is largely responsible for this practice. Books, journals, conferences, and political science curricula are rigidly categorized according to subfield, and little encouragement is offered for researchers to venture into another area of study. The complex and interrelated nature of today's environmental issues, however, requires knowledge of a variety of theoretical and empirical approaches if they are to be properly understood (Kamieniecki and Sanasarian 1990). Clearly, important relationships exist between movements, parties, national governments, international organizations, and policy, and only by reading works in both comparative politics and international relations can they be fully known (Rosenau 1980).

A recent and growing body of literature in international relations actually seeks to sort out the linkages between domestic and international politics. While Peter Katzenstein (1978) and Stephen Krasner (1978) analyze the important influence of domestic factors on foreign economic policy, for instance, Peter Evans (1979), Peter Gourevitch (1986), and James Alt (1987) examine the impact of the international economy on domestic politics and domestic economic policy.[1] Robert Putnam's (1988) study, which attempts to account for reciprocal causation between domestic and international politics, employs a theory of "two-level games" to explain the ratification of various international agreements. In so doing, considerable emphasis is placed on "parties, social classes, interest groups (both economic and noneconomic), legislators, and even public opinion and elections, not simply executive officials and institutional arrangements" (1988, 432). The approach taken by Putnam and others has forced them to draw upon important concepts in comparative politics and international relations. In noting this, Putnam says that "the most portentous development in the fields of comparative politics and international relations in recent years is the dawning recognition among practitioners in each field of the need to take into account entanglements between the two" (1988, 459).

The primary objective of this book is not to advance a new theory of domestic-international interactions nor to test directly existing linkage theory. Rather, the book has a more modest goal: to bring together works written by prominent researchers in comparative politics and international relations that address important aspects of global environmental politics. Central principles of linkage theory were used as a guide in organizing the book and selecting the topics on which contributors were asked to write. The intention is to provide readers with a broader and richer understanding of the dynamics underlying global environmental issues than they would normally receive by reading essays written solely from a comparative politics or international relations perspective.

The present chapter provides background information and raises critical issues that are addressed later in the book. The chapter begins with a discussion of the reasons for the growth of the environmental movement and how changes in value orientations over time may account for the expansion of the movement. This section is followed by an examination of the role ecological parties play in Western democracies. Next, the chapter addresses international organizations and environmental regimes. Various issues concerning international law and policy are analyzed at the end of the discussion.

REASONS FOR INCREASED APPREHENSION

The environmental movement is having a growing impact on national and international politics, and there is little evidence to suggest that the movement's momentum will slow in the near future. Nationally, surveys indicate a sharp rise in public concern over environmental problems in Western countries, which has contributed to the emergence of citizens' groups and ecological parties in those countries (Milbrath 1984; also see Rosenau's chapter in this book). Feeling intense pressure from various quarters, policymakers are enacting stringent regulations designed to abate pollution. Internationally, a sense of urgency about the deteriorating condition of the earth's ecological system is sweeping the capitals of foreign governments, and nations are now working together that have never worked together before. While most countries initially confined their attention to specific environmental problems inside their borders, they are now focusing on transnational issues such as biodiversity, the depletion of the ozone layer, and global warming. Given the traditional political and economic barriers inherent in international relations, a remarkable number of environmental agreements have been implemented (Young 1989). As Caldwell observes, "The growth of the environmental movement to international and global proportions has been a historical development. . . . Understood in its full context, it may be seen by subsequent generations as a major change-of-state in human affairs—an awakening of modern man to a new awareness of the human predicament on earth" (1990, 9).

Several factors account for these trends in international environmental politics and policy. Rapid industrialization and economic growth have increased the number and seriousness of pollution problems. Regardless of where people reside, nearly everyone has experienced threats to the environment and his or her health. Often, these problems are transnational and require binational or even multinational cooperation to solve them. As a result, policymakers have become increasingly aware of the vulnerability of the ecosystem and of the need to take immediate bilateral and multilateral action.

Apprehension about pollution can also be traced to the cumulative impact of major news stories and events in recent years. The chemical accident at Bhopal, India, the release of radiation resulting from the fire at the Chernobyl nuclear power plant, the huge oil spill by the *Exxon Valdez* tanker in Prince William Sound in Alaska, the toxic chemical spills at Seveso, Italy, and Basel, Switzerland, and the release of oil into the Persian Gulf and the burning of Kuwait's oil wells during the war with Iraq were widely covered by the media. With the aid of advanced communications technology, millions of people quickly became aware of the magnitude of these catastrophes. Coming one after another, these and other news stories, drawing heavily upon scientific facts, pointed to the fragility of the natural environment and forced the international community to take note of the vital interrelationships which exist between humans and other life forms.

Porter and Brown (1991) further point out that additional scientific data on environmental problems have led to increased awareness and concern about the present condition of the earth's ecosystem. Compared to ten years ago, for example, scientists have a much better understanding of the causes and effects of acid precipitation, the depletion of the ozone layer, and global warming. While more research must be done before effective long-term policies can be enacted, the findings of preliminary studies suggest serious cause for alarm and, in some cases (e.g., the case of wildlife extinction), the need for immediate action.

New scientific information and increased pressure for action at the international level undoubtedly explains why the Group of Seven (G7) placed considerable emphasis on global environmental issues at their annual summit meeting in Paris in 1989. The heads of state of the G7, which includes the United States, Canada, the United Kingdom, Japan, Germany, France, and Italy, reached agreement on a number of general principles and possible policy strategies concerning the release of chlorofluorocarbons (CFCs) into the atmosphere, the burning of fossil fuels, and other matters. The fact that environmental issues received a great deal of attention in the final communiqué of this powerful economic organization made a strong impression on the rest of the world. For this and other reasons Porter and Brown conclude that "the global environment has emerged as a third major issue area in world politics, along with international security and the global economy" (1991, 2).

To a large extent, the withering away of superpower competition in the early 1990s has redirected attention away from strictly military issues and towards global environmental problems. It is quite possible that by the year 2000 most nations, affluent or less affluent, will have redefined or expanded their definition of national security to include natural resource issues. Whether nations will actually begin to form security pacts to the extent they did during the cold war, however, remains to be seen. While such pacts can help conserve the earth's natural resources, they also may lead to large-scale conflict over natural resources, similar to the way in which military agreements contributed to world wars in the past. Just as it is for peace and arms control, truly international cooperation is required to protect the global environment. Additional social learning and value transformation must first take place before effective cooperation at the international level is possible.

VALUE ORIENTATIONS AND ENVIRONMENTAL PROTECTION

Inglehart's (1981) work provides theoretical insights into why industrialized nations—or at least the advanced ones—are now closely attuned to "new politics" issues, including those related to the conservation of natural resources. According to him, postindustrial societies are undergoing a slow, fundamental shift in their value orientations. The major features of postindustrial societies include a large percentage of people working in the service sector, the service sector contributing a greater portion of the gross national product (GNP) than the agricultural and manufacturing sectors combined, a high level of affluence and mass material well-being, and the national economy becoming more driven by knowledge, information, and technology. Extending Maslow's "hierarchy of human needs," Inglehart distinguishes between "materialist" and "postmaterialist" values. The former set of values is predicated on basic needs and desires, and priorities reflect scarcity in the socioeconomic environment. The latter set of values is present in societies that have already achieved a long period of peace and prosperity. Postmaterialist orientations tend to reflect satisfaction with higher-order needs.

Inglehart believes that postmaterialist value orientations are most common among postindustrial generations. In theory, the younger generational cohorts raised during the period of affluence are more likely than older cohorts to exhibit value orientations reflecting higher-order needs. Thus, individuals raised during the Great Depression and World War Two who hold political values that reflect the basic needs of security, safety, and sustenance are slowly being replaced in the population by people who have experienced widespread affluence and a relative absence of large-scale military conflict. As far as the environment and quality of life are concerned, the young are rejecting the central elements of the Dominant Social Paradigm, which emphasizes economic growth, and are adopting a New Environmental Paradigm to replace it. As Lester Milbrath explains in chapter 1, this is primarily occurring through socialization and learning.

THE ENVIRONMENTAL MOVEMENT

As one might expect, the recent transformation in values among citizens in advanced industrialized societies has led to increased public involvement which, in turn, has significantly colored environmental politics and policy at all levels of government. To a large extent, the increasing number of citizens who are deeply troubled about declining levels of environmental quality helps explain the rapid growth of environmental groups and the successful election of Green party candidates to legislative bodies in Western Europe. The demands of citizens, often channeled through local environmental groups and political parties, have resulted in the enactment of strict pollution control regulations over the strong objections of labor and industry.

5

In an early study, Milbrath (1984) argued that environmentalists represent a vanguard, using education, persuasion, and politics to try to lead people to their vision of a new, sustainable society.[2] In this they are opposed by a rearguard, best represented by Julian Simon and Herman Kahn, which contends that modern industrial societies are working quite well, that there is no limit to human ingenuity, and that industrial societies produce the greatest wealth and the most equitable social, economic, and political conditions. While the rearguard prefers that society continue to follow the Dominant Social Paradigm, the vanguard favors the adoption of the New Environmental Paradigm reflecting carefully considered production and consumption, resource conservation, environmental protection, and the basic values of compassion, justice, and democracy. Citizen activists and grass roots groups, as the frontline soldiers of the vanguard, initiate political battles to promote the ideals of the New Environmental Paradigm within the domestic and international arenas.

With this in mind, this book analyzes various aspects of the environmental movement. Russell Dalton's chapter provides a comprehensive examination of the early roots and historical development of the environmental movement in Western Europe. His study draws a distinction between two waves of environmental mobilization. The first wave at the turn of the century focused on issues of wildlife protection and the preservation of a nation's natural resources, whereas the second wave of the 1960s and 1970s centered on the new environmental problems and quality-of-life concerns of advanced industrial societies. Bron Taylor and his colleagues then follow with a careful investigation of the divergent and sometimes radical elements of the movement as well as the ethical and moral dilemmas faced by environmental activists in non-Western countries.

THE EMERGENCE OF ECOLOGICAL PARTIES

In the early 1980s most citizens' organizations and new political movements attempted to develop a closer relationship with the Social Democrats and other established left-wing parties in Western Europe. They hoped these parties would act as an effective force against unlimited economic growth, nuclear power, the deterioration of the environment, and the deployment of nuclear weapons. For various reasons, they were not able to influence significantly the policy stands of the Social Democrats and other labor and socialist parties in Western Europe on these issues.[3] The lack of action on the part of the established parties, along with the perceived inability of political parties and other political institutions to develop an alternative policy approach, is a major reason for both the growth and electoral success of ecological parties in

Europe. Despite the fact that ecological parties have attracted only a small percentage of voters in most elections, established parties now feel they must take positions on major environmental questions or risk losing voter support to the Greens.

A Profile of Ecological Parties

Ecological parties tend to have similar types of programs and operate in different political systems and cultures. Today they are active, at least at the local level, in Canada, the United States, Japan, and Western Europe. Ecological parties are currently represented in several national parliaments in Europe as well as in the European Parliament.[4] In a few countries the Green parties already have a significant effect on the process of coalition building, while in other countries they challenge traditional institutions and attempt to persuade conventional parties to change their policy. In some cases, small liberal parties view the Greens as a serious challenge to their continued electoral survival.

While the precise issues of interest and policy positions differ from country to country, common elements are present in their party platforms. First and foremost, Green parties believe that their nations are in the midst of an ecological and economic crisis which threatens the future of the world. The symptoms of this crisis are human exploitation and environmental degradation, which are manifested in capitalism and uncontrolled economic growth. In addition to demanding strict environmental regulations, they favor just distribution of goods and services to those socially disadvantaged. The ecological parties often take strong stands on sexual discrimination, nuclear energy, and disarmament. Some promote the rights of foreign workers, gypsies, homosexuals, disabled people, prisoners, the elderly, and animals. Greens generally voice concern about problems in poverty-stricken countries, and they support a more equitable distribution of wealth between affluent and less affluent nations. Moreover, they favor decentralization and individualistic, self-determined participation. They have a grass roots orientation and closely adhere to egalitarian and democratic principles and practices. Overall, the issues that comprise ecological party platforms in Europe reflect the "new politics" of the postmaterialist era and are broader in scope than those addressed by environmental groups in the United States.

Although ecological parties share a wide range of characteristics and positions on important "new politics" issues, there are also substantial differences between them that have led to fierce conflicts in the European Parliament and have seriously blocked efforts to promote international Green cooperation. In Poguntke's (1989) view, these divisions have less to

7

do with the traditional left-right dimension and more to do with disagreements over strategies for accomplishing common goals.

Major internal conflicts have also characterized the development of ecological parties and still prevent them from achieving increased electoral success. The most intense debates have occurred over participation in coalitions, expansion from local and state to national party competition, adoption of positions on issues outside the environmental policy sphere, and party governance. Conflicting personalities, a lack of leadership, and country-specific legal and political barriers have hindered the growth of Green parties as well.[5] In this book Herbert Kitschelt presents a realistic assessment of the Green party phenomenon in Western Europe in general, while James Lester and Elfar Loftsson analyze the activities of the Scandinavian ecological parties in particular.

INTERNATIONAL REGIMES AND INTERNATIONAL LAW

As argued at the outset, movements and parties frequently play an important role in influencing international politics, including international regimes and policy. Movements and parties, ecological or otherwise, often dictate election issues, who runs for public office, and who wins elections. As James Rosenau (1980) explains, which party controls the national legislature and who is elected or appointed to the highest political offices will largely determine the nature of both domestic and foreign policy. Whether certain international agreements are pursued and consummated will undoubtedly depend upon who controls government and to what degree. According to Rosenau (1980), the Vietnam War closely linked national and international politics and policy.

In between elections, movements and parties also help shape national and international issue agendas. Using the media and other means, movements and parties can bring vital issues to the attention of the masses. Sometimes they can be instrumental in promoting a particular position or blocking a certain proposal. Whether a country participates in or abstains from an international regime often depends upon these kinds of internal pressures (see Putnam 1988).

An international regime is generally defined as "a set of norms, rules, or decision-making procedures, whether implicit or explicit, that produces some convergence in the actors' expectations in a particular issue area" (Porter and Brown 1991, 20). (In contrast, those in comparative politics and other areas normally define regime as the government in power.) The concept may be applied to a broad range of international arrangements, from coordination of trade relations to superpower security relations. This way of conceiving regimes has been criticized by Strange (1982) for including arrangements that are only agreements to disagree and have no predictability or stability. In the international environmental arena, nearly all norms or rules are defined by an explicit agreement.

With this in mind, Porter and Brown alternatively define an international regime as "a system of norms and rules that are specified by a multilateral legal instrument among states to regulate national actions on a given issue" (1991, 20). The convention is the main form of multilateral legal instrument used to address global environmental problems. A given convention may contain all the binding obligations expected to be negotiated, or it may be accompanied by a more detailed instrument elaborating on its rules and guidelines. A framework convention is negotiated in anticipation of later elaborating texts, and it is intended solely to provide a set of principles, norms, and objectives relating to the issue. It usually imposes few, if any, specific and binding obligations on the nations involved. Protocols are negotiated within the context of a framework convention, and they detail the particular, binding obligations of the parties to the framework convention.

Haggard and Simmons (1987) have analyzed a number of theoretical approaches that have been used to explain why international regimes in a given issue area come into existence and why they change. Their analysis includes the structural, game theoretic, institutional bargaining, and epistemic communities approaches. Of course, no one theoretical approach explains the development and transformation of all international regimes. It is clear from the literature, however, that international organizations often play a central role in institutional bargaining regarding environmental affairs. Oran Young's chapter examines how international organizations figure prominently in international environmental negotiations and the formation of international environmental regimes.

While it is clear to most that transboundary environmental problems require international solutions, such agreements are often difficult to reach. Regardless of the issue area, the sovereignty of nation states has proved to be a major obstacle to arriving at international agreements. No country is willing to relinquish completely its freedom of decision making to obtain security from common threats. Bargaining and compromise are therefore necessary in order to reach meaningful arrangements. Even then, the question of effective enforcement still looms. In this volume, Lettie Wenner's discussion of the important role the principle of national sovereignty plays in international law in general, and in air and water pollution control in particular, is enlightening in this respect. In concluding, she reviews possible techniques for dealing with transboundary environmental problems.

Sheldon Kamieniecki

INTERNATIONAL ORGANIZATIONS
AND ENVIRONMENTAL POLICY

International governmental organizations (IGOs) have worked hard to conserve the earth's natural resources, including those found in less affluent countries.[6] Beginning with the Conference on the Human Environment held in Stockholm, Sweden, in 1972 and the creation of the United Nations Environment Programme (UNEP), the United Nations has been fairly successful in raising vital environmental concerns and bringing together diverse nations with competing interests. Global warming, the pollution of the oceans and protection of marine life, and the transportation and disposal of toxic substances and radioactive materials are among the major issues on which the UN and its specialized agencies have forged agreements.

As a result of a resolution passed in 1989 by the United Nations General Assembly, the twentieth anniversary of the Stockholm conference was marked by the 1992 United Nations Conference on Environment and Development in Rio de Janeiro, Brazil. The "Earth Summit," as it was called, brought together 178 nations and more than 115 heads of state. In the absence of leadership from the United States, the European nations, especially The Netherlands, pushed for strong initiatives to protect the environment, Japan offered financial and technological assistance, and India became the most effective negotiator for the less affluent nations (Dolan and Abramson 1992). More than one hundred countries signed both a treaty to curb future global warming and a biological diversity pact to conserve plants, animals, and their habitat. The People's Republic of China, which signed both measures, agreed to compromises it had opposed only a few years previously for fear that such actions would hinder its future development. In contrast, the United States succeeded in diluting the conference's global warming convention by insisting upon the elimination of specific targets for the reduction of carbon dioxide from the final draft. Moreover, it refused to sign the biological diversity agreement. As a result, President Bush's last minute proposal to increase funding for forest preservation in less affluent nations was greeted with considerable cynicism by most of the participants at the meeting.[7] Despite America's recalcitrance, the "Earth Summit" adopted a nonbinding agreement (Agenda 21) that outlines environmental action plans for the next century. Perhaps most importantly, the United Nations-sponsored conference brought critical natural resource issues before the entire world for consideration.

At the regional, governmental level, the European Community, whose membership had grown to twelve nations by the 1980s, has become deeply involved in harmonizing environmental regulations among its member states. The governing bodies established by the EC, namely the European Parliament and the EC headquarters, have been relatively responsive to pressures from interest groups. In fact, David Vogel states that "in a number of cases, environmental organizations and national regulatory officials enjoy more influence over [EC] policy makers . . . than they do with their own national governments" (1990, 271). Pressure by environmental groups has resulted in the adoption of stricter regulations than those enacted at the national level in such areas as air and water pollution; the marketing, use, and labeling of pesticides; and the disposal of toxic wastes. How effectively the EC will be able to enforce these tough standards, however, is uncertain. Specific questions concerning the formulation and implementation of environmental policy in Western Europe are discussed in Vogel's chapter in this book.

The Green wave has added members, money, and clout to numerous environmental INGOs. The International Union for Conservation of Nature and Natural Resources (IUCN) and the International Council of Scientific Unions (ICSU) have worked endlessly on various kinds of environmental programs and projects. While national governments remain the ultimate engine of international action, the IUCN, ICSU, and other nongovernmental transnational organizations are frequently able to influence governments through their members and sympathizers within individual nations. As Caldwell correctly observes, "Concerted pressure by national members of these organizations upon their respective governments may induce a readiness of those governments to cooperate toward implementing a common environmental policy" (1990, 13). INGOs also regularly participate at major international conferences and lobby international funding agencies, such as the World Bank, to help reduce the impact of economic development on the environment. The role and influence of INGOs is examined by John McCormick in this volume.

ISSUES CONCERNING LESS AFFLUENT NATIONS

Perhaps the major obstacle to achieving international agreements on global environmental issues is the growing gap between less affluent and wealthy nations, and the strong conviction on the part of many leaders that economic growth will improve the standard of living and quality of life of their nations. The advanced industrialized nations, too, are deeply concerned about maintaining their economic well-being and have demonstrated resistance, on occasion, to conserving natural resources. Politics aside, the finite nature of natural resources and the vulnerability of the earth's ecosystem make it virtually impossible for every nation to achieve the kind of economic

11

growth the West has experienced since World War II. Those who recognize this have therefore begun to call for the adoption of sustainable development as an alternative to unmanaged and uncontrolled economic growth and population growth.

The concept of sustainable development was discussed in *Our Common Future*, the report of the World Commission on Environment and Development (1987). In what is more commonly known as the Brundtland Report (named after the commission's chair, Norwegian prime minister Gro Harlem Brundtland), sustainable development is defined as "development that is consistent with future as well as present needs." In redefining the concept of "development," the report stated that the continuation of present economic policies, which tend to place heavy emphasis on economic growth, risks irreversible damage to and depletion of the earth's natural resources. According to Porter and Brown (1991), this suggests the need to limit global economic activities and the need for greater equity not only between affluent and less affluent nations but also within societies and between generations. Affluent countries that now use a disproportionate share of the earth's natural resources are inherently unsustainable, as are nations in which the distribution of land and other resources is seriously unequal. No doubt, the policies of development assistance agencies of affluent nations, multilateral financial institutions such as the World Bank and the International Monetary Fund, and the General Agreement on Tariffs and Trade (GATT), as well as the central characteristics of the international market system, will have to be significantly altered to achieve sustainable development—not an easy task in an increasingly chaotic and turbulent world (Rosenau 1990).

Any international effort to approach sustainable development must seriously address the economic, political, and environmental problems of the majority of the world's nations.[8] Air and water pollution, toxic waste disposal, the rapid depletion of rain forests, and the extinction of certain species of wildlife are among the major environmental problems that are not being effectively addressed. Clearly, the economic and political conditions commonly present in most less affluent nations severely hinder efforts to conserve natural resources and abate pollution. Dictators and authoritarian governments do not tolerate public protests against their policies, and they often resort to force to prevent them from occurring. The poor economic conditions and heavy debt load in many less affluent countries place a great deal of pressure on leaders to sell off their nation's natural resources quickly in return for hard currency. While some leaders recognize the vulnerability of the global ecosystem, most reject calls by Westerners to limit their economic growth. In many cases less affluent nations are controlled by a single family or a small group of wealthy landowners who see little benefit in conserving their country's natural resources for possible future use.

It is unrealistic to expect less affluent countries to adopt the radical political and economic reforms being called for by the West. The most effective strategy, at least in the short run, is for Western nations and international organizations to provide the necessary (and less controversial) scientific and technical expertise needed to encourage both economic growth and environmental protection. Future economic assistance, regardless of the source, must also contain stipulations for the conservation of natural resources. No doubt, the pressure for economic development in less affluent nations poses the toughest challenge for the environmental movement in the 1990s and beyond. This and other issues are explored in depth in Steven Sanderson's chapter on Latin America and in Louis Schubert's chapter on Asia. While environmentalists have been rather successful in influencing the agendas and policies of Western nations, they are likely to achieve fewer victories in other countries.

THE SOVIET REPUBLICS AND EASTERN EUROPE

The sweeping political changes that have taken place in the Soviet republics and Eastern Europe have resulted in the discovery of numerous severe pollution problems in those countries.[9] Pollution problems are particularly acute in Poland, Romania, Czechoslovakia, and parts of former East Germany. Obviously, previous Communist leaders sacrificed air and water quality and public health in favor of industrial production. Perhaps the movement by parts of Eastern Europe and by the newly independent republics in what was once the Soviet Union (and what is now referred to as the Commonwealth of Independent States) toward capitalist-style economies will also hasten an imitation of Western-style environmental politics and policies.[10] Environmental organizations have already begun forming in the individual republics of the C.I.S. and in other nations, and the newly elected political leaders have made natural resource conservation a high priority. The cleanup will be very expensive and, no doubt, take years to complete. The newly formed political units of the C.I.S. and Eastern Europe will have to receive financial assistance and advanced pollution control technology from the West if they are to improve their environmental quality. These and other issues are addressed in this volume by Barbara Jancar-Webster.

Support for granting such aid is likely to come from environmental groups and ecological parties in the West. Unless the political landscape radically changes, however, various barriers will prevent ecological parties from acquiring true positions of power in advanced industrialized societies in the 1990s (Kitschelt 1988). In former West Germany, where the Greens had been most successful, internal bickering, the continued dominance of the

Christian Democrats and Social Democrats, and reunification with East Germany present them with an uncertain future (Webb 1990).[11] Although the reunification of Germany has brought the environmental problems of former East Germany to the forefront, high unemployment and the high cost of modernizing old industries will place serious economic pressures on Germans, possibly undercutting environmental appeals. The end of the cold war, the declining importance of the peace issue, and the addition of millions of new voters will require unprecedented cohesiveness and the adoption of clever strategies for maintaining and enlarging the base of support for environmental groups and ecological parties. Of course, as Kitschelt observes in his chapter, how well the Greens do will also depend a great deal on the tactics employed by the other parties.

CONCLUSION

It is somewhat ironic that the bourgeoisie of the postwar era created the affluence and political conditions conducive to nurturing an environmental movement in the advanced industrialized societies. As a consequence, a significant portion of the masses now question the pretexts on which unlimited economic growth was originally based. If Inglehart (1981) is correct, the transformation from materialist values to postmaterialist values in Western society is likely to continue and support for "new politics" issues is likely to grow. As the New Environmental Paradigm finds wider acceptance and greater numbers of disciples infiltrate the halls of government, tough national and international environmental policies will perhaps follow.

Movement towards more democratic forms of government in Asia, Latin America, Eastern Europe, the republics of the former Soviet Union, and other nations of the world may lead to increased environmental protection nationally and internationally as well. Free and open debate should help educate the masses and result in a new awareness of the need to conserve natural resources as nations attempt to increase their standard of living. Newly formed environmental groups, both radical and nonradical, are likely to be the vanguard in this debate. Severe economic crisis, ethnic turmoil, and regional conflict, however, may seriously restrict what most nations can and cannot do, at least in the short term.[12] A growing acceptance of capitalism and an increased desire for economic growth around the world pose new and even more difficult challenges for those who wish to establish international environmental regimes. At some point leaders and citizens will have to weigh priorities and decide on what courses of action should be taken to protect the natural environment.

The chapters in this volume provide a starting point for future leaders and citizens in this regard by addressing central questions that are relevant to conflicts between capitalism, economic growth, democracy, and environmental protection. It is impossible to cover completely every issue dealing with natural resource conservation in a single book, and an effort has been made instead to touch upon the major topics and issues in the most important controversies by drawing upon the thoughts and ideas of distinguished researchers in comparative politics and international relations. If this ambitious effort succeeds, readers will come away with a broad and deep understanding of the complex dynamics underlying global environmental issues and problems.

NOTES

1. In addition, see Katzenstein's (1985) study.

2. This point is addressed in great depth in Milbrath (1989).

3. The specific reasons why they were not successful are discussed in Müller-Rommel (1989).

4. For a comprehensive examination of ecological parties in individual European nations, see Müller-Rommel (1989).

5. The obstacles ecological parties face are discussed in Milbrath (1989). Also see Vedung (1988).

6. For an extensive account of the role of international organizations in environmental policy-making, consult McCormick (1989) and Caldwell (1990).

7. In fact, William Reilly, the administrator of the Environmental Protection Agency (EPA) and the head of the United States delegation at the conference, later stated in a memorandum to EPA employees that the Bush White House had actively undermined his efforts in Rio de Janeiro. He wrote, "For me personally, it was like a bungee jump. You dive into space secured by a line on your leg. . . . It doesn't typically occur to you that someone might cut your line!" (*Los Angeles Times*, 2 August 1992).

8. This point is made in Goodman and Redclift's (1991) volume on Latin America.

9. Rosenau (1990) offers an in-depth and insightful analysis of the upheaval taking place in world politics today.

10. Since the Havel government took power, however, there has been a sharp increase in air pollution in the industrial heartland of Czechoslovakia. Strong economic pressures have forced the government to increase the mining and burning of brown coal, which results in the emission of extremely high concentrations of sulfur dioxide and other pollutants. Officials are now seriously considering introducing nuclear power on a broad scale in order to

improve air quality in the country. It could very well be that environmental conditions will first become worse before they become better in this and other Eastern European nations.

11. United in their doubts about German reunification, West Germany's Green party and East Germany's Alliance 90, a far-left party, ruled out cooperation with the Social Democrats and joined forces for the all-German elections in December 1990. While both parties contain environmentalists, pacifists, and feminists, members of Alliance 90 were most concerned about the threat of mass unemployment following reunification.

12. For instance, see O'Brien's (1991) analysis of the impact of the debt crisis on environmental policy in Latin America.

REFERENCES

Alt, James E. 1987. Crude politics: Oil and the political economy of unemployment in Britain and Norway, 1970–1985. *British Journal of Political Science* 17 (April): 149–99.

Caldwell, Lynton K. 1990. *International environmental policy: Emergence and dimensions*, 2d ed. Durham, N.C.: Duke University Press.

Dolan, Maura, and Rudy Abramson. 1992. Earth Summit ends on note of hope, not achievement. *Los Angeles Times*, 14 June.

Evans, Peter B. 1979. *Dependent development: The alliance of multinational, state, and local capital in Brazil.* Princeton: Princeton University Press.

Goodman, David, and Michael Redclift, eds. 1991. *Environment and development in Latin America: The politics of sustainability.* New York: Manchester University Press.

Gourevitch, Peter. 1986. *Politics in hard times: Comparative responses to international economic crises.* Ithaca, N.Y.: Cornell University Press.

Haggard, Stephan, and Beth A. Simmons. 1987. Theories of international regimes. *International Organization* 41 (Summer): 491-517.

Inglehart, Ronald E. 1981. Postmaterialism in an environment of insecurity. *American Political Science Review* 75 (December): 880–900.

Kamieniecki, Sheldon. 1991. Political mobilization, agenda building and international environmental policy. *Journal of International Affairs* 44 (Winter): 339–58.

Kamieniecki, Sheldon, and Eliz Sanasarian. 1990. Conducting comparative research on environmental policy. *Natural Resources Journal* 30: (Spring): 321–39.

Katzenstein, Peter J., ed. 1978. *Between power and plenty: Foreign economic policies of advanced industrial states.* Madison: University of Wisconsin Press.

————. 1985. *Small states in world markets: Industrial policy in Europe.* Ithaca, N.Y.: Cornell University Press.

Kitschelt, Herbert P. 1988. Left-libertarian parties: Explaining innovation in competitive party systems. *World Politics* 40 (January): 194–234.

Krasner, Stephen D. 1978. *Defending the national interest: Raw materials investments and U.S. foreign policy.* Princeton: Princeton University Press.

McCormick, John. 1989. *Reclaiming paradise: The global environmental movement.* Bloomington: Indiana University Press.

Milbrath, Lester W. 1984. *Environmentalists: Vanguard for a new society.* Albany: State University of New York Press.

————. 1989. *Envisioning a sustainable society: Learning our way out.* Albany: State University of New York Press.

Müller-Rommel, Ferdinand, ed. 1989. *New politics in Western Europe: The rise and success of Green parties and alternative lists.* Boulder, Colo.: Westview Press.

O'Brien, Philip J. 1991. Debt and sustainable development in Latin America. In *Environment and development in Latin America: The politics of sustainability,* ed. David Goodman and Michael Redclift, 24–47. New York: Manchester University Press.

Poguntke, Thomas. 1989. The "new politics dimension" in European Green parties. In *New politics in Western Europe: The rise and success of Green parties and alternative lists,* ed. Ferdinand Müller-Rommel, 175–94. Boulder, Colo.: Westview Press.

Porter, Gareth, and Janet Welsh Brown. 1991. *Global environmental politics.* Boulder, Colo.: Westview Press.

Putnam, Robert D. 1988. Diplomacy and domestic politics: The logic of two-level games. *International Organization* 42 (Summer): 427–60.

Rosenau, James N. 1980. *The scientific study of foreign policy.* Revised and enlarged edition. London: Frances Pinter.

————. 1990. *Turbulence in world politics: A theory of change and continuity.* Princeton: Princeton University Press.

Strange, Susan. 1982. Cave! Hic dragones: A critique of regime analysis. *International Organization* 36 (Spring): 479–96.

Vedung, Evert. 1988. The Swedish five-party syndrome and the environmentalists. In *When parties fail: Emerging alternative organizations,* ed. Kay Lawson and Peter H. Merkl, 76–109. Princeton: Princeton University Press.

Vogel, David. 1990. Environmental policy in Europe and Japan. In *Environmental policy in the 1990s,* ed. Norman J. Vig and Michael E. Kraft, 257–78. Washington, D.C.: Congressional Quarterly Press.

Webb, Adrian. 1990. German.politics and the Green challenge. *Economist Intelligence Unit Briefing, Special Report No. 2032*, March, 1–44.

World Commission on Environment and Development. 1987. *Our common future.* New York: Oxford University Press.

Young, Oran R. 1989. *International cooperation: Building regimes for natural resources and the environment.* Ithaca, N.Y.: Cornell University Press.

SECTION ONE

Environmental Movements

1 The World is Relearning Its Story about How the World Works

LESTER W. MILBRATH

All societies develop a story about how the world works. Primal people often attribute planetary forces and natural events, such as droughts, to the power and whim of spirits or gods. In modern society, we turn to science and abstract theories, such as that of "the market," for our story. The point remains that, in all cases, there is a story.

In this chapter, I first discuss the role stories play in defining ourselves and our society. Many scholars believe that a new story about the relationship between humans and nature is emerging in Western societies that contrasts sharply with the story that currently dominates public discourse. I review how people are learning and adopting this new story; I present evidence showing that many parts of the new story are widely accepted, even though it has not yet had much impact on public policy. I conclude with a brief look at the future of environmental learning/thinking.

The stories that dominate the interpretation of reality in each society might be thought of as sets of cultural lenses; they provide the structure for social learning. Reality does change, however: populations grow, economies grow, new technologies are deployed, and humans do alter their physical environments—too often in a degrading way. When reality changes, those cultural lenses may lead observers to ignore emerging aspects and reality is seriously distorted. Our interpretations of reality also change as we learn more from science and experience. The chapter by Dalton in this volume, which reviews the history of the environmental movement, illustrates how our interpretations change with experience and learning. The recent growing tendency to perceive humans as harmonious participants in biocommunities, rather than as dominating exploiters, is an example of such a reinterpretation that carries us back to beliefs widely held in earlier centuries.

Stories that become dominant in a society are so universally accepted that most people are not aware that they are following a story. In the modern age of the ascendancy of science, we are not very conscious of our story and of the way it guides our lives. Part of our story is the constant assertion that science is the source of truth. Our story also assumes the primacy of the human being, whose welfare must come before that of other creatures; our species asserts the right to dominate nature for its own benefit. We additionally believe that we can multiply our numbers without limit and that our economic growth has no limit. This story ignores the reliance of humans on having the ecosphere continue to function well and on the intimate connection between the human story and the cosmic story.

This particular belief structure (cultural lens) dominating thought in a society, then, may be made up partly of images that reflect reality and partly of images that are myth. As reality grows further and further out of synchrony with dominating images, the gap between reality and image creates a tension leading some people to change their beliefs while others stubbornly hold on to their beliefs. Berry said it eloquently:

> It's all a question of story. We are in trouble just now because we do not have a good story. We are in between stories. The old story—the account of how the world came to be and how we fit into it—is not functioning properly, and we have not learned the New Story. The old story sustained us for a long period of time. It shaped our emotional attitudes, provided us with life purpose, energized action. It consecrated suffering, integrated knowledge, guided education. We awoke in the morning and knew where we were. We could answer the questions of our children. . . . Everything was taken care of because the story was there. It did not make men good, it did not take away the pains and stupidities of life, or make for unfailing warmth in human association. But it did provide a context in which life could function in a meaningful manner. (Berry 1988, 123)

As some people think about the deficiencies of the old story, they develop new ideas that are closer to the reality they see and which depart in crucial ways from the old story. This process eventually takes the form of a new belief structure that challenges the old; some might call it a new worldview. The emerging story may be hidden from public consciousness for a time. At the public level, many people continue to use the old political rhetoric that is embedded in the old story—probably because everybody understands the old story and it is the "only game in town," even though their inner thoughts already are moving on to a new story and a new politics.

A story about how the world works, held by a single individual, may be called a *worldview*; if the story is agreed to by lots of people, scholars usually call it a *social paradigm*. A worldview does not become a paradigm until it is widely shared. A dominant social paradigm (DSP) may be defined as a society's dominant belief structure that organizes the way people perceive and interpret the functioning of the world around them. A social paradigm incorporates beliefs about how the world works physically, socially, economically, and politically. From time to time a dominant paradigm is challenged so fundamentally that it gives way to a new paradigm that seizes dominance;

this process is called *paradigm shift*. A defining characteristic of paradigms is that changes of paradigms occur in discontinuous revolutionary breaks (Kuhn 1972). This distinguishes paradigm shifts from more gradual kinds of social change.

Many scholars who study beliefs and values, myself included, perceive that the whole Western world is currently undergoing paradigm shift. This shift has not progressed far enough that the key concepts of the challenging paradigm can regularly enter our public discourse; those desiring to be understood must continue to use the language of the old but still dominant paradigm. Dominant paradigms are so fundamental a part of social architecture that most people take them for granted; they are not aware they are using a paradigm. Perlmutter and Trist discuss this characteristic as part of their definition of the concept:

> Paradigms are the "logics" or "mental models" that underlie the missions, systems of governance, organizational character and structures (including socio-technical systems) which are the parameters of the social architecture of institutions. . . . A paradigm expresses a self-consistent world view, a social construction of reality widely shared and taken for granted by the members of a society, most of whom are aware only to a limited extent of the underlying logic, which is implicit rather than explicit in what they feel and think and in the courses of action they undertake. A paradigm provides, as it were, the medium in which they exist and tends to become explicit only when the need for a new overall perspective arises through increasing dysfunction in the prevailing paradigm. (1986, 2–3)

Cotgrove has done some of the clearest thinking about paradigm shift:

> A paradigm is dominant not in the statistical sense of being held by most people, but in the sense that it is the paradigm held by dominant groups in industrial societies; and in the sense that it serves to legitimate and justify the institutions and practices of a market economy. . . . it is the taken-for-granted common-sensical view which usually determines the outcome of debates on environmental issues. Paradigms then provide maps of what the world is believed to be like. They constitute guidelines for identifying and solving problems. Above all, paradigms provide the framework of meaning within which "facts" and experiences acquire significance and can be interpreted.
>
> Paradigms are not only beliefs about what the world is like and guides to action; they also serve the purpose of legitimating or justifying courses of action. That is to say, they function as ideologies. Hence, conflicts over what constitutes the paradigm by which action should be guided and judged to be reasonable is itself a part of the political process. The struggle

to universalize a paradigm is part of a struggle for power.

The protagonists face each other in a spirit of exasperation, talking past each other with mutual incomprehension. It is a dialogue of the blind talking to the deaf. Nor can the debate be settled by appeals to the facts. We need to grasp the implicit cultural meanings which underlie the dialogue. It is because protagonists to the debate approach issues from different cultural contexts, which generate different and conflicting implicit meanings, that there is mutual exasperation and charges and counter charges of irrationality and unreason. What is sensible from one point of view is nonsense from another. It is the implicit, self-evident, taken-for-granted character of paradigms which clogs the channels of communication. (1982, 26–27, 33, 82, 88)

In the early 1980s, I participated in a three-nation (England, Germany, and the United States) comparative study of environmental beliefs and values. One of our purposes was to study the contrasting beliefs and values of the current dominant social paradigm (DSP) and a challenging environmental paradigm. (Cotgrove was our collaborator in England and scholars at the Science Center in Berlin made up the German team.) Questionnaires were filled out by a random sample of the public and also by samples of the following elites: environmentalists, business leaders, labor leaders, and elected and appointed officials (see Milbrath 1984 for details). That study provided solid evidence that a new environmental paradigm is emerging, one that differs significantly from the dominant social paradigm.

This emerging paradigm is being developed by environmentally oriented thinkers who constitute a kind of vanguard. They advocate a new set of beliefs and values that people have begun referring to as a "New Environmental Paradigm" (NEP) (Dunlap and Van Liere 1978). Naturally, those who believe in the wisdom of the DSP wish to defend it; they have become a rearguard in opposition to the challenging vanguard with its NEP. The labels *rearguard* and *vanguard* are my own. I do not intend for these labels to be pejorative. The outstanding characteristic of the rearguard is that these people are defenders of the DSP, and the outstanding characteristic of the vanguard is that these people are trying to bring about a new society with a new paradigm (in his chapter, Dalton refers to this perspective as the *ecologist orientation*). The people in the rearguard and vanguard may not perceive themselves as playing out these roles though from the perspective of the social analyst they are doing so as social change is worked through.

MAJOR DIFFERENCES BETWEEN DSP AND NEP

The NEP is not a minor modification of the DSP; rather, it is a fundamental and profound challenge to some of the central premises of the

DSP. A society operating on NEP values and beliefs would be strikingly different from modern society. To understand better how a new society that orders itself according to the NEP would be different from contemporary society, which orders itself according to the DSP, those differences are highlighted in tables 1.1 and 1.2. These tables partly derive from the three-nation study of environmental beliefs and values, discussed above, but are supplemented by the thinking of contemporary environmental writers. The most fundamental differences center upon the role of economic activity.

Table 1.1. Fundamental Value and Belief Differences between the DSP and the NEP

Dominant Social Paradigm (DSP)	New Environmental Paradigm (NEP)
priority on economic growth and development, focus on short-term or immediate prosperity	priority on ecosystem viability, focus on long-term sustainability
continuation of economic growth justifies dangers of perturbing bio-geo-chemical systems	perturbing bio-geo-chemical systems is rarely, if ever, justifiable
perpetual economic growth; unrestricted population growth	growth rates are sustainable only if limited
accept risks to maximize wealth	avoid risks to the ecosystem and over all societal well-being
reliance on markets to spur growth and ensure a bright future	reliance on foresight and planning to ensure a bright future
emphasis on immediate materially oriented gratification	emphasis on simplicity and personal enrichment
emphasis on hierarchy and centralization	emphasis on horizontal structures and decentralization
centralized decision making and responsibility	greater personal and local responsibility
emphasis on private over public goods	ensure meeting public goods
enormous faith in science and technology	skepticism and critical evaluation of science and technology
reliance on mechanistic simple cause/effect thinking and narrow expertise	recognition of need for holistic/integrative thinking
emphasis on competition, domination patriarchy	emphasis on cooperation, partnership, egalitarianism
violence needed to maintain dominance and social order	aversion to violence—seen as destructive of social order
subordinate nature to human interests	place humans in ecosystemic context
emphasize freedom so long as it serves economic priorities	emphasize freedom so long as it serves ecological and social imperatives

15٬٩٫٩٥٩

25

College of St. Francis Library
Joliet, Illinois

Table 1.2. Contrasting Policies/Strategies/Approaches

Dominant Social Paradigm (DSP)	*New Environmental Paradigm (NEP)*
maximize growth even at the cost of polluting	reduce waste and avoid pollution even at economic cost
encourage conspicuous consumption	discourage conspicuous consumption
emphasize work to fill economic needs	emphasize fulfillment in work
utilize whatever resources needed to maximize current economic activity to benefit current generation	conserve and maintain resource stocks for future generations
emphasize profitable use of non-renewable resources; rely on market to resolve resource shortages	emphasize renewable resources; plan for resource shortages
encourage development and virtually unrestricted deployment of science and technology	critically evaluate and, at need, restrict deployment of science and technology
use hard/large-scale technology	use soft/ "appropriate" technology
emphasize development of nuclear energy	phase out nuclear energy
sacrifice other species for economic gain	protect other species, even at economic cost
encourage monocultures to maximize output and wealth for humans	restore/preserve ecosystem diversity and resilience
emphasize high-yield (intrusive) agriculture	emphasize regenerative/appropriate agriculture
rely on markets; minimal use of planning	utilize both planning and markets

The currently dominant paradigm promotes economic growth as an unquestioned good that also is the preferred means to reduce poverty and inequality. Faith in growth extends to population growth that is believed not only to be possible but also useful in spurring economic development. (In less developed countries, having large numbers of children reassures parents that they will be cared for in their old age.) Believers in the DSP assume that markets are the best mechanism for maximizing economic growth and human welfare; they reject most planning, especially by government. High consumption is encouraged to spur further growth and jobs. The long-term future is given little thought, and it is blithely assumed that future generations will find new ways to continue high production and consumption.

The vanguard advocates of the NEP see the world very differently. They argue that the presumptions that economic growth, high consumption, and unrestrained growth in population can continue indefinitely are dangerously fallacious. Such life patterns will swiftly deplete resources and, more importantly, are likely to alter bio-geo-chemical earth systems so that they behave unpredictably and injure life systems. Unpredictability of earth systems, such as the climate, would have devastating consequences for the society and economy; turbulent earth systems could not only spoil the dreams of the growth advocates but could also destroy much of our civilizational infrastructure, causing poverty and death around the globe (Kassiola 1990). The vanguard argues further that unfettered markets do not protect ecosystems and that we must use foresight and planning to get to the future we want. Environmentalists would gladly abandon highly consumptive ways of life and point out that life-styles with less material consumption can be equal in quality, if not actually superior, to life-styles seeking persistently to consume more and more.

Many of the remaining contrasts derive from the basic one just discussed. Hierarchy and centralization are advocated by the DSP to maximize efficiency and growth. Environmentalists point out that the DSP also promotes patriarchy, domination, and large-scale elite-dominated technologies. The vanguard believes that horizontal and decentralized structures can be equally efficient economically, and even more efficient socially; they are also more likely to be innovative and resilient to failure. Structuring society in this way would give more power to those lower in society's strata and encourage more local and personal responsibility. These structural changes cannot be promoted and managed by the market; they can only be instituted and managed by governmental coordination of disparate entities.

The two paradigms weight public goods quite differently. The DSP emphasizes market mechanisms to maximize private goods and gives little weight to public goods (which always raises hated taxes). Environmentalists perceive environmental public goods (e.g., clean air, water, and soil) to be absolutely essential. In general, they perceive public goods to be just as important for quality of life as private goods and desire public action (planning), as well as taxes, to insure that public goods are well provided.

Adherents of the two paradigms also have different perspectives on science and technology. DSP adherents have great faith in the capacity of science and technology to solve almost any problem that arises. They believe science and technology cannot only be relied on to solve practical physical problems but also are more likely to be helpful in solving social ills than many of the welfare schemes we have tried (we should emphasize science and technology to keep growing economically, which will resolve many other social problems without governmental programs). They assert that science and technology have been so wondrously helpful that they should be strongly promoted; and they will develop much more effectively if they are left unsupervised.

NEP adherents, however, point out that science and technology have become the servants of those who provide money for their development and control their deployment—i.e., the establishment. Some technologies are now so powerful that they can change the way the world works; they have the potential to destroy everything we have built. Furthermore, despite built-in safeguards, technologies do fail (Chernobyl, Bhopal, *Exxon Valdez*, etc.) and wreak great havoc on humans and the ecosystem. Environmentalists value scientific inquiry because new knowledge is needed to solve many urgent problems, but they urge careful evaluation of possible future consequences before a technology is developed and deployed. Environmentalists are more likely to view the future with an holistic, systemic, and integrative perspective; they decry simple mechanistic cause-effect thinking (mainly used within the DSP) that cripples estimation of the systemically generated second-, third-, and fourth-order consequences of a proposed action.

If economic efficiency and growth play a lesser role in life, a society can more easily reject patriarchy and domination of the weak by the strong. NEP adherents urge partnership (mutually advantageous relationships) in marriage and in the workplace. They even urge that this perspective should become the accepted mode in the relationships among nations. Environmentalists strive to avoid violence and seek policies that alleviate the sources of violence.

This new ecological way of thinking makes clear that humans are part of the larger ecosystem and that all humans (in fact, all creatures) are linked in the earth system. Individuals, firms, and nations must come to recognize their interrelatedness and realize that they must reduce conflict and work together if they are to protect the functioning of planet earth's life systems. The old belief that the strong should be able to dominate nature, other species, and other humans is no longer tenable for solving today's global environmental problems.

The perspective on freedom also differs in the two paradigms. The dominant paradigm emphasizes freedom in the market and urges unfettered opportunities to develop and deploy whatever people can dream up. Environmentalists point out that this type of freedom gives great advantage to the strong, who are usually well-situated in the establishment, and deprives the weak and less fortunate of opportunities for meaningful expression. Freedom for the strong generally results in exploitation of the weak as well as injury to life systems. NEP advocates also love freedom and would nurture it, but they recognize the necessity for society to restrict actions that would injure communities, ecosystems, and earth systems. Economic freedom would not be allowed to override society's top priority of ecosystem viability. The NEP features a society that empowers individuals and localities to adopt greater autonomy and that would try to reduce the impersonal economic processes that characterize the huge economic structures erected under the dominant paradigm. Economics will not become unimportant, but maximizing output will no longer serve as the predominant value by which we measure our rights, our successes, and our options.

Table 1.2 illustrates some of the more specific policies that the two paradigms would promote. This table does not introduce new concepts; the contrasted policies are consistent with the differing fundamental values and beliefs of the two paradigms presented in table 1.1. One could say in summary that DSP defenders highly value economic wealth, power, and control of their environment (including control of other people); they would expand throughput of all materials and would willingly risk ecosystem degradation and disruption of global bio-geo-chemical systems to maximize those values. They see the world and how it works very differently from advocates of the NEP, who place top priority on protecting the proper functioning of planetary life systems and would limit human population, economic activity, and waste to achieve that protection. The NEP vanguard would live more lightly on the earth, would conserve and husband resources, would cherish other species and other humans, and would use regenerative methods to nourish uncultivated ecosystems (e.g., forests) and to restore the productivity of soils and cultivated ecosystems.

HOW CAN/DO PEOPLE ADOPT
A NEW SOCIAL PARADIGM?

How did environmental problems move from being of such little concern over the years leading up to the 1960s to the status of being a high-priority policy concern by the late 1980s? How do people learn, adopt, and practice a new social paradigm?

Everyone knows that individuals learn, but societies also learn. Our personal learning is always intimately intertwined with social learning. In modern society, most social learning is stimulated by the mass media. News events are a strong stimulus to learning. The breakup of the hegemony of the Communist party over Eastern Europe and the disintegration of the Soviet Union helped us learn that the cold war is over. The *Exxon Valdez* oil spill helped us learn how oil transport accidents injure ecosystems. In these cases, our personal learning was significantly amplified by social learning as we shared images and interpretations.

Social learning is shaped by cognitive images at the conscious level and subliminal messages that deeply affect our emotional makeup. Modern advertising is especially adept at reaching us at the emotional level, and is a

29

powerful force in social learning. Dramatic presentations also reach deeply into our unconscious; they constitute powerful reinforcers or challenges to our beliefs about how the world works. In the days before humans had mass media, and especially before they had printing, much of the social learning was developed and reinforced through storytelling. Of course, formal education and scientific developments also play a strong role in personal and social learning.

Social learning about the environment does not progress very fast or very far if people are not aware of crucial phenomena or that there is a problem that must be solved. Environmental learning has been hampered by the fact that in recent centuries most people simply did not think about it. Even today, the environment does not enter the consciousness of certain types of thinkers and writers. Most contemporary economists still conduct their analyses and make projections without considering the environment. Most educational administrators and planners, especially in the U.S., are not yet conscious that young people should learn about the environment. The commissioner of education in New York State recently published and promoted a "New Compact for Learning" that purported to prepare young people for life in the twenty-first century—yet he displayed no awareness of a need for youth to learn about the environment.

EVOLUTION OF ENVIRONMENTAL LEARNING/THINKING

Much of this book is devoted to describing the environmental movement. I invite the reader to view the development of environmentalism as a prime example of social learning. European culture spawned industrial society and led in its development. Ironically, that same culture spawned and led the environmental movement, which was stimulated by people witnessing the destructive excesses of industrialism and seeking correctives to curb the dangers they perceived in it (see Dalton's chapter). European settlers in North and South America, Africa, Australia and New Zealand were ruthless in thrusting aside and killing indigenous people. They were equally ruthless with nature: forests were cut over and/or burned; unsuitable lands were plowed and frequently abandoned; wildlife was exploited, diminished, and sometimes exterminated; local climates were inadvertently changed (Cronon 1983). There was a callous disregard for natural beauty and nature preservation.

A little more than a century ago, a small but influential group of people (mostly from the upper classes) became concerned that some of the world's most beautiful creatures and places would be desecrated. They began the conservation movement in North America and Europe by organizing numerous conservation groups. They had friends in high places and were able to get the U.S. government to set aside the first national park, Yellowstone, in 1872. The conservation efforts undertaken (parks, preserves, regulations, new bureaucracies) were remarkably similar in North America and Europe. The U.S. conservation movement can be credited with establishing the U.S. National Park Service, the U.S. Forest Service, and a network of wildlife refuges and wilderness areas. These conservationists on both continents still believed in their present societal thrust (the DSP), but they wanted natural resources to be used efficiently and to be preserved for the enjoyment of future generations of humans (Hays 1959).

Meanwhile, industrial activities accelerated with little thought being given to pollution and resource depletion. By the 1950s, air, water, and soil pollution became visibly evident in numerous industrial locales. The new science of public health began to link pollution to adverse effects on human health. Rachel Carson's *Silent Spring* (1962) alerted the Western world to the fact that many well-intentioned efforts to dominate nature were having unanticipated deleterious consequences. Carson's book constituted the first major successful effort to alert ordinary citizens to environmental danger and to help them think systemically and in the long term. With these new stimuli, a new environmental movement began to develop alongside the older conservation movement, with which it collaborated on many issues.

Many people participated in environmental learning even though they did not join environmental groups. The new environmental movement was, at first, mainly an antipollution movement. Governments responded to popular demand by creating antipollution laws and agencies which, in some places, have had considerable success in forcing industry to clean up. Environmental agencies in most countries are still predominantly antipollution agencies. Growth in population and economic activity overwhelms these efforts, however, and pollution is worsening all over the planet. In recent decades, pollution has reached alarming levels in many Third World countries; but most of those societies do not have appropriate traditions or institutions for registering political discontent. Usually, conditions must get very bad before the victims rise up in protest, sometimes violently; most Third World environmental movements can be called "victims' movements."

During the 1970s and 1980s the thinking of the worldwide environmental movement was transformed even further, partly due to learning from experience and partly due to new scientific findings. Concerns about the dangers of nuclear power enlisted vigorous activism like no other issue and colorful mass demonstrations brought worldwide media attention. A book sponsored by the Club of Rome, *The Limits to Growth* (Meadows et al.

1972), spread alarm around the globe and sparked a furious public debate about the characteristics of economic and population growth—a debate which continues to this day.

Many environmentalists developed new modes of thinking that can be characterized as holistic, systemic, integrative, long-term, and planet-wide; they recognized that societal transformation would be necessary to preserve the viability of the planet's life systems. They would subscribe to most of the beliefs and values listed under the NEP in table 1.1. Ordinary people had not yet come to think that way, but by the late 1970s and 1980s they could perceive with their own senses that environmental conditions had gotten bad and were getting worse; they mainly blamed industry (and governments for not controlling industry). This translated into a strong reservoir of public support for environmentalists, but it did not translate easily into meaningful political action. Activists in many developed countries formed Green political parties to be able to exert greater political leverage for societal transformation. Also during the 1980s, accruing scientific and field evidence of such global threats as acid rain, desertification, deforestation, loss of the ozone layer, and global warming led all shades of environmentalists to call for swift and deep social change. The formerly valid distinction between conservation and environmental organizations began to disappear as both types of groups recognized the need to work together for societal transformation to avert dire global environmental perils.

Surveys of environmental beliefs and values have been conducted in many countries; these constitute the clearest evidence that people are relearning their story about how the world works.

Lessons from the Three-Nation Study of Environmental Beliefs and Values

Our three-nation study conducted in the early 1980s, mentioned earlier, not only provides clear evidence for the DSP-NEP differences outlined in tables 1.1 and 1.2, but also shows how far different kinds of people in developed countries have progressed in relearning their story about how the world works. We found the sharpest difference of belief and value to be between environmental and business leaders. Environmentalists were a vanguard pushing for a new society, the NEP, while business leaders were staunch defenders of the DSP. Governmental leaders were divided but, on balance, were closer in their views to business leaders than to environmentalists. At that time the public was not sufficiently aware of the problems of global warming and loss of the ozone layer, and we could not get meaningful responses to questions about them.

The public was so varied that they could not be neatly characterized. Roughly 20 percent in the U.S.A. were strong believers in the NEP (the percentages were a bit higher in England and Germany); their beliefs and values correlated into a paradigmatic structure. Another 20 percent held the structure of beliefs characterizing the DSP. Most of the public selected views from both structures, or had given very little thought to the matter. For example, when we asked if people would prefer to live in a society that emphasized economic growth versus one that limited economic growth, they overwhelming chose an emphasis on economic growth. In a later question we asked if they would prefer a society that emphasizes environmental protection *over* economic growth to a society that emphasizes economic growth *over* environmental protection. In this trade-off, the U.S. public chose environmental protection over economic growth by a ratio of 3 to 1 in both 1980 and 1982 (a U.S. poll in 1990 showed the ratio to be greater than 4 to 1); in Germany the ratio was 3 to 1 in 1980 and 2 to 1 in 1982; in England the ratio was 5 to 1 in 1980 and 3 to 1 in 1982. This general preference for environmental protection over economic growth has been confirmed in several other studies in thirteen countries (Milbrath 1989, 120–24). Business leaders were more likely to choose economic growth, as we expected, but we were surprised that their most popular category was a middle position, indicating ambivalence between the two values.

Accepting or rejecting the idea of limits to growth was one of the few issues on which there were clear differences by country. People in the United States were strongly divided on the issues, about half saying there are limits and the other half denying it, whereas in Germany a big majority accepted the idea of limits. The proportion accepting limits in England fell between that in the U.S.A. and Germany. As expected, environmental leaders were most inclined to believe in limits, while business leaders were least inclined; but the country differences just mentioned held within each group of leaders as well.

Publics in most countries have only a fragmentary knowledge of environmental principles. Very few people have systematically studied the environment. If we pay close attention to the content of their knowledge, we can discern a pattern of developmental learning. People learn first those things they can observe with their own five senses. These senses are sharpened if people experience a degradation or loss of something they have normally counted on (like clean water). It is little wonder that pollution was an early and dominant theme in environmental protection thinking. Millions of people today still equate the environmental problem with pollution.

People learn, almost without conscious awareness, from the general aura of perceptions that surround them. The mass media, especially television, play the central role in creating that aura. Hundreds of direct and subliminal messages instill a general awareness and, if the awareness is of a problem, they also arouse a sense of concern. We recently conducted a study of the levels of environmental knowledge, awareness, and concern among eleventh graders in New York State schools (Milbrath, Hausbeck, and Enright 1990). We found high levels of environmental awareness and concern, but low levels of knowledge. Most students reported that they learned about the environment mostly from television. Hardly any mentioned learning about it in school—little wonder, since most schools do not teach about it. Television is deft at raising awareness and concern, but is not very effective at systematic transmittal of knowledge. The latter is a job for the schools which they have not yet accepted.

The ability to think holistically, systemically, and in the long term is rarely developed in modern society. This ability is crucial, however, for understanding the probable causes and consequences of such global problems as acid rain, loss of the ozone layer, global warming, extermination of species, and desertification. The concepts are not difficult to understand; they could be taught to fourth or fifth graders. They do require, however, that the learner follow abstract theory and accept its validity even when it cannot be confirmed by the five senses.

As might be expected, people have been especially slow to appreciate the consequences of global environmental problems. When recent opinion polls report that a much lower percentage of the public (about 40 percent) want the government to take vigorous action to forestall global warming than want the government to take vigorous action to reduce toxic pollution (about 80 percent), we should not infer that people have thought equally about both matters and have made an informed judgment about priorities. A more valid inference is that most people know about pollution from having seen it with their own eyes, whereas very few understand the workings of physical systems and are able to foresee a threat that is not yet visible, especially if it is denied by many leaders.

Results of a Recent United Nations Survey

The largest recently completed environmental opinion study[1] was conducted for the United Nations Environment Programme (UNEP) by the Louis Harris Organization in fourteen countries, including nine less-developed countries (LDCs), between February and June 1988. Fifty leaders were interviewed in each country in addition to a sample of the public. The study measured environmental awareness, concern, and behavioral potential, but it was not a thorough study of environmental learning and belief structures. The samples of both leaders and the public were too small for safe generalizations about small differences. Nevertheless, many of the findings were so sweeping that we can be quite sure that environmental learning is taking place rapidly. In the following paragraphs I will rely heavily on the Harris/UNEP study. I will also draw on recent travel experiences in the East and West, on participation in international conferences, and on a variety of other studies.

High levels of awareness and concern about environmental problems have now spread worldwide, with concern in LDCs being as high as in the more developed world. A majority (often a high majority) of people in thirteen countries in the UNEP/Harris survey perceived that their environment had become worse over the past ten years; only in Saudi Arabia did a majority believe it had become better. Furthermore, most people did not expect improvement; rather they saw the present course leading to calamity. Young people and women, especially, predicted a dire future. In every country, huge majorities wanted their government to give higher priority to environmental protection, including vigorous action on new laws and stronger enforcement of them.

Most people blamed first their government, then industry, for the worsening environmental situation. They were not likely to see environmental problems as stemming from societal belief systems and life-styles. People were asked whether they saw population growth as a cause of environmental problems, but in no country did a majority perceive it as an important cause. Respondents were not even asked if energy overuse was a cause of environmental problems.

There was high anxiety everywhere about the threat pollution poses to public health, especially among young people. Majorities in each country said they would accept a lower standard of living if they could have an environment that was safer for health. Sizable majorities also perceived the following problems as very serious: loss of good farmland, deforestation, radioactivity from nuclear plants, desertification, toxic wastes, and acid rain. Global problems that required theoretical knowledge to understand, such as global warming and loss of the ozone layer, were perceived to be serious by only a minority in 1988. In the U.S. in the early 1990s, both of these problems were perceived as serious by about 75 percent of the public.

Most people believed that solutions were possible if environmental protection became a national and world priority. They looked to their governments and the United Nations to do this. They also wanted governments to ensure that business and farmers made the necessary changes. They wanted stricter enforcement of environmental laws. A majority in most countries believed that effective action would require the cooperation of other countries. Most people were willing to contribute time or money to help make things better. The ratios saying they were willing to pay higher taxes if the money would be used for environmental protection ranged from 2-to-1 to 3-to-1 across these countries. Older people were more likely to perceive major environmental problems, and to hold the culprits responsible, but young people were more willing to take personal action to make things better. Women were more aware of environmental problems than men; they saw environmental problems as more serious than men did, and they were more critical of institutional failures, and they were more willing to accept a lower standard of living if health risks could be lessened.

Country differences can be interesting, but good data are not available for many countries. Learning about the environment has probably progressed furthest in Western Europe (especially Germany, The Netherlands, and Scandinavia), Canada, New Zealand, and Australia. In these countries there is greater recognition of the gravity of global problems and of the origin of those problems in socioeconomic-political systems, and higher readiness to express that concern through political action. The United States lags behind, not because of a lack of knowledge but because of (1) insufficient recognition of the gravity of the problems by the public and the leaders, (2) insufficient attention to the deep nature of the problems by the mass media and by educational institutions, and (3) the structure of the political system, which frustrates attempts by concerned citizens to express meaningfully their concerns via the electoral process.

The people of Eastern Europe and the former Soviet Union clearly recognize how devastated their environments have become under their previous insensitive regimes. However, they have not progressed very far in defining their environmental problems in order to bring their socioeconomic-political resources to bear on them. They look to the West for knowledge, technology, and money, and seem to perceive themselves as helpless without them.

A high percentage of people in less developed countries sense that their environment is deteriorating and that the problem is serious. They may blame the government for inaction, but they have no effective way to pressure their governments to act. The governments place the highest priority on economic development and the people seem to agree. Both the governments and the people recognize that this victimizes some people. Sometimes those feeling abused rise up in protest; thus, environmental movements in LDCs are best characterized as victims' movements. There is little recognition that environmental problems originate in the socioeconomic-political system (e.g., population growth, energy use, farming techniques, and land-use practices), and that some problems have global dimensions. The same is true for environmental learning in the newly industrialized countries, such as South

Korea and Taiwan—even Japan.

A BRIEF LOOK AT THE FUTURE OF
ENVIRONMENTAL LEARNING/THINKING

A surge of environmental learning was underway during the latter part of the 1980s. Media coverage increased dramatically as several magazines with worldwide circulation featured cover stories, and sometimes full issues, focusing on environmental problems, especially global problems. The number of environmental conferences rose significantly and many nonenvironmental organizations devoted special programming to the environment. Greenpeace, which began as a small Canadian group in 1972, acquired affiliates in twenty-four countries and Antarctica. Friends of the Earth, also founded in 1972, had organizations in thirty-three countries. More than six thousand nongovernmental organizations (NGOs)—half of which are from developing countries—are represented at the Environmental Liaison Centre in Nairobi, which works with the United Nations Environment Programme. Many of the NGOs were formed in the last fifteen years (Caldwell 1988). Earth Day was celebrated worldwide on 22 April 1990.

As we began the last decade of the millennium, a World Conference on Environment and Development was held in Rio de Janeiro on 1–14 June 1992. In 1987, the U.N.-sponsored World Commission on Environment and Development recommended "sustainable development" as the primary goal for the future; it became the theme of the Brazil conference. This slogan can be interpreted numerous ways and has served as an umbrella under which people of disparate views can gather. Peoples eager for development are reassured that their dream can come true. Business and corporate leaders believe they can continue to grow so long as they try hard not to pollute unnecessarily. Affluent people believe they will not have to change their life-styles so long as they cut down on wastes and carefully dispose of them.

A few people, most of them environmentalists, caution that sustainable development must not be confused with sustainable growth, which is a contradiction in terms; persistent growth is simply not sustainable. Granting that poverty is desperate and must be reduced, environmentalists urge reduction of throughput in the more developed countries and use of our creativity to learn how to develop without growth in economic throughput. They also insist that population growth must be curbed, although discussion of the topic was anathema to many attending the U.N. conference in Brazil in 1992.

Our learning and thinking have not progressed far enough for the people

37

of the world to deal effectively with the grave global environmental problems on the horizon. Affluent people resist any thought of giving up comfortable life-styles while poor people aspire to them. Both groups would consider it a calamity to slow down economic growth. We do not even discuss population curbs at world conferences. Arguments, public debates, propaganda, and public education only reach people who are listening, a small minority. Most people want government, industries, and engineers to take care of environmental problems they consider to be dangerous. Only a handful feel any personal responsibility to act.

Obviously, considerable learning is required; ironically, most people and governments do not recognize that environmental learning is a high priority. Much of the knowledge needed to deal with environmental problems is already available and more is being rapidly generated. We already know a great deal about how societies and people learn. Why is it so difficult for us to focus on our environmental learning task? What does it take to get people to listen? Nature can use its fury to get us to listen, even when we do not wish to. Must we always learn the hard way, by death and destruction?

NOTES

1. In January 1992 the George Gallup International Institute fielded a thirty-nation study of environmental opinion; findings from this study were not available at the time of this writing.

REFERENCES

Berry, Thomas. 1988. *The dream of the earth.* San Francisco: Sierra Club Books.

Caldwell, Lynton K. 1988. Beyond environmental diplomacy: The changing institutional structure of international cooperation. In *International environmental diplomacy,* ed. John Carroll, 13–28. Cambridge: Cambridge University Press.

Carson, Rachel. 1962. *Silent spring.* Cambridge, Mass.: Riverside Press.

Cotgrove, Stephen F. 1982. *Catastrophe or cornucopia: The environment, politics and the future.* Chichester and New York: John Wiley and Sons.

Cronon, William. 1983. *Changes in the land: Indians, colonists, and the ecology of New England.* New York: Hill and Wang.

Dunlap, Riley, and Kent Van Liere. 1978. The new environmental paradigm. *Journal of Environmental Education* 9, no. 4:10–19.

Hays, Samuel P. 1959. *Conservation and the gospel of efficiency.* Cambridge: Harvard University Press.

Kassiola, Joel J. 1990. *The death of industrial civilization: The limits to economic* growth and the repoliticization of advanced industrial society. Albany: SUNY Press.

Kuhn, Thomas S. 1970. *The structure of scientific revolutions.* 2d ed. Chicago: University of Chicago Press.

Meadows, Donella, Dennis Meadows, Jorgen Randers, and William W. Behrens III. 1972. *The limits to growth.* New York: Universe Books.

Milbrath, Lester W. 1984. *Environmentalists: Vanguard for a new society.* Albany: SUNY Press.

————. 1989. *Envisioning a sustainable society: Learning our way out.* Albany: SUNY Press.

Milbrath, Lester W., Kathryn Hausbeck, and Sean Enright. 1990. Levels of knowledge, awareness, and concern about the environment: An inquiry into environmental education. Paper presented at the annual meeting of the International Society for Political Psychology, Washington, D.C.

Perlmutter, Howard V., and Erick Trist. 1986. Paradigms for societal transition. *Human Relations* 39, no. 1:127.

2 The Environmental Movement in Western Europe

RUSSELL J. DALTON

Writing a decade ago, the American sociologist Robert Nisbit observed that "it is entirely possible that when the history of the twentieth century is finally written, the single most important social movement of the period will be judged to be environmentalism" (1982, 101). That observation is even more appropriate today.

In the 1980s environmental issues arrived at the center of the political stage in virtually all advanced industrial democracies, and this attention has continued into the 1990s. Environmental reform has an extensive popular base in most West European states, and these results easily apply to North America. Certainly, one can speak of a fundamental shift in citizen values when a majority of Europeans and Americans prefer strict environmental regulations over policies aimed at ensuring continued economic growth. Although environmental issues were once stigmatized as only relevant for radicals or eccentrics, they now play a significant role in the policy decisions of governments and the life-style choices of many individuals. There has been a greening of Western society.

The environmental issue is often equated with the "new" political controversies of advanced industrial societies, but the origins of the movement date back at least to the 1800s. The period from 1880 to 1910 saw the first major wave of environmental action in Western Europe. Citizens in several nations formed new voluntary groups to protect wildlife, preserve natural areas of national significance, and conserve nature. Many of the first major pieces of environmental legislation and land-use planning also date from this era. After a long period of relative dormancy, a second wave of environmentalism swept across Europe beginning in the 1970s. New environmental groups emerged to deal with current problems and get their concerns on the political agenda. In many areas, these new groups moved beyond the issue interests and social base of traditional conservation groups, but the basic interests of the old and new groups often overlapped and their efforts frequently reinforced one another.

This chapter[1] examines the historical evolution of the environmental movement from its initial wave of mobilization in the late 1800s to the emergence of contemporary environmental groups. Following the historical development of the environmental movement enables us to identify how the movement has changed over the years—how it expanded its social base and also expanded its range of political interests and styles of political action. In fact, much of the current literature on European environmental groups shows the differences between old, established conservation groups and the newer, more politically assertive ecologist groups (Brand et al. 1986; Dalton and Kuechler 1990; Cotgrove 1982; Lowe and Goyder 1983). Thus, we use the historical record to identify the differences that now exist between various environmental organizations and to discuss the implications of these differences for organizational values and behaviors.

THE BEGINNINGS OF NATURE CONSERVATION

The modern nature conservation movement began to develop in Western Europe in the latter half of the 1800s, though an exact date is difficult to pinpoint.[2] Several factors produced the first stirrings of the movement. In most nations, the environmental consequences of the Industrial Revolution were beginning to become manifest during this period. Urbanization and industrialization had transformed landscapes, and the harmful effects of these processes were destroying "natural" areas and wildlife, as well as polluting the environment. Historical accounts of the period stress the scale of industrial pollution, the impact of railroad expansion, the construction of public sanitation facilities, and similar developments as factors that focused on environmental matters.

The growth of the natural sciences during the century also stimulated awareness of environmental problems. Biologists and botanists studied and catalogued the natural environment, documented the loss of habitats and species, and traced these problems to industrialization. The German botanist Ernst Haeckel first used the term "ecology" in 1866. The natural sciences developed a formal standing in Europe during the latter half of the century, and the growing membership of natural history societies provided a popular basis for environmental action.

These changes in the objective circumstances of life were complemented by an even more important shift in the cultural environment of the upper class in most European societies. European intellectuals increasingly challenged the belief in rationalism and progress that was identified with the Enlightenment. In France, a romanticist trend developed by midcentury (Duclos and Smadja 1985; Vadrot 1978). Authors such as Chateaubriand, Hugo, and Vigny reflected the rural and pastoral tradition *(champêtre)* of

Rousseau and presented an idealized view of nature. Similar romantic notions of the natural order and a longing for a return to nature developed within Belgium and Holland (Tellegen 1981). In Britain, Victorian romanticism replaced the Darwinist view of nature identified with laissez-faire political economists (Weiner 1981; Lowe 1983; Thomas 1983). Instead of dominating nature, Victorians saw the protection of nature and wildlife as a measure of humankind's higher order. Thus, some of the leading British philosophers of the period—John Stuart Mill, John Ruskin, and Lord Avebury—were founding members of conservation groups. Romantic sentiments also ran as an undercurrent through German society at the end of the late 1800s, perhaps best typified in the *Wandervogel* movement that enabled upper-class urban youth to relish the joys of nature through weekend hikes in the country. The last decade of the century was a period of general cultural criticism in Germany *(Zivilisationskritik)* that idealized nature and the goal of returning to the land (Linse 1983; Sieferle 1984). Only southern Europe, which had not yet experienced the full force of industrialization and modernization, did not share in this critique of modernity.

These romantic currents within Europe were both a reaction to the tremendous social changes that these societies were experiencing (an early version of "future shock") and a criticism of the direction these societies were taking. The economic depression of the late 1800s further heightened these anti-industrial sentiments. An idealized view of nature provided a source of stability and reassurance in a rapidly changing world; these sentiments also stimulated actions to protect (or create) this image of the natural order.

These forces combined in different ways in different nations. In some cases, objective conditions and national economic needs prompted the first conservation activities. In other nations, moral and aesthetic values seemed more important in stimulating action. But in almost all of northern Europe, the common result was the proliferation of conservation groups and public pressure for conservation legislation throughout the later 1800s and early 1900s.

One component of the conservation movement, and probably the largest, dealt with the protection of birds. The first wildlife campaign in Britain, for example, sought to protect nesting seabirds from wanton slaughter by sportspersons (Sheail 1976; Lowe 1983). Hunters used the birds as live targets as the birds congregated along the Yorkshire coasts during breeding season. The hunters killed hundreds a day and left the bodies where they fell. Led by the local clergy, residents of the area protested this destruction and formed a society for the protection of seabirds in 1867. This citizens' lobby eventually pressured its MP into introducing a protection bill for seabirds that was passed in 1869. This action was pursued for basically altruistic reasons: to avoid unnecessary harm to wildlife and to protect whole species of seabirds from possible extinction.

On the European continent, concern over bird protection was also spreading (Hayden 1942). In 1868, a group of German farmers and foresters petitioned the Austro-Hungarian foreign office to protect migratory birds that benefited German agriculture. This petition led to a series of international conferences where the issue was debated and possible solutions were discussed. Finally, the participating nations reached an agreement in 1902 that specified a list of "beneficial" birds which the signatories would protect.[3]

A further stimulus for the bird protection movement was the growing use of feathers and other forms of bird plumage in women's dress fashions (Doughty 1975). Around the turn of the century, the dictates of fashion created a large international market in bird feathers centered in Paris, London, and New York. Exotic species, such as the osprey and birds of paradise, as well as common birds such as the robin and hummingbird, were sacrificed to ladies' fashions. Bird preservationists claimed that upwards of two hundred million birds were killed for their feathers each year at the beginning of the twentieth century.

This wanton destruction of wildlife for nonessential reasons violated the humanist and Victorian sensibilities of many upper-class women in Europe. These sentiments were perhaps most obvious in Britain, where reactions to the plumage trade led to the proliferation of bird protection groups (Doughty 1975; Sheail 1976). The Plumage League and the Selbourne Society were separately formed in 1885 to oppose the feather trade; shortly thereafter they merged under the Selbourne Society title. In 1889, a group of women in Manchester who had been unable to join the all-male British Ornithological Union established the Society for the Protection of Birds (SPB). By 1893, the SPB boasted a national membership of nine thousand. The Selbourne Society and the SPB often differed in tactics and competed for political influence, but both groups pressed for an end to the exploitation of birds for fashion. The Society for the Protection of Birds developed its social and political contacts more rapidly, and received a royal charter in 1904 to become the Royal Society for the Protection of Birds (RSPB). The dramatic and emotional appeals of the RSPB on behalf of bird protection were very effective in mobilizing public opposition to the killing of birds for their plumage. Newspaper stories depicted the barbarity that accompanied massive bird kills, and public letter-writing campaigns preached that feather fashions violated the Victorian norms of compassion and refinement. Even so, bird protection groups faced several decades of lobbying until the plumage trade was effectively halted by proclamation during World War I and then by legislation in 1921.

The public discussion of the plumage trade diffused public interest in the bird protection issue throughout Europe. The Dutch Association for Bird Protection *(Vereniging tot Bescherming van Vogels)* and the German Federation for Bird Protection *(Deutscher Bund für Vogelschutz* [DBV]) were both established in 1899; at about the same time, the Irish Society for Bird Protection was formed. Denmark passed its first bird protection legislation in 1894, and this was followed by the establishment of the Danish Ornithological Society *(Dansk Ornitologisk Forening)* in 1906. With the creation of the French League for Bird Protection *(Ligue pour la Protection des Oiseaux)* in 1912, a national lobby for bird protection existed in nearly every northern European nation.[4] Even though these groups were almost exclusively concerned with bird protection issues, their activities contributed to the general conservationist spirit of the times.

Preservationist groups constituted a second component of the early conservation movement. A variety of organizations emerged throughout Europe to preserve national historical sites and areas of natural or environmental significance. In Britain, efforts to protect open spaces and common lands eventually led to the formation of the National Trust in 1895. The Trust was to act as a holding company for those wishing to donate land for preservation as part of Britain's national heritage. Parliament recognized the Trust as a unique statutory body in 1907, and charged it with permanent preservation of property for the benefit of the nation. Besides acting as a land-holding company, the Trust also formed a voluntary association that pressured policymakers on conservation issues. The National Trust initially focused its attention on the protection of historical sites rather than areas of natural beauty or environmental importance. Thus, the Society for the Promotion of Nature Reserves (SPNR) was formed in 1912 to work with the National Trust in developing nature reserves that would protect wildlife and preserve areas of Britain in their natural state (Sheail 1976).

Germany was another early leader in the preservationist movement, but the German experience differed from that of the rest of Europe in two important ways. First, government assumed responsibility for preservation of significant national sites. Conservation was the responsibility of the state governments, and many states actively worked to protect areas of historical or environmental importance. Prussia, for example, created an office for the protection of national monuments in 1904—the forerunner of the modern environmental ministry—and appointed an internationally renowned conservationist, Hugo Conwentz, to the office. Second, the federal structure of policy-making led to the regionalization of the conservation movement. There was no equivalent to the national organizations in Britain and other European democracies; instead, conservation organizations tended to form at the state level. The German Federation for Protection of the Homeland *(Deutscher Bund Heimatschutz)* was formed in Dresden in 1904; the Nature Protection Federation of Bavaria *(Bund Naturschutz Bayern)* was established in 1913; and the Nature Protection Ring *(Naturschutzring)* was founded in Berlin. Groups also formed in other states and at the local level. Preservation of the nation's heritage became a measure of German national patriotism, leading to the early creation of nature preserves and the passage of conservation legislation (Wey 1982).

Comparable preservationist groups developed in most other northern European nations. Residents of Amsterdam established the Dutch Association for the Preservation of Natural Monuments in 1905 to protect the Naarder Sea; the organization continued to develop nature preserves throughout Holland. It presently manages roughly two hundred reserves amounting to over fifty thousand hectares. In 1911 another organization, *Heemschut,* was formed to protect cultural monuments in Holland, such as old buildings and historical sites. Around the turn of the century, French and Belgian citizens created societies to protect places of cultural significance and natural beauty—the *Société pour la Protection des Paysages* and *the Société Nationale pour la Protection des Sites,* respectively. The forerunner of the Danish Association for Nature Conservation *(Naturfrednings Forening)* was established in 1911; in 1925 it became a national organization promoting the conservation of nature and public education on conservation issues.

Although many preservationist groups were also interested in the protection of wildlife, a third distinct component of the conservation movement focused exclusively on the protection of non–avian species. Indeed the oldest of all major existing European conservation groups is the French National Society for the Protection of Nature *(Société Nationale de Protection de la Nature* [SNPN]). The society was originally formed in 1854 as the *Société Impériale Zoologique d'Acclimation.* It was an association of zoologists who wanted to protect the wildlife of France and its empire, both through legislation and the establishment of nature preserves. A similar organization, the Society for the Preservation of Wild Fauna of the Empire (SPWFE), was formed in Britain in 1903 (Fitter and Scott 1978).[5] The early leadership of the SPWFE described itself as "a modest and unpretentious group of gentlemen of wide experience of the outposts of the Empire and a common enthusiasm for the preservation from destruction of many of its fauna."

Despite the commendable goals of these two wildlife organizations, their ultimate aim was not the protection of species from human assault, but the preservation of species for hunting and other uses. The French society, for instance, celebrated wildlife preservation at their annual meeting with a dinner of exotic game; one could hardly imagine a contemporary conservation group performing the same ritual. Similarly, the British society was largely composed of royalty and former colonial administrators who had enjoyed the safari experience and wanted to create big-game preserves. Critics of the SPWFE lampooned it as a group of "penitent butchers," a nickname that stayed with the group because its members seemed to develop a concern with the protection of wildlife only after they had finished their own hunting.

Although we can distinguish between separate components of the conservation movement, in actual practice their actions were often complementary. Just as the National Trust and SPNR worked together on historical and landscape preservation in Britain, the Association for the Preservation of Natural Monuments and *Heemschut* cooperated in the same way in The Netherlands. National societies for the prevention of cruelty to animals (pets and domesticated animals) facilitated the development of bird and wildlife preservation associations, such as the RSPB in Britain and the Association for Nature Conservation in Denmark. Different groups often had the same wealthy benefactors and board members, and the voluntary associations often drew upon the same popular base of upper-class European society. Thus together, these separate organizations combined to produce a general mobilization period for conservation issues.

Almost as quickly as the conservation movement grew in the early 1900s, its momentum began to ebb a short time later. In part, this decline resulted from the movement's own success. National legislation and international agreements on bird protection at least partially addressed the problems that had initially led to the formation of the bird protection lobby. Conservationists also made progress on wildlife preservation. By the 1910s, there were organizations aimed at the preservation of historical landmarks and the "natural" environment in most northern European nations. In short, policy success partially obviated the rationale for additional political efforts. World War I and its consequences further undercut the momentum on conservation issues. The war not only undermined the groundwork for international environmental action but also shifted public attention from conservation issues to matters of greater immediacy: postwar reconstruction. Historical accounts of the SPNR, for example, note that the organization stagnated because it was formed just two years before the outbreak of war.

The interwar years were a period of relative dormancy for the conservation movement. Old environmental problems certainly had not ended, and a series of new ones surfaced during this period (such as oil pollution at sea and newly endangered species). But public interest in conservation issues slackened. Postwar reconstruction and then the Great Depression focused public interest on more immediate economic difficulties. Although most of the major national conservation groups discussed above continued to exist, their membership roles stabilized at a fairly modest level.[6] In fact, only one of the major contemporary environmental groups in Europe, the Council for the Protection of Rural England (CPRE), was established during the inter-war period (1926). At the international level, some agreements were reached on pollution from shipping, protection of whales, and the protection of African wildlife. But Lynton Caldwell (1990) concludes that these agreements represented very small gains, and subsequent events showed that their provisions were inadequate or soon overtaken by new environmental threats. The international momentum that had been drained by World War I was never reestablished. In summary, the mobilization wave of 1880 to 1910 had raised the European environmental movement to a certain level and created the organizational infrastructure necessary to remain at this level, but the interwar years generally represented a continuation on the same plateau.

THE MODERN REVIVAL OF CONSERVATIONISM

The conservation movement began to reestablish itself following the Second World War. In Britain, for example, wartime destruction created new opportunities for conservationists. Britain's wartime needs for agricultural products had temporarily transformed the landscape of rural England; conservationists saw postwar planning and reconstruction as an opportunity to preserve what was left of the natural British countryside. In addition, popular sentiments toward government had changed as a result of the war; Britons attributed greater responsibility to the state in addressing social needs. One illustration of this new sentiment was the passage of the Town and Country Planning Act in 1947, which granted the state control over planning for all land in Britain. Legislation in 1949 established the Nature Conservancy as a government agency charged with establishing a national system of publicly owned nature reserves.

This same conservationist revival occurred in other West European nations. The Dutch conservation movement rapidly reinstituted itself after the war was over. Belgian and French groups similarly reestablished themselves after the war. As in Britain, these organizations were motivated by a reaction to the war's destructive impact on the environment and by the need for environmental planning in postwar reconstruction. The modern Italian conservation movement began in 1951 with a protest by a group of writers and artists opposed to the destruction of the *Tevere* in the Spanish square. These efforts led to the establishment of *Italia Nostra* in 1955, an organization dedicated to the preservation of Italy's cultural heritage in its architecture, museums, and rural areas. Perhaps the greatest change came in postwar West Germany, where the new democratic climate led to the reemergence of conservationist and nature protection groups (Rucht 1988). Older groups, such as the *Bund für Vogelschutz* and the *Bund Naturschutz Bayern* again became politically active, and new conservation groups were formed. In 1960, the German Nature Protection Ring *(Deutscher Naturschutzring* [DNR]) was created as an umbrella group to unite many of these diverse organizations within a single conservationist lobby. The DNR now boasts a membership of ninety-five different organizations with a combined individual membership of 3.3 million.

Another impetus for the postwar conservation movement came at the international level (Boardman 1981; Caldwell 1990). The Swiss League for the Protection of Nature sponsored a conference in 1946 that assembled the leading conservationists in Europe, such as P.G. van Tienhoven from Holland and Julian Huxley from Britain. This meeting helped to reestablish old networks of international support and cooperation. Under the auspices of UNESCO, European conservationists worked toward the development of a new international conservation body. In 1948, a charter established the International Union for the Conservation of Nature (IUCN) as an international association of government conservation offices and nongovernmental conservation organizations.[7]

With a growing international element to many conservation and environmental issues, the IUCN became a central actor in the international conservation network. The IUCN facilitated the exchange of scientific information and policy advice between governments and other international organizations. But these administrative functions limited the IUCN's ability to mobilize public opinion and financial support on behalf of conservationist causes. The IUCN's limitations (and its tenuous financial situation) led European conservationists to create a new organization designed to involve the public in conservation issues: the World Wildlife Fund (WWF). The British national branch was established in 1961 and was soon followed by WWF affiliates in France (1963), Germany (1963), Belgium (1965), Italy (1966), The Netherlands (1972), and Denmark (1973). WWF became the popular arm of the international conservation movement; it was the first multinational environmental group, and it dramatically expanded the financial and popular support for international conservationist issues (Boardman 1981, 108–10; Nicholson 1970).

Despite this progress, the postwar years were a difficult period of rebuilding for the conservation movement overall. Membership in conservation groups grew, but only slowly, and financial resources remained limited. New legislation was passed and new members joined these organizations, but the most important actions by the movement were its efforts to restore environmental issues to the public agenda. Its greatest accomplishment was the development of an organizational base that was to support a dramatic new surge in the movement.

A NEW ENVIRONMENTAL WAVE

In the late 1960s, the Green movement again began to bloom. Public interest in conservation and environmental issues surged. A host of new environmental organizations emerged within a few years, often attracting widespread support from new sectors of society, as well as stimulating involvement in already established conservation groups. The public's growing environmental consciousness frequently concerned the unresolved problems long discussed by conservationists, but just as often the issues involved the new environmental problems experienced by advanced industrial democracies: nuclear power, resource shortages, toxic waste, acid rain, and protection of the quality of life. Environmental problems again became a salient issue to the European public and political leaders.

This new wave of environmental mobilization differed in important ways from the earlier conservation movement; but like the mobilization wave at the turn of the century, it resulted from the convergence of several factors. One major contributing factor was the scientific and educational network created by conservation organizations. This network initially provided the information that alerted citizens and public officials to the world's growing environmental problems. The clearest example is the writing of Rachel Carson, a former biologist at the U.S. Fish and Wildlife Service. Her book, *The Silent Spring* (1962), sounded the warning of an impending environmental crisis; it had an enormous impact on both sides of the Atlantic. It was followed by a host of other books from European and American authors (such as Stuart Udall, Barry Commoner and Paul Ehrlich) that stimulated this growing environmental consciousness. Few of the issues raised by these authors were new. The problems of indiscriminate use of DDT, for example, were well-known by specialists in advance of Carson's book; but governments were slow to act until *The Silent Spring* awakened the public to the menace. The primary impact of these books was to draw public attention to these unresolved problems.

The writings of the conservationists took on added force because of several dramatic environmental crises that befell Europe in the later 1960s. In 1967 the supertanker *Torrey Canyon* ran aground in the English channel and spilled millions of gallons of crude oil into the sea. The enormous oil spill fouled the coasts of Cornwall and Brittany, destroying birds and aquatic life and causing millions of dollars in damages. Two years later, a leak of toxins into the Rhine River produced a massive fish kill. The source of drinking water for millions of Europeans had its banks covered with the bodies of rotting, poisoned fish. The blowout of an oil drilling platform off the Santa Barbara coast in early 1969, and the subsequent destruction of the beautiful California coastline, produced reverberations that reached all the way to Europe. Then late in 1969, thousands of dead birds mysteriously washed up on the banks of the Irish Sea, generating front-page headlines in the London newspapers and governmental inquiries that eventually attributed the problem to the side-effects of industrial pollution. Environmental problems were no longer something that affected only bird-watchers or rural preservationists; the potential threat to even the average individual was becoming obvious. Moreover, these spectacular mega-events stimulated greater public awareness of other environmental problems within a nation or local area, which further heightened popular demands for new environmental protections.

For at least some parts of the modern environmental movement, the growth of environmentalism also reflected a cultural criticism of advanced industrial societies that arose from Europe's cultural ferment in the late 1960s (a new form of *Zivilisationskritik*). European youth attacked the insatiable materialism and excess consumerism of advanced industrial societies—and environmental problems illustrated their radical commentary. Scholars trace the origins of the modern French environmental movement and anti-nuclear power movement to the forces spawned by the May Revolts in 1968 (Vadrot 1978; Chafer 1982). The revolts gave environmentalism an ideological theme: the deterioration of the environment reflected the inevitable consequences of unbridled economic growth and the overcentralized French state. Similarly, the social criticisms of the Provo movement (1965–67) and the Kabouter movement (1968–70) provided a political and ideological starting point for a modern environmental movement in Holland (Tellegen 1981 and 1983; Jamison et al. 1990, chap. 3). Dutch youth cited the problems of pollution and other environmental deterioration as examples of the failures of the economy and the bureaucratic elitism of Holland's consociational democracy. The formative influence of the student movement and the protests of the late 1960s is equally prominent in accounts of the beginnings of the ecology movement in West Germany and Denmark (Brand et al. 1986; Kitschelt 1989; Jamison et al. 1990, chap. 4). In Belgium, youth protests for regional decentralization and democratization of society gradually broadened their scope to include environmental issues. In addition, Flemish environmentalism developed as an offshoot of a charismatic Catholic movement called Live Differently *(Anders Gaan Leven);* it encouraged its adherents to adopt a lifestyle of voluntary simplicity and reject the dominant social paradigm of industrial society (Kitschelt and Hellemans 1990, chap. 2).

The overlap between the student movement and environmental movement was also important in defining the activists and supporters of environmentalism. The student movement spawned a new generation of young, assertive political activists who provided a leadership cadre and activist core for many of the newly forming environmental groups. Similarly, a large part of the social base for the new wave of environmental action was initially drawn from the young university graduates of the 1960s and 1970s. The children of Europe's postwar economic miracle provided a base for modern environmentalism.

The public discussion of conservation and environmental issues was further stimulated by governmental actions. The Council of Europe declared 1970 the "European Conservation Year" in an effort to stimulate public awareness. Even more important was the convocation of the United Nations Conference on the Human Environment held at Stockholm in 1972. The conference culminated several years of international meetings and environmental studies (Caldwell 1990). The Stockholm Conference assembled officials from 114 nations, scientific experts, and an exceptionally large number of conservationists and environmentalists. It produced specific proposals for governmental action in the form of a United Nations Environment Program (UNEP). The primary accomplishment of the Stockholm Conference, however, was that "it legitimatized environmental policy as a universal concern among nations, and so created a place for environmental issues on many national agendas where they had been previously unrecognized" (Nicholson 1970, 110; also see Caldwell 1990, chap. 3).

Action on environmental issues was also spurred along by new books and television productions on environmental topics. The most influential publication was the Club of Rome's *Limits to Growth* (Meadows et al. 1972), with its dire forecasts for humans and the environment. This, along with the Stockholm meetings, stimulated many public figures to accept finally environmentalism as a significant issue. At the same time, a multitude of other books stimulated public interest with more popular accounts of the problem.

In the years immediately before and after the Stockholm Conference, many European governments initially took up the challenge of addressing the environmental problems of advanced industrial societies. In 1970, Georges Pompidou introduced a host of measures in response to the growing demand for environmental protection in France; the government followed this action with the creation of the Ministry of the Environment in January 1971 (Vadrot 1978, chap. 1). The West German government strengthened its commitment to environmental protection in the wake of the Stockholm Conference; it revised the Basic Law in 1972 to grant the federal government jurisdiction on environmental matters, and then implemented twenty-six major pieces of legislation during the 1972–76 session of parliament—more environmental legislation than was passed in the first two decades of the Federal Republic. The establishment of a Danish ministry for the environment in 1971 was followed by the passage of major new legislation in 1973 (the Act for the Protection of the Environment and the Land and Regional Planning Acts). Environmental policy gained increasing attention from Dutch politicians, especially among political figures on the Left (Tellegen 1981). This official recognition of the environmental issue by a number of European governments further stimulated demands for environmental action.

THE NEW ECOLOGIST MOVEMENT

The synergistic influence of these multiple forces produced a dramatic surge in the environmental movement beginning in the late 1960s and continuing into the 1970s. One of the most significant consequences of this surge was the establishment of organizations that represented a new ecologist consciousness born during the 1960s protest movements. These are the groups that are generally identified with the predictions of New Social Movement theory, because these groups presented a challenge both to the dominant social paradigm of advanced industrial societies and to the established political methods of Western democracies.

At the forefront of this new assault was Friends of the Earth (FoE). David Brower, a renowned American naturalist, established the first FoE organization in San Francisco in 1969. Brower created the new organization after failing to convince the Sierra Club (of which he was an officer) to adopt a more activist strategy on environmental issues, especially nuclear power. Friends of the Earth wanted to address with an assertive political style the new environmental problems of advanced industrial societies and the social structures that gave rise to these problems. Brower spread the news of his new organization on a trip through Europe the following year. Several British environmentalists formed FoE-UK in London in 1970; the success of their early campaigns prompted local FoE groups to spring up independently throughout Britain.[8] French environmentalists established a branch of FoE *(Les Amis de la Terre* [AdlT]) in 1970, drawn from the counterculture forces of the May Revolts. Established politicians on the Left and Right criticized AdlT for politicizing the environmental issue and for its American origins (some critics even suggested that this meant it must have CIA ties); but AdlT rapidly attracted public support. The Dutch affiliate of FoE, the Environmental Defense Association *(Vereniging Milieudefensie* [VMD]), was established in 1972 in reaction to the conventional tactics and moderate

53

goals of the existing Dutch environmental groups. VMD soon became nationally prominent for its actions on nuclear power, recycling, resource management, and other modern environmental issues. FoE groups gradually spread to most other European democracies and many non-Western nations. By the end of the 1970s, FoE International claimed affiliates in over two dozen nations, including the above groups and active FoE organizations in Ireland (formed in 1974), Belgium (1976), Italy (1977), Greece (1978), Sweden (1979), and Switzerland (1980).

Friends of the Earth illustrates a new model of citizen action on environmental issues. FoE politicized environmentalism by discussing issues that government officials and established conservation groups often ignored, such as nuclear power, industrial pollution, and quality of life issues. In debating these topics, moreover, FoE groups frequently challenged the dominant social paradigm of Western industrial democracies: they said that industrial pollution occurred because big business had thwarted control mechanisms, that nuclear power represented the dominance of technocracy and large corporate interests over small-scale renewable forms of energy, and that waste problems arose from indifference to earth's resource limits. Friends of the Earth activists were not just environmentalists, they were social critics. FoE groups also developed a new action repertoire, using tactics that combined confrontation with the authorities and events that would spark the public's interest (Dalton n.d., chap. 8; Lowe and Goyder 1983, chap. 7). The environmental crisis called for immediate action, and FoE existed to stimulate this action.

Greenpeace constitutes another important international network of ecologist groups (Brown and May 1989). The original Greenpeace organization was formed in Canada in the early 1970s as a protest against a planned nuclear test on the Aleutian island of Amchitka. The campaign united both environmentalists (Green) and opponents to nuclear weapons (peace), giving the organization its name. In their next major campaign David McTaggart led Greenpeace's opposition to French nuclear testing in the South Pacific. McTaggart moved to Paris in 1974 to sue the French government for injuries he suffered when French naval personnel tried to expel him from the testing zone, and he created a bridge between Greenpeace activities in North America and Europe. Working from his Paris base and with the support of Friends of the Earth chapters in Europe, McTaggart helped to establish a Greenpeace office in London and Paris in 1977. Greenpeace affiliates then quickly spread across the map of Northern Europe: Holland (1978), Belgium (1979), Luxembourg (1980), Denmark (1980), West Germany (1980), Sweden (1983), Norway, Italy (1986), Spain (1987) and Ireland (1988).

Other national groups advocating this new ecologist orientation emerged during the 1960s and 1970s. In Britain, for example, the

Conservation Society was formed in 1966 (Cotgrove 1982). The society advocated population control and other measures to produce a British society that could sustain itself with available resources; its populist goals were also displayed in a decentralized, antibureaucratic organizational structure. The ecology movement developed an especially rich organizational base in Holland (Tellegen 1981; Jamison et al. 1990). Student activists formed Action Group Straw *(Aktie Strohalm)* in 1970 to focus greater public attention on the social aspects of environmental problems; it now works together with the Foundation for Environmental Education *(Stichting Milieu-educatie* [SME]), which developed educational and public information materials that stress a holistic view of nature and the environmental problem. The Small Earth society *(De Kleine Aarde)* was established in 1972; it maintains that only a change in life-styles can resolve problems such as pollution or energy shortages. The Foundation for Alternative Life *(Stichting Mondiaal Alternatief)* promotes the concept of a sustainable society, where resources and societal needs are brought into balance. German environmentalists developed an extensive network of new groups, often beginning with local citizen action groups *(Bürgerinitiativen)*. In 1971, the Federal Association for Citizen Action Groups for Environmental Protection *(Bundesverband Bürgerinitiativen Umweltschutz* [BBU]) united several hundred of these local groups under its umbrella. The BBU quickly established itself as a representative of the new wave of environmental activists. Other groups such as Robinwood, which was formed in 1982, mount campaigns to draw public attention to environmental problems, and research centers, such as the Öko-Institut, provide a research base for environmental action. In Denmark, an informal weekly colloquium between students and university professors evolved into NOAH, a loosely knit federation of local groups that advocate an ecologist viewpoint on environmental issues (Jamison et al. 1990). In summary, the mobilization wave of the 1960s and 1970s created a new generation of European environmental groups, dedicated to a more ideological and politicized view of environmental policy and willing to use more assertive tactics in support of their cause.

A CONSERVATIONIST EXPANSION

In addition to the creation of new groups, the environmental surge of the 1970s stirred a parallel growth in support for traditional nature conservation organizations. The membership rolls of the RSPB, for example, virtually exploded, increasing from an average of about ten thousand members throughout the 1950s, to thirty thousand by the end of the 1960s, past one hundred thousand in 1971, two hundred thousand in 1975, and now over four hundred thousand members. Membership in Britain's National Trust skyrocketed to nearly one million members by the end of the 1970s. Similarly, the membership rolls of most other major European conservation groups increased dramatically during this decade (the Dutch Association for the Preservation of Natural Monuments boasted over two hundred thousand members and the Danish Association for Nature Conservation included over one hundred thousand members). In France, these forces led to a reorganization of conservation groups under the new structure of the French Federation of Societies for the Protection of Nature *(Féderation Française des Sociétés de Protection de la Nature* [FFSPN]), which consolidated several dozen groups with over half a million members. A variety of new French environmental groups were also founded during this period. Because of the regional nature of Belgian politics, separate environmental federations formed in Flanders, Wallonia, and Brussels in the early 1970s. Membership in the newly established World Wildlife Fund organizations throughout Europe also shot upward. Citizens of various political viewpoints were being mobilized into different sectors of the environmental movement.

This mobilization period also helped to institutionalize the environmental movement in Mediterranean Europe (Diani 1990). In Italy, the Fund for the Italian Environment *(Fondo per l'Ambiente Italiano)* was established in 1975 following the model of the British National Trust. Its efforts to protect Italy's cultural heritage reinforce the activities of *Italia Nostra* and *Pro Natura.* The ecologist wing of the movement is represented by the League for the Environment *(Lega per l'Ambiente—Arci),* the Italian branch of the Friends of the Earth, and the League for the Abolition of Hunting *(Lega per l'Abolizione Caccia)* (also see Diani and Lodi 1988). The major Greek conservation organization, the Hellenic Society for the Protection of Nature (HSPN), was joined in the 1970s by several other environmental groups and research institutes.

RETRENCHMENT AND RESURGENCE

After the surge in environmental action during the late 1960s and early 1970s, government efforts on behalf of environmental protection began to wane in the late 1970s. A worldwide recession shifted the attention of political elites toward mounting economic problems, and many government officials and representatives of the established political parties saw environmental protection as a potential brake on economic recovery. Indeed, some environmentalists challenged the belief in economic growth as the driving force of social progress, a belief that is shared by traditional economic interest groups and political parties of the Left and Right. When environmentalists opposed a nuclear energy plant, for example, they often faced a united front of business leaders, union officials, and their party allies. The French government committed itself to a nuclear power program as the basis of national energy independence (Nelkin and Pollack 1981); a pragmatic West German government headed by Helmut Schmidt lacked enthusiasm for environmental reform and allowed environmental legislation to stagnate. In some cases, government ambiguity on environmental policy seemingly turned to enmity. The Thatcher government elected in 1979 was openly hostile to most environmental initiatives; conservative Dutch governments in the 1980s repeated this pattern of environmental retrenchment. In 1985, agents of the French government bombed a Greenpeace ship in New Zealand, killing one crew member and illustrating the failure of government in the worst possible terms. The Greenpeace bombing was an extreme case of government overreaction, but European governments and the established political parties generally became unresponsive to the environmental movement as a consequence of renewed economic problems and mounting opposition from traditional economic interest groups.

The general withdrawal of support for environmental reform by governments and political parties was widely interpreted at the time as a sign of the passing of the environmental movement, but this has clearly not occurred. The mobilization wave of the preceding decade created an infrastructure of environmental groups that continued to draw attention to these issues and press for environmental action. The popular concerns that initially gave rise to these groups were not erased by economic recession; in fact, the debate over measures to stimulate economic growth often sensitized the public to the costs of economic development. Moreover, when governments were unwilling to deal with environmental issues, the assertive style of environmental groups kept these issues before the public. Similarly, when the leadership of the established parties ignored the environmental issue, small minor parties catered to the environmental constituency or new Green parties formed (see chapter 4 in this volume; Müller-Rommel, 1989). As these Green parties won representation to the national legislature, first in Belgium and West Germany, they had another political forum for the environmental movement.

The efforts of established political leaders to downplay or discount the claims of environmentalists were also undercut by a continuing stream of environmental crises. In July 1976, a chemical plant in Seveso, Italy, exploded, exposing thousands to cancer-causing dioxins. The supertanker *Amoco Cadiz* broke in half off the coast of Brittany in March 1978, spewing 68 million gallons of oil into the sea. Thousands of seabirds were killed and other aquatic life was severely damaged by the oil spill. It took several years for the environment of the Brittany coast to return to normal. The accident at Three Mile Island in 1979 created substantial public doubts about nuclear reactors in those European nations that were pressing forward with nuclear power as a method of energy independence (see, e.g., Nelkin and Pollack 1981; Hatch 1986). One could travel to the Alps, the Black Forest, or Scandinavia in the early 1980s and see how acid rain was causing the death of the forests. In 1986, a chemical spill at a Swiss industrial firm killed millions of fish in the Rhine River and threatened local drinking water supplies from Switzerland to Holland. In addition, local development projects (such as the Rhine-Danube Canal and proposed airport expansions) or past errors (e.g., hidden toxic waste dumps) stimulated continuing environmental action at the local level throughout Europe. This seemingly unending stream of events in the media kept the public aware of Europe's persisting environmental problems so that environmentalism did not slip from the political agenda.

The Chernobyl nuclear disaster in 1986 may be the event which finally changed the course of contemporary European politics on environmental issues. When the fallout spread to West Europe, government agencies in West Germany told parents to keep their children indoors and to avoid certain foods; border guards throughout Europe checked shipments of agricultural produce with Geiger counters; and even the reindeer herders in Lapland could not eat venison because of the excessive radioactivity levels. Scientists estimated that anywhere between a few thousand and tens of thousands of Europeans will eventually die from cancers produced by Chernobyl radiation. Chernobyl thus created widespread public recognition that acid rain, dying forests, a deci- mated ozone layer, and nuclear fallout are threats comparable to the economic problems facing advanced industrial societies. Moreover, these environmental problems pose threats that cannot be avoided by individuals because of a privi- leged social position or geographic location. In short, Chernobyl and its by- products convinced many Europeans that the environmentalists' claims were not mere political rhetoric, and this forced political leaders to respond to pub- lic demands for environmental reform (Dalton n.d., chap. 3).

Over the last few years, Western governments have displayed a renewed awareness of the environmental issue. The commission of the European Community declared 1986–87 the European Year of the Environment, and the Single Europe Act of 1987 modified the Treaty of Rome to grant the Community new legislative authority on environmental issues. Individual national governments also became visibly active on environmental matters (see chapter 9). The Kohl government in Germany instituted new measures to protect environmental quality and pressed the Community to adopt poli- cies aimed at reducing acid rain. The Greek government finally took strong measures to address Athens's extreme smog problems, passing legislation to limit automobile traffic in the city center. Even the Conservative government in Britain gradually responded to the pressure for environmental reform, and in late 1988 Margaret Thatcher declared herself a born-again environmentalist (repeating a conversion that George Bush had undergone a few months earlier during the American presidential elections). Green parties posted broad advances in the 1989 European Parliament election, winning more than 10 percent of the vote in Britain, Germany, France, and Belgium; the rainbow coalition within the new parliament includes deputies from ten nations. Western leaders toasted their newly found environmentalism by transforming the 1989 Paris Economic Summit into an "Environmental Summit" *(Economist,* 15 July 1989).

It is likely that the ebb and flow of environmentalism will continue during the 1990s, as Western democracies confront these problems and political conditions change. Solutions will be difficult, and so attention to environmental issues will not be sufficient to ensure their resolution. In other words, the issues which stimulated the contemporary environmental movement will be difficult to resolve, and they are therefore likely to remain potential sources of social and political conflict for a substantial period of time. Equally important, the successful institutionalization of the movement, in its various forms, provides the basis for the continuation of environmentalism as a force in European politics.

TWO SHADES OF GREEN

We have shown that the history of environmentalism includes two distinct waves of environmental mobilization. The first wave at the turn of the century focused public attention and organizational efforts on issues of wildlife protection and preservation of a nation's cultural and natural treasures. The second wave of the 1960s and 1970s addressed the new environmental problems and quality of life concerns of advanced industrial societies.

In broad terms, these two waves of environmental mobilization have much in common. The characteristics of both mobilization waves suggest that an unusual combination of social ferment and political events might be required to first create new political organizations (see, e.g., Tarrow 1983). Changes in social conditions, and more importantly the social climate (Zeitgeist), were important contributors to both mobilization waves. In addition, there were institutions and individual entrepreneurs who could mobilize this potential for political action. The convergence of these factors at two periods enabled the environmental movement to overcome the hurdles facing any prospective organization, and develop an institutional infrastructure for the movement.

The two mobilization periods also share similarities in their consequences. Both waves, truly international in scope and representing reform,
washed across Europe and North America, diffusing new issue interests and
new interest groups across national borders. Both waves spawned groups concerned with similar collective goods: the protection of nature, preservation of
fauna and flora, and improving the quality of life. Environmental groups of
all colors share a common bond when compared to economic interest groups
(such as unions and business associations) or other public interest lobbies.
The political interests of different environmental groups routinely overlap,
even if they begin from separate starting points. Bird protection groups, for
example, now realize that the destruction of habitats by industrial pollution
should be a concern of their members, just as modern environmental groups
structure their campaigns to tap widespread public support for nature conservation issues. Formal and informal patterns of cooperation interrelate a broad
range of different groups. The available evidence also suggests a substantial
overlap in their membership and funding bases (Dalton n.d.; Lowe and
Goyder 1983; Diani 1990). At one level, it does make sense to talk of a single
environmental movement, especially if we want to be inclusive in studying
the sources and forms of environmental action.

At the same time, the two waves of environmental mobilization should
not be treated as two examples of an identical phenomenon, separated only
by several decades. Each wave produced a different orientation toward what
environmentalism entails, and how it relates to the prevailing social norms of
Western industrial democracies. The crucial starting point for these differences, we will argue, lies in the "ideology" or "collective identity" of each
wave of the environmental movement.

The first mobilization wave emphasized a shade of environmentalism
that we will call a *conservation orientation*. At this stage, environmentalism
meant a concern with the perpetuation of species, the protection of habitats,
and the preservation of a nation's heritage represented by its cultural monuments and environment. Just as a philatelist might save a rare stamp for his
or her collection, conservationists wanted to save fauna, flora, and cultural
sites for themselves and others to enjoy.

In addressing these interests, conservationists generally accept the existing
sociopolitical order and accept the norms of this social system.
Conservationists are pursuing *consensual social goals* within the existing socioeconomic structure; it merely requires that an organization bring attention to
an unrecognized need that society already supports. In a similar classification
of environmental groups, Philip Lowe and Jane Goyder (1983, 35) refer to
conservationists as "emphasis groups . . . whose aims do not conflict in any
clear-cut way with widely held social goals or values but which are motivated

by a belief in the importance of certain values and the need for vigilance on their behalf."

The various bird societies, wildlife protection, and cultural preservation groups formed during the first mobilization wave generally reflect a conservationist perspective. The conservation movement was also supplemented by new groups which formed during the second mobilization wave—such as WWF, DNR and FFSPN—and which broadened public support for conservation issues. Few would question the labeling of bird protection organizations as conservation groups, even if some members and activists in these groups do critique the prevailing social order for the destruction of habitats and feeding grounds for birds. Similarly, when an organization labels itself as a "royal society" there can be little doubt about its acceptance of the prevailing social order.

The second mobilization wave created a new ecologist orientation that differs from conservationism in its issue interests and fundamental political ideology.[9] New organizations formed in the 1970s and 1980s, such as Friends of the Earth and Greenpeace, focus public attention on issues such as nuclear power, industrial pollution, acid rain, carcinogens, and the other new environmental problems of advanced industrial societies. These issue interests reflect a more basic critique of the values of the prevailing social order of advanced industrial democracies. Ecologists are attempting to develop a new societal model—what is called a New Environmental Paradigm (Dunlap and van Liere 1978; Milbrath 1984, chap. 2). This ecologist orientation represents an eclectic humanist philosophy rather than a rigid ideological framework. Instead of stressing (or even accepting) the accumulation of wealth and unrestrained economic growth as societal goals, ecologists advocate an economy in harmony with nature and the personal needs of its citizens. The writings of E. F. Schumacher (1973) often provide a beginning reference point. The materialism and excess consumerism of modern societies are roundly criticized as causes of resource shortages and sources of pollution. Ecologists advocate a sustainable society, in which consumption patterns are balanced against the world's natural productive capacity (Manes 1990; Brown 1981; Milbrath 1989; Porritt 1984). These sentiments imply a restructuring of the economic system of Western industrial societies, substituting for the domination of the environment a nature-friendly economic order.

The alternative social paradigm of ecologists also emphasizes the value of the individual and the need for a more humane social order. Modern societies are highly structured and bureaucratized *(Gesellchaft* model), and ecologists advocate a pattern of social relations that harks back to small-scale communal life *(Gemeinschaft* model). The acceptance of status differences in

61

the dominant social paradigm is replaced by a sense of egalitarianism and the importance of individuals. This pattern of social relations allows a sense of collective identity to coexist with a tolerance of individual life-style choices. A stress on participation and self-direction is another trait identified with ecologist groups. Drawing on the traditions of Kropotkin and Thoreau, the new environmental paradigm contends that personal fulfillment and self-expression should be maximized. Individuals must control society, rather than society controlling the individual. Thus nuclear power is criticized not just for its environmental consequences, but also because it signifies the domination of industry and technology over the individual. This orientation leads ecologists to advocate changes in the political structure of Western democracies, leading to a more open political system, a greater opportunity for citizen input, and a more consensual style of decision making.

In short, ecologists do not see current environmental problems as an aberration of the socioeconomic order but as a direct consequence of this social system. The solution of environmental problems would therefore require changes in this order. Instead of merely trying to preserve parts of the natural world, as is the conservationist goal, ecologists question the economic and social structures that are seen as the sources of contemporary environmental problems.

ENVIRONMENTAL IDEOLOGIES AND POLITICAL ACTION

The dichotomy between conservationists and ecologists is useful in describing the historical evolution of the environmental movement and for categorizing the various elements of the environmental movement. This framework is even more important, however, in providing a basis for explaining the behavior of environmental groups and their potential impact on contemporary politics. The ecologists' commitment to an alternative social paradigm should lead them to adopt a range of organizational and political behaviors that distinguish them from conservation groups—even though both share a broad concern for environmental reform. Elsewhere (Dalton n.d.), we have argued that this ideological divide structures the political orientations and political actions of environmental groups.

The process of resource mobilization provides some of the clearest evidence of how a group's environmental identity is reflected in its actions. Virtually all environmental interest groups recognize the need to mobilize resources to support the organization and its goals, but resource mobilization is not a value-free process. Because conservation groups, such as Britain's National Trust or Holland's *Natuurmonumenten,* emphasize issues and values that are widely shared by most Europeans, these groups are able to generate larger memberships, larger budgets, and larger staffs. More important, conservation groups are able to go where the money is and draw significant support from parts of the political establishment: government agencies, businesses, and foundations. In contrast, the challenging political orientation of ecologist groups, such as Greenpeace or FoE, means that they often must find their support outside the political establishment; membership fees, the sale of group materials, and individual gifts thus rank more prominently among ecologists' source of funds. These different sources of funding lead, we would argue, to different strategies of political action and different capabilities for action.

The role of ideology in creating the context for political action is further seen in how groups perceive the world of environmental politics. There is clear evidence that a conservationist/ecologist orientation frames a group's definition of what environmental issues are of greatest importance, what actions are necessary to address these issues, and what factors stand in the way of environmental reform (Dalton n.d.). Moreover, a group's ideological orientations influence its evaluations of potential allies and opponents in the policy process (Dalton 1991). For example, European environmental groups are generally critical of the environmental records of most political actors, but ecologist groups are significantly more critical of establishment institutions, such as the office of prime minister, business interests, or conservative political parties. They are also more positive toward Green/New Left parties.

Thus even if an environmental interest group pragmatically pursues its goals as social movement theory suggests, its actions are conditioned by judgments about what issues are important and how these goals may be achieved—and these, in turn, are influenced by the environmental orientations of the group. In creating these perceptions of the political world, whether they are accurate or not, ideology defines the context for environmental action. Moreover, often more than mere perceptions are involved. The views of conservation groups and ecologist groups reflect the real potential for political cooperation that exists for groups holding certain goals and political orientations. Ecologists do not just perceive that businesses are generally opposed to their goals; business interests *are* opposed. Thus, ideology can structure the choices facing a social movement organization.

The influence of environmental orientations cumulates in the political activities of environmental interest groups. The choice of action strategies is influenced by the goals, resources, and opportunities facing an environmental group. These contextual factors are partially defined by the conservationist/ecologist orientation of a group. In addition, a group's environmental orientation has a strong and independent impact on the choice of

63

action strategies. Because of its own identity and its closer ties with the political establishment, a group like the RSPB is more likely to engage in conventional political activities such as sitting on government commissions, meeting with government ministers, and meeting with members of Parliament. Conversely, a group like FoE might also engage in these conventional activities, but to a more limited extent. Ecologist groups balance these conventional activities with an almost equal level of unconventional political action: protests, spectacular actions, public demonstrations, and the like. The identity of ecologist groups such as NOAH or Greenpeace is linked to their status as challengers to the political establishment, and the best way to illustrate that identity is through protest activities. Thus even if a conservationist group and an ecologist group are interested in the same issue and have access to similar resources, their differing environmental orientations will lead them toward different action strategies.

This diversity among environmental groups is, we would argue, a common characteristic of citizen action groups in contemporary democracies; it can be seen with women's groups, self-help groups, and other public interest lobbies. It reflects the ideological differences between conservation and ecologist groups, the range of issues which touch environmental themes, and the pragmatic needs for rival public interest groups to establish their own political identities. We see this diversity as a source of the movement's basic strength and vitality. The diversity of environmental groups enables the movement to expand its resource base and membership base. A 1985 estimate held that more than ten million Europeans belonged to one or more of the national environmental groups discussed in this chapter, and two to three times as many may be active in local environmental action groups. Similarly, a diverse repertoire of action provides the movement with many options in challenging the political establishment. The different ideological views underlying this diversity press the government for policy reform on several fronts. To government policymakers, the environmental movement must appear as a many-headed Hydra, pressing for environmental reform from all sides. Consequently, the spreading network of environmental legislation at the national and European level adds credence to claims that the 1990s will be the environmental decade.

NOTES

1. This research was supported by a grant from the National Science Foundation (SES 85–10989). Portions of this chapter are drawn from a forthcoming larger study (cited as "Dalton n.d.") of environmental interest groups in Western

Europe. I would like to thank Yale University Press for allowing me to publish materials from this study.

2. Almost every nation stakes some claim to being at the vanguard of the environmental movement. English authors note that Henry VIII passed a law to protect "wilde fowle" in 1534; French environmentalism began with water quality legislation in 1669; and the Germans claim that early legislation protecting the continental forests stimulated the industrial revolution by necessitating the development of iron and steel as building products. Others such as Nicholson (1970, chap. 6) and Boardman (1981, chap. 1) trace the environmental movement back to the ancient Egyptians and Greeks.

3. The signatories were: Switzerland, Germany, Austria-Hungary, Belgium, Spain, France, Greece, Luxembourg, Monaco, Portugal, and Sweden. Absent from the signatories, though they participated in the conferences, were Great Britain, The Netherlands, Italy, Russia, and Norway. See Hayden (1942, chap. 2) for additional details.

4. Similar forces existed on the other side of the Atlantic. The American Audubon Society was founded in 1886, the Sierra Club in 1892, and the Boone and Crockett Club was established as a nature conservation lobby in 1887 (see Hayden 1942; Petulla 1988).

5. The organization has evolved over the years, shifting from a concern with wildlife in British colonial holdings to nature conservation issues in Britain. Instead of protecting the African big-game animals, its recent campaigns have aimed at protecting British hedgehogs, toads and bats. It is now known as the Fauna and Flora Preservation Society (FFPS).

6. The one exception to this pattern is Germany, where the "coordination" policies of the Third Reich led to the outlawing of the German Federation for the Protection of the Homeland and the Nature Protection Ring in 1933. They were replaced by the National Socialist organization entitled People's Federation of Nature Protection (*Volksbund Naturschutz*); see Wey (1982, 138).

7. The organization was originally called the International Union for the Protection of Nature, but its name changed in the 1950s to reflect a broadening of its concerns to conservation of natural resources and other environmental issues.

8. Since the FoE label was the licensed company name of the national office, this led at first to an awkward relationship with autonomous local groups using the FoE name. The national office resolved this situation by offering a "franchise" to local FoE organizers for a nominal fee. The present organizational structure of FoE-UK reflects the legacy of the dual national/local base (Wilson 1984; Lowe and Goyder 1983).

9. The central distinction between conservation and ecologist orientations represents an ideological cleavage within the environmental movement that is widely observed. Stephen Cotgrove (1982) similarly emphasizes the distinction between conservationists and "new environmentalists" in his research on British environmental groups. Lester Milbrath's (1984) study of environmental groups in three nations uses the classification of "nature conservation" and "environmental reformer" groups. Dieter Rucht (1989) classifies German and French environmental groups as either

representing a "nature conservation" or a "political ecologist" orientation; Vadrot (1978) uses a conceptually similar classification of French groups as *syndicalistes* or *libertaires.* Diani and Lodi (1988) distinguish between the "conservationist," "environmentalist," and "political ecology" currents of the Italian environmental movement (also see Diani 1990).

REFERENCES

Boardman, Robert. 1981. *International organization and the conservation of nature.* Bloomington: Indiana University Press.

Brand, Karl-Werner, Dieter Rucht, and Detlef Busser. 1986. *Aufbruch in eine andere Gesellschaft: Neue soziale Bewegungen in der Bundesrepublik.* Revised ed. New York: Campus Verlag.

Brown, Lester. 1981. *A sustainable society.* New York: Norton.

Brown, Michael, and John May. 1989. *The Greenpeace story.* Scarborough, Ont.: Prentice-Hall Canada.

Caldwell, Lynton. 1990. *International environmental policy: Emergence and dimensions.* 2d ed. Durham, N.C.: Duke University Press.

Carson, Rachel. 1962. *The silent spring.* Boston: Houghton Mifflin.

Chafer, Tony. 1982. The anti-nuclear movement and the rise of political ecology. In Philip Cerny, ed., *Social movements and protest in France.* London: Pinter.

Cotgrove, Stephan. 1982. *Catastrophe or cornucopia: The environment, politics and the future.* New York: Wiley.

Dalton, Russell. 1991. Alliance patterns of the European environmental movement. In Wolfgang Rüdig, ed., *Green politics II.* Edinburgh: University of Edinburgh Press.

————. n.d. *The green rainbow: Environmental groups in Western Europe.* Yale University Press. Forthcoming.

Dalton, Russell, and Manfred Kuechler, eds. 1990. *Challenging the political order.* New York: Oxford University Press; Cambridge: Polity Press.

Diani, Mario. 1990. The Italian ecology movement: From radicalism to moderation. In Wolfgang Rüdig, ed., *Green politics I.* Edinburgh: University of Edinburgh Press.

Diani, Mario, and Giovanni Lodi. 1988. Three in one: Currents in the Milan ecology movement. In Bert Klandermans, Peter Kriesi, and Sidney Tarrow, eds. *From structure to action.* Greenwich, Conn.: JAI Press.

Doughty, Robin. 1975. *Feather fashions and bird protection: A study in nature conservation.* Berkeley: University of California Press.

Duclos, D., and J. Smadja. 1985. Culture and the environment in France. *Environmental Management* 9:135–40.

Dunlap, Robert, and K. Van Liere. 1977. The new environmental paradigm. *Journal of Environmental Education* 9:10–19.

Fitter, Richard, and Sir Peter Scott. 1978. *The penitent butchers.* London: The Fauna Preservation Society.

Hatch, Michael. 1986. *Politics and nuclear power: Energy policy in Western Europe.* Lexington: University of Kentucky Press.

Hayden, Sherman. 1942. *The international protection of wildlife.* New York: Columbia University Press.

Jamison, Andrew, Ron Eyerman, Jacqueline Cramer, and Jeppé Laessøe. 1990. *The making of the new environmental consciousness: A comparative study of environmental movements in Sweden, Denmark and The Netherlands.* Edinburgh: University of Edinburgh Press.

Kitschelt, Herbert. 1989. *The logics of party formation.* Ithaca, N.Y.: Cornell University Press.

Kitschelt, Herbert, and Staf Hellemans. 1990. *Beyond the European Left.* Durham, N.C.: Duke University Press.

Linse, Ulrich. 1983. *Zurück o Mensche zur Mutter Erde: Landkommunen in Deutschland 1890–1933.* Munich.

Lowe, Philip. 1983. Values and institutions in the history of British nature conservation. In A. Warren and F. Goldsmith, eds., *Conservation in perspective.* New York: Wiley.

Lowe, Philip, and Jane Goyder. 1983. *Environmental groups in politics.* London: Allen and Unwin.

Manes, Christopher. 1990. *Green rage: Radical environmentalism and the unmaking of civilization.* Boston: Little, Brown.

Milbrath, Lester. 1984. *Environmentalists: Vanguard for a new society.* Albany: SUNY Press.

————. 1989. *Envisioning a sustainable society.* Albany: SUNY Press.

Müller-Rommel, Ferdinand, ed. 1989. *New politics in Western Europe: The rise and success of Green parties and alternative lists.* Boulder, Colo.: Westview Press.

Nelkin, Dorothy, and Michael Pollack. 1981. *The atom besieged.* Cambridge: MIT Press.

Nicholson, Max. 1970. *The environmental revolution: A guide for the new masters of the world.* New York: McGraw-Hill.

Nisbit, Robert. 1982. *Prejudices: A philosophical dictionary.* Cambridge: Harvard University Press.

Petulla, Joseph. 1988. *American environmental history.* Indianapolis: Bobbs-Merrill.

Porritt, Jonathan. 1984. *Seeing green: The politics of ecology explained.* London: Basil Blackwell.

Rucht, Dieter. 1989. Environmental movement organizations in West Germany and France. In B. Klandermans, ed., *Organizing for change.* Greenwich, Conn.: JAI Press.

Schumacher, E.F. 1973. *Small is beautiful.* New York: Harper & Row.

Russell J. Dalton

Sheail, John. 1976. *Nature in trust: The history of nature conservation in Britain.* London: Blackie.

Sieferle, Rold. 1984. *Forschrittsfeinde? Opposition gegen Technik und Industrie von Romantik bis zur Gegenwart.* Munich: Beck.

Tarrow, Sidney. 1983. *Struggling to reform.* Western Societies paper no. 15. Ithaca, N.Y.: Cornell University Press.

Tellegen, Egbert. 1981. The environmental movement in the Netherlands. In T. O'Riordan and R. Turner, eds. *Progress in resource management and environmental planning.* New York: Wiley.

Tellegen, Egbert. 1983. *Milieubeweging.* Utrecht: Aula.

Thomas, Keith. 1983. *Man and the natural world.* London: Allen Lane.

Vadrot, C. 1978. *L'ecologie: Histoire d'une subversion.* Paris: Syros.

Weiner, Martin. 1981. *English culture and the decline of the industrial spirit, 1850–1980.* Cambridge: Cambridge University Press.

Wey, Klaus. 1982. *Umweltpolitik in Deutschland: Kurze Geschichte des Umweltschutzes in Deutschland seit 1900.* Opladen: Westdeutscher Verlag.

Wilson, Des, ed. 1984. *The environmental crisis: A handbook for all friends of the earth.* London: Heinemann.

3 Grass-Roots Resistance: The Emergence of Popular Environmental Movements in Less Affluent Countries

BRON TAYLOR
HEIDI HADSELL
LOIS LORENTZEN
RIK SCARCE

The emergence and proliferation of grass-roots environmental groups in the developing world has been a striking feature of the past two decades. Although there are differences in the social contexts and characteristics of these movements, it is possible to discern commonalities in the social contexts from which they have emerged, similar characteristics in these movements themselves, and patterns to the resulting social conflicts. Our goal is to examine a number of grass-roots environmental movements in less affluent countries on several continents, and to articulate common patterns we have found in the emergence of these movements. No claim is made that these generalizations apply to all grass-roots, "popular environmental" movements—partly because most of them are relatively new and have received little or no scholarly attention.[1] Rather, we offer our observations and analysis hoping to encourage further research into the objectives, impacts, and future prospects of such movements.

TRENDS AND TENDENCIES IN POPULAR ENVIRONMENTAL MOVEMENTS

Few environmental movements in less affluent countries have their primary origins in ecological concerns or focus exclusively on environmental issues. Most commonly, such groups have their genesis in the survival efforts of persons and communities living at the margins of existence, especially peasants and indigenous peoples in rural areas. Popular grass-roots environmental movements often begin with efforts promoting community development, literacy, and political empowerment. But it is the battles over who owns and/or controls the use of land that are the most characteristic of the emerging popular environmental movements.

Such battles take one of two forms: struggles to overturn current owner-ship patterns and to reform current land uses, or efforts to preserve tradition-al land ownership and use patterns against the encroachment of the industrialized world. The crucial issue is land reform or land defense. Struggles over land shape popular movements into environmental move-ments, because generally speaking the land-use plans of poor people living in the specific sites of their activism are more ecologically sustainable than the more centralized ownership and mechanized land-use patterns they are try-ing to overturn or prevent. In rural areas, the (usually accurate) perception within popular environmental movements is that the land is being exploited for and by outsiders—either multinational commercial interests or, more commonly, commercial elites within the nation in question—interested in quick profits and not the ecologically sustainable use of land.

Much of the commercial enterprise carried out or planned in rural areas displaces long-term inhabitants, or at least threatens to do so. Thus, the fear of displacement is another source of popular environmental resistance. Another form of displacement, and just as pernicious, is the division of fami-lies when fathers and sons leave to seek employment in urban centers (or other countries) after their traditional livelihoods are destroyed by changing land-use patterns.

Displacement fears aside, commercial development threatens traditional ways of life and means of subsistence. The process usually begins with road building, followed by logging, mining, and industrialized agriculture (ranch-ing and farming). The usual result is the increasingly centralized ownership of land by outsiders. Such threats contribute to the proliferation of grass-roots popular movements stressing self-reliance, resistance to outside com-mercial interests, and often the pursuance of ecologically sustainable practices as central goals.

Popular environmental groups in less affluent nations are, generally speaking, radical in their genesis, or tend to become increasingly radical through the experience of social struggle. By radical we mean one or more of three things. First, these movements often threaten private ownership of property; they seek either to prevent private ownership of commonly used lands, or to overturn current private land ownership patterns. Some are self-consciously socialist in orientation. Second, these movements increasingly critique industrial development and mechanized agriculture, thereby placing themselves in opposition to elites who usually hope to emulate the more technologically advanced societies. Movements influenced by such a critique seek to prevent or overturn Western-style, mechanized forms of develop-ment.[2] Third, radicalism is also found in the increasingly militant tactics that many of these groups employ, including illegal actions, from civil disobedience to sabotage (sometimes called "ecotage" or "monkeywrenching" when the purpose of the sabotage is to protect the natural world). Such militancy has even, occasionally, involved homicide, justified as self-defense.

Not surprisingly, this radicalism is often met by violence—sometimes governmental, often private, and seldom prosecuted. Such reactionary violence far outpaces in scope and brutality the more occasional, poorly armed, and usually defensive violence of those involved in popular environmental movements. The efforts of most popular environmental groups to institute land reform (and/or to keep possession of ancestral lands) goes a long way toward explaining the brutality of the violent response.

Obviously, the above patterns suggest that popular environmental movements operate under difficult circumstances. It is important to note, therefore, two key forces driving and buttressing these movements. First, women play important and often decisive roles. This is remarkable given the traditional subjugation of women in most of these countries. Various observers have even concluded that some of these movements are essentially women's movements. Second, increasingly these movements articulate moral rationales beyond self-interest for their activism. Such rationales are often based on religious sentiments, and thus religion is frequently central for those involved. This is often overlooked. Moreover, these movements usually rely exclusively on nonviolent tactics, for either pragmatic and/or moral and spiritual reasons.

Survival, on the one hand, and the prospects for the success of these movements, on the other, are greatly enhanced through the strategic building of coalitions. Often, previously antagonistic local groups are brought together in a common cause against the perceived "outside" interests; just as importantly, solidarity is sought from international environmental groups which help apply political pressure on national governments.

These movements have had successes, usually small-scale, but sometimes shaking the corridors of power in the international business, finance and political sectors. Some groups, for example, have formed coalitions with environmental activists in more affluent countries and have secured changes in the lending practices of certain international lending agencies.

Yet despite the proliferation of such groups and their notable successes, the ecological and social context that gave rise to them remains so grave, the economic interests so intransigent, and the need for a comprehensive restructuring of political, social, economic and ecological relations so fundamental, that it appears naïve to anticipate enduring successes, or even to hope for the long-term survival of the peoples, and the places, at stake in these struggles.

The following analysis of popular environmental movements around the world will illustrate the preceding characterizations. Among the best-known and globally influential are those originating in India.

SARVODAYA MOVEMENTS IN INDIA AND SRI LANKA

With empty water pots, women gathered in Tehri, India, on World Environment Day in 1979, protesting water scarcity and the failure of water supply projects. "We have come to tell you that nature is the primary source of water, and we are the providers for our families. Unless the mountains are clothed with forests, the springs will not come alive," they declared (Shiva 1988, 211). Peasants gathered to protest the damming of the Ganga and Narmada, sacred rivers whose shores and river valleys were home to thousands. If completed as they were planned, the dams would have displaced more than one million people, mostly peasants and tribals (Kendell and Buivids 1987, 153–54). Peasant women in the hills of Garhwal refused to sell milk from their cows, protesting social conditions which made milk a market commodity while local children went hungry. In 1987 rural women, with some men and their children, blockaded mining operations destroying forests and streams in the Doon Valley. The blockade continued even after they were beaten by two hundred men hired by the quarry contractor (Shiva 1988, 209). All were manifestations of a movement known as Chipko Andolan—literally the "hugging-the-trees-movement." Chipko is based, Vandana Shiva writes, on the realization that "the right to food today is inextricably linked to the right of nature to conserve her ability to produce food sustainably" (1988, 178).

This movement is often and properly described as a self-help, survival-oriented, environmentally conscious movement. But such a description can oversimplify the motivations of its people. Understanding this movement first requires some understanding of Mahatma Gandhi's philosophy of conflict; and second, an understanding of how the major religions originating in India—Hinduism, Jainism, and Buddhism—can promote intraspecies compassion. These religions provide fertile ground for viewing all life as intrinsically valuable, regardless of its usefulness to human beings. Such moral sentiments and environmental ethics are now called "deep ecology" (especially in the West). The term was coined by the Norwegian eco-philosopher Arne Naess, and is juxtaposed with "shallow" environmental ethics that ground ecological concern exclusively on human needs and desires.

We cannot here describe in detail the mythic, religious resources for environmental ethics embedded in these traditions.[3] A couple of examples must suffice to provide a "feeling" for the Indian worldview and the deep ecological ethics which can be derived from it. Beginning with the *Jataka*

Tales, which were later recast by Buddhism into more philosophical form in The Diamond Sutra (Schelling 1991, 10–12), we can find a basis for a "deep ecological" concern for the natural world. These tales register what one Buddhist scholar calls "the first written literature [promoting] cross-species compassion" and a sense of "kinship that sweeps across animal species" (Schelling 1991, 11). For example, in one well-known tale, the Buddha, in an early incarnation, compassionately sacrifices himself as food for a hungry tigress about to eat one of her cubs (Schelling 1991, 10–11).

Probably more important is the image of the "Jewel Net of Indra." This myth expresses a cosmology generally shared by the religions originating in India—a cosmology that surely informs the religious sentiments of the more spiritually inclined Chipko activists. Francis Cook aptly describes this myth-metaphor:

> Far away in the heavenly abode of the great god Indra, there is a wonderful net which has been hung by some cunning artificer in such a manner that it stretches out infinitely in all directions. In accordance with the extravagant tastes of the deities, the artificer has hung a single glittering jewel in each "eye" of the net, and since the net itself is infinite in dimension, the jewels are infinite in number. There hang the jewels, glittering like stars. . . . If we now arbitrarily select one of these jewels for inspection and look closely at it, we will discover that in its polished surface there are reflected *all* the other jewels in the net. . . . Not only that, but each of the jewels reflected in this one jewel is also reflecting all the other jewels, so that there is an infinite reflecting process occurring. [This image] symbolizes a cosmos in which there is an infinitely repeated interrelationship among all the members of the cosmos. This relationship is said to be one of simultaneous *mutual identity* and *mutual intercausality*. (Callicott 1989, 214)

Such cosmology, along with the *Jataka Tales,* tends to enhance feelings of kinship with everything else in the universe, and thus provides a basis for deep ecological moral sentiments and activism. Such myths provide moral rationales beyond survival or self-interest for Chipko-style activism, and thereby may buttress the courage and determination of at least some of the Chipko activists. To the extent that people believe they are acting in harmony with the structure of a divine universe, they will be strengthened in their struggle.[4]

Mahatma Gandhi (1869–1948), best known for pioneering nonviolent tactics that were eventually successful in overturning British colonial rule in India, seemed to combine such typically Indian religious sentiments (often expressed in the ideal of *ahimsa,* meaning "no harm" or "no wanton killing") with the conviction that through social struggle truth will eventually emerge,

73

as long as at least one party to the struggle remains committed to the truth as such and seeks to align herself with it (Bondurant 1965). Gandhi and the independence struggle inspired many of the "Sarvodaya" self-help workers who, after independence, established cooperative, self-help groups in rural communities. It was as a direct result of the leadership of such Gandhian workers, and in some cases directly out of cooperatives they established, that the Chipko movement emerged (Shiva 1988, 68–77).

"Sarvodaya" can be rendered differently. Berreman renders it "building a just society" (1989, 246). A. T. Ariyaratne, who in the late 1950s founded the Sarvodaya Shramadana Movement (another self-help and development movement, but in Sri Lanka), writes that Sarvodaya "signifies the awakening or liberation of one and all, without exception" and then adds the common Sarvodayan slogan, "May all beings be well and happy" (Macy 1983, 13, cf. 12; cf. Ingram 1990, 123–39). As with Chipko, this movement "in formulating its philosophy and goals . . . took inspiration from the Gandhians, as the name it adopted attests" (Macy 1983, 29). Religion provides the Sarvodaya Shramadana Movement with one—if not the—central resource and moral basis for its goals and tactics (Macy 1983). As with Chipko, the liberation goal is inclusive of nonhuman life, and thus is deep-ecological in orientation.

Finally, the people of India, with their ancient religious roots and diverse tribal religions, often view specific creatures or places as sacred. Thus, when peasants and tribals protest the damming of the sacred rivers Ganga and Narmada, they believe they are defending sacred values. Some Chipko activists hug trees to protect Aranyanik, goddess of the forest. Western observers of non-Western environmental movements often fail to appreciate the site-specific nature of the spirituality of many groups, and thus miss altogether how the defense of such places is a religious-moral duty.[5]

With these impressions in mind regarding the religious sentiments common in India, and the inspirational role of Gandhi in these movements, we can now sketch the development of the Chipko movement itself. Anthropologist Gerald Berreman recounts how the movement

> began in 1972 among the people of the central Himalayas in India, as an effort utilizing nonviolent direct action to prevent the destruction of their forests and thereby save their environment, their livelihood, their ways of life, and ultimately life itself in their homeland. The characteristic method employed by those participating in the movement . . . is to interpose themselves bodily between tree cutters and the trees—a tactic in the Gandhian tradition. (Berreman 1989, 240, 246)[6]

After its initial campaigns, its methodology and philosophy quickly spread to

Himachal Pradesh in the north, Karnataka in the south, Rahasthan in the west, Orissa in the east and to the Central Indian Highlands (Shiva 1988, 67).

In the early stages of the Chipko movement, the exploitation of forest resources by outside contractors was the primary concern of local villages (Pearce 1991, 267). Such villages are often populated primarily by women, as able-bodied men seek work in urban areas (Berreman 1989, 243, 253; cf. Harrison 1987, 61, 332). By 1975, three hundred villages in the hill districts of Uttar Pradesh faced severe erosion and landslides due to deforestation by non-local commercial interests (Shiva 1988, 74; Berreman 1989, 244–45). Widespread, organized protests against the commercial exploitation of forests by outside contractors eventually led the government to a new strategy: using local labor and forest contractor cooperatives (Shiva 1988, 76).

This strategy contributed to a schism in the Chipko movement. One faction was more pragmatic and development-oriented, supporting local sawmill cooperatives, the other less compromising and more explicitly environmentalist, feminist, and antimarket—in a word, more radical. The more radical faction resists market-driven forest exploitation regardless of who profits, even if it is the local men and the husbands of Chipko activists (Shiva 1988, 76, cf. 71–72). Pearce sees the schism as a battle between deep ecologists and anthropocentric environmentalists: "While Bahuguna pledged himself to saving the ecosystem of the Himalayas, Chadi Prasad Bhatt said, 'Saving trees is only the first step in the Chipko movement. Saving ourselves is our real goal'" (Pearce 1991, 268).[7]

All observers agree that women have been very important in the genesis and impact of these movements, but differ on how to characterize women's contributions. Berreman credits two men, Chandi Prasad Bhatt (a Sarvodaya worker who organized a self-help cooperative in the 1960s) and Sunderlal Bahuguna with helping found the movement (1989, 246–47). He implies that it is inaccurate to label it a "women's movement"—as Shiva comes close to doing—since men are involved "in similar ways and to a similar extent" (1989, 252). Shiva and Pearce emphasize the critical role of women in founding and empowering the movement, and how these women inspired both Bhatt and Bahuguna (Pearce 1991, 266–67; Shiva 1988, 70). Both men eventually became the highest profile Chipko spokespersons, Bhatt of the more anthropocentric faction, Bahuguna of the more deep-ecological one. But Shiva well argues her view by quoting Bahuguna himself: "We are the runners and messengers—the real leaders are the women" (1988, 70).

In the years since its founding, Chipko has precipitated major and minor confrontations, "each exemplifying its nonviolent method and each impressively effective" (Berreman 1989, 247). The focus of the movement broadened in the 1980s, and now expresses concern over mining, the damming of India's rivers (Pearce 1991, 205–6), and control over dairy production. In 1983 it spawned "Appiko Chaluvali," another antilogging movement, this time in the Western Ghats, and there have been Chipko-style campaigns in defense of urban parks in India, and even far away in the forests of North and South America (Berreman 1989, 251). Chipko's spiritual politics and militant tactics have become a permanent feature of many popular environmental struggles around the world.[8]

THE PACIFIC RIM

Just before the winter solstice of 1991, ninety Nobel Prize winners debated the proposition that "mankind [sic] is, on balance, harnessing its intelligence to build a better world" (*Spokane Spokesman Review*, 20 December 1991). Only half of these renowned figures agreed, ecological anxieties prompting much of the pessimism. Henry Kendall, who won the physics prize in 1990 "warned of an 'environmental disaster' if mismanagement of resources and overpopulation persist" (*Spokane Spokesman Review*, 20 December 1991).

Nowhere are the twin specters which haunted the pessimists among the Nobel laureates—population growth and natural resource depletion—more pressing than along the western edge of the Pacific Rim. Here, survival and environmental conflicts often become Manichean struggles between industrial and tribal lifeways. Those resisting industrial and commercial incursions often turn to mass civil disobedience, but in the absence of the deep Gandhian influences found in India, sometimes tactics have become even more militant. Ecotage is increasingly common, sometimes carried out by large, riotous crowds, and resistance has even been expressed in armed rebellion or unorganized acts of violence. The results of these struggles have been mixed, but the tenacious ties between peoples and their lands, often grounded in spiritual beliefs about the sacredness of certain places, are exhibited again.

One of the most tragic campaigns by an indigenous people for its land has occurred in the Malaysian state of Sarawak. There, the Penan, the last nomadic, hunter-gatherers in Southeast Asia, have fought since 1987 to end the destruction of the tropical hardwood forests on which their physical and spiritual existence depends (*Earth Island Journal* 5, no. 3 [1990]: 8). Other Sarawaki tribes have managed to keep their land free of loggers, in part through ecotage. For example, the Iban tribe blew up twenty-five bulldozers and logging trucks in 1982, repeating such tactics four years later (Scarce 1990, 151). But the Penan will not resort to destructive tactics, while the Malaysian government has refused to halt the destruction of the forest upon which the Penan's survival depends—even when presented with a petition signed by seven thousand persons and fourteen organizations in 1986. In *Earth Island Journal* (5, no. 3 [1990]:8), anthropologist Bruno Manser is reported as saying, "The reaction of the Sarawak authorities was nil," and adding, "the destruction of the land went on even faster."

In 1987 Manser, a Swiss citizen living among the Penan since 1984, persuaded them to blockade logging roads leading into their forests, hoping the world would rally to their support. The Penan have now continued this struggle for more than five years. They have been beaten and often jailed, sometimes for months, all in response to their nonviolent acts of civil disobedience. But little of the hoped-for international support has materialized.

The roots of the ecological and cultural war against the Penan is in part private economic interest—the environment and tourism minister for the Sarawak region, Datuk Amar James Wong, is reported to own more than seven hundred thousand acres of the Penan's homeland, as well as many of the logging companies that cut the timber. The other central cause is the international demand for wood products. The Japanese purchase most of the Penan's wood—often for wasteful conveniences such as disposable wood chopsticks, now produced at the rate of 20 billion pairs each year (Pearce 1991, 230), but cf. Weisenthal 1990, 15)—while simultaneously revering and preserving their own forests much better than most countries (Pearce 1991, 227–29).[9]

Environmental groups such as the grass-roots, Australian-based Rainforest Information Center and the U.S.-based spin-off, the Rainforest Action Network (RAN), have tried to reduce the demand for tropical hardwoods through an international boycott.[10] The boycott has slowed the cutting and road building, which has decimated one-third of the Penan's historical food-gathering grounds and opened up two-thirds for further exploitation (*Earth Island Journal* 5, no. 3 [1990]: 8). Nevertheless, the deforestation continues.

SOUTHEAST ASIA

Rain forest dwellers are not always as committed as the Penan to nonviolent resistance to logging. In Burma (which was recently renamed Myanmar), along the Salween River border with Thailand, three tribal peoples have launched a guerrilla war against those invading their forest. Since Burma gained its independence from British colonial rule in 1948, the Karen National Union has struggled alongside their blood relatives, the Karenni, and another neighboring tribal group, the Moi, for autonomy and for their traditional lifeways in their ancestral territories. They have been fighting a brutal government, led by autocrat Ne Win, that came to power in 1962 through a coup overthrowing Burma's first democratic government.

Spectacular teak forests hide the rebels, while revenue from rebel logging is used to purchase arms and ammunition. Eric Ransdell claims that the rebels log carefully, viewing the forest as "their heritage, the only home they had ever known. Parents . . . plant teak trees as a kind of living inheritance for newborn children, who, despite the fighting, [grow] up believing that the forest [is] eternal" (Ransdell 1991, 90).

Maintaining this faith was made even more difficult in 1988, however, when the Burmese government sold the rebel forest to Thailand. "In less than two years, an estimated four million acres fell to the chainsaw. The world's last great teak forest was [rapidly] disappearing" (Ransdell 1991, 90).

Shortly after the 1962 coup, Ne Win had employed similar tactics to prop up his regime, selling Burmese fishing rights. Cutting the forests also provided financial resources to help maintain social control. The Thais coveted the Karen timber enough to pay 200 million dollars for it. Ironically, this sale made possible an environmental victory in Thailand: the 1989 banning of all commercial logging. This ban was precipitated by ecological disasters such as flooding and mudslides, and the grass-roots activism of a coalition of "poor peasant hill-farmers . . . and the students and intellectuals of Bangkok" (Pearce 1991, 190–92).

Today the Karen's war has become desperate—and the fate of six hundred forest-dependent endangered species is linked to the outcome. Previously, the Karen were able to sell their trees to the Thais—only the mature ones were cut and only Karen workers could do the felling. The money from one hundred-year-old tree would feed ten thousand tribe members and equip a quarter of their six thousand troops. But this source of revenue dried up in 1988 when the Burmese began to attack the Karen from Thai territory. Moreover, "now, the . . . Burmese military . . . protect[s] loggers who are clear-cutting [the] forests" (Ransdell 1991, 94).

Little concern from the international community has been forthcoming. The U.S. Congress voted in 1990 to prohibit the importation of Burmese teak, but with little impact (Ransdell 1991, 146). The Karen, Karenni, and Moi, weighing their options, increasingly consider attacking the loggers directly, as Korubo and Kayapo warriors have already done in Brazil (*Spokane Spokesman Review*, 20 December 1991; Hecht and Cockburn 1989, 140, 143). Since the rebels are defending the forests in favor of their more traditional and sustainable lifeways, they properly can be considered both a cultural survival movement, as well as a popular-environmental one.

The government of Thailand has also faced environmental direct action *within its borders*, on Phuket, a small offshore island. On 1 June 1986, fifty thousand of the island's two hundred thousand inhabitants demonstrated to halt the construction of a tantalum refinery. Anxiety about the safety of the plant had been fueled by grass-roots environmental activists showing a video-tape of the Bhopal disaster. Two weeks later seventy thousand people attend-ed a meeting with the Thai industry minister. The minister arrived to find the crowd enraged, however, and he quickly fled. Receiving no assurances from the government, the crowd torched the plant and prevented fire trucks from responding to the construction site. Damage was estimated at 25 mil-lion dollars—the most expensive act of ecotage in history. Afterward, the Thai government began to review its environmental planning laws with an eye toward more public input (Sachs 1988; Scarce 1990, 154).

AFRICA

By 1989, two-thirds of all refugees were in Africa (Matthews 1991, 24). Most of these are environmental refugees, victims of soil erosion, desertification and devegetation. Often environmental decline displaces only part of the family, as able-bodied men seek work in urban areas (Harrison 1987, 61, 332). Africa, self-sufficient in food as late as 1970, now fails to feed many of its people.

Given the enormity of African environmental decline and its conse-quences for survival, one might expect a proliferation of grass-roots environ-mental groups in Africa. Most of the evidence, however, seems to confirm Harrison's claim that "Africa is weaker than any other continent in popular grass-roots organizations of every kind" including those with ecologically sus-tainable development objectives (1987, 278). Pearce agrees that "Africa is a desert for environmental groups," and attributes this to "the unhealthy domi-nation of governments over every aspect of the lives of their peoples" (1991, 258). Eco-philosopher Baird Callicott suggests that there is a deeper cultural reason for the dearth of environmental activism in Africa: its indigenous spiri-tualities rarely view animals as kindred peoples and nonhuman life as intrinsi-cally valuable.[11]

Kenya has many grass-roots self-help groups, and thus provides at least one "partial exception" to the usual lack of such groups in Africa (Pearce 1991, 258). Kenya's "green belt movement," moreover, is an *explicitly envi-ronmental* self-help group that has gained international recognition (Pearce 1991, 258–62). Started in 1977 by Kenya's National Council of Women, the movement enlists rural peoples as tree planters in the fight against deser-tification and soil erosion. Local communities establish tree plantations on open spaces, school grounds, and roadways. Pearce notes that by 1990 over ten million native trees had been planted, very possibly doing more to stall desertification than the U.N. environmental program (1991, 259). The project is headed by a woman, Wangari Maathai, a former anatomy professor. Harrison notes that women continue to be the backbone of Kenya's popular environmental movements, and suggests that this tradition of women's self-help efforts can be traced to the time when men were away fighting British rule (1987, 279).

The green belt movement worked well with the government for many years, but became more militant in 1989 over the government's plans to chop down trees in Uhru Park in the capital of Nairobi. The repression that followed included the eviction of the green belt movement from its offices and accusations that it was trying to destabilize the government (Pearce 1991, 261–62). Maathi's rising international status (in 1989 she was named "Woman of the World" by the princess of Wales) may have helped insulate the movement from more serious repression.

A similar movement exists in Senegal, and is labeled, literally, "women's gardening groups"—even though men participate. These groups have become a major force for reforestation. They plant gardens and trees and engage in projects that protect the environment while reducing the work of rural women involved in subsistence agriculture (Timberlake 1986, 212).

Zimbabwe's Organization of Rural Association for Peasants (ORAP) is yet another movement which grew out of women's groups. ORAP groups engage in income-generating projects and "service projects" promoting environmental improvement and restoration, especially related to water and sanitation. The "self-help" and decentralized nature of these organizations is evident in group names such as *Siyazenzela* (We're doing it for ourselves) and *Vusanani* (Support each other to get up) (Timberlake 1986, 212).

Despite the efforts of those involved in Africa's popular environmental movements, it is hard to be optimistic. Not only is grass-roots activism exceptional, but Africa has "the harshest of habitats," which makes sustaining large numbers of people on it more difficult than on any other densely populated continent (Harrison 1987, 27–46). Just as problematic is the prevalence of development policies modeled after and promoted by Western countries. These policies exacerbate environmental decline in many ways, especially by encouraging the expansion of multinational rather than locally based firms and through the planting of ecologically destructive monoculture "cash crops" when more—not less—peasant farming is needed (Pearce 1991, 104–6). Despite the various cultural obstacles to the emergence of popular environmental movements in Africa, however, it is reasonable to speculate that Africa's fragile ecosystems, droughts, and survival struggles will precipitate increasing environmental activism, and possibly militant action, even on this distressed continent.

SOUTH AMERICA—THE BRAZILIAN AMAZON

In February 1989, one thousand warriors from twenty previously warring Indian groups, in traditional tribal regalia and war paint, met with Brazilian government officials to protest plans to dam and flood seven thousand square kilometers of land adjacent to the Xingu River. The project would displace seventy thousand forest inhabitants near the Amazon boom town of Altimura (Pearce 1991, 133). Many environmentalists and First World celebrities were present in solidarity with the Indians. The meeting nearly turned violent after a Kayapo woman ritually threatened a government official with her machete, threatening to kill any dam builders entering the forest (Hecht and Cockburn 1989, 212; Pearce 1991, 134).

Indians had been fighting against various invaders for nearly five hundred years. By the time of the Altimura confrontation, many tribes had disappeared, and many others were nearly exterminated by the invader's diseases and violence. The occupation of the Indians' lands had accelerated in the 1960s following intensified road building into the forest. This led to increasing collaboration among Indian tribes, culminating in the founding of the Indigenous Peoples' Union in 1980. Supported by Western solidarity groups such as Survival International (in England) and Cultural Survival (in the United States), the Indians are becoming skilled at coalition building and lobbying, even succeeding in 1987 in overturning their status under Brazil's constitution as "wards of the state" (Hecht and Cockburn 1989, 175, cf. 193). During the 1980s, they increased their use of direct action resistance to the invasions. In several different incidents, warriors from different tribes killed loggers and miners found in their traditional forest areas (Hecht and Cockburn 1989, 140, 143; *Spokane Spokesman Review,* 20 December 1991).[12]

Perhaps better known are the efforts of members of the rubber tappers' union to preserve their traditional forest lifeways and livelihoods. Beginning in 1976, the tappers began resisting rancher and miner incursions into their areas through direct action occupations of the disputed areas. Many murders of rubber tappers and their union leaders went largely unreported until the assassination of Chico Mendes in late 1988 (Pearce 1991, 140–41; cf. Hecht and Cockburn 1989, 171–73). With international concern about Amazonian deforestation mounting, Mendes had become well-known within international environmental circles as a forest defender and promoter of "extractive reserves": the tappers' own ecologically sustainable proposal for the Amazon.

Extractive reserves set aside the forests for gathering, hunting, and sustainable, rotating small-plot planting, while precluding mining or large-scale ranching or farming (Hecht and Cockburn 1989, 181). Most observers miss or underplay the "profoundly radical" nature of the extractive reserve proposals, which favor "some form of communal land ownership, [attacking] . . . private property and hence capitalism" (Hecht and Cockburn 1989, 182).[13] This certainly explains some of the violence against those promoting extractive reserves, including, perhaps, the suspicious 1987 bombing of an aircraft carrying the Brazilian agrarian reform minister, who had just signed the enabling legislation for the reserves (Hecht and Cockburn 1989, 182).

By the late 1980s, a scientific consensus had emerged that the traditional lifeways of many forest peoples—especially Indians and other long-term inhabitants such as rubber tappers and river dwellers—provide models for sustainable ways of life in the forest (Hecht and Cockburn 1989, 155; Pearce 1991, 138). Thus it makes sense to view these particular groups as popular environmental movements, even though in the heat of survival struggles they have not always viewed themselves as such.

There are, however, many obstacles to understanding grass-roots popular environmental movements in the Amazon. The best way to proceed is to analyze the complex social life in the region, including groups not involved in practicing or promoting ecologically sustainable lifeways. Such analysis can overturn misperceptions about the causes of the ecological destruction and equally serious misunderstandings regarding the best prospects for ecosocial protection and restoration in the Amazon.

Since the word "Amazon" has become almost synonymous with dense and largely unpopulated rain forests, it may be surprising to note that in the legal jurisdiction of the Brazilian Amazon, which is 57 percent of the Brazilian national territory, 13 million people live.[14] There is great variety among the inhabitants in terms of what they do, how much they earn, and how they relate to their natural environment. Indigenous peoples today number between 140,000 and 190,000.[15] Besides the rubber tappers and river dwellers, there are hundreds of thousands of small farmers, some of whom own the land they work, most of whom do not; in addition, there are large ranchers involved mainly in cattle ranching, land speculators, miners, private national and international business concerns, Brazilian government-owned businesses, and the Brazilian military.

Often obscured by the trees is the social drama in which these actors are involved. A major characteristic of this drama is conflict and violence over access to and use of land among groups in the region, and often between these groups and the Brazilian government. Particularly noteworthy (especially when contrasted with Africa) is the degree of organization among many of the actors. Not only have Indians and rubber tappers organized themselves, but so have peasant farmers, rich landowners, ranchers, and so on. Brazil in the 1970s and 1980s was the scene of a considerable multiplication of urban and rural popular organizations that have, in turn, formed innumerable networks and coalitions.

A poor peasant, for example, may belong to his local rural workers union. This rural workers union helps organize this peasant and others for land occupations, supports their self-defense against the land owners and their gunmen, and fights the ensuing legal and media campaigns, often with the support of regional and national union groups. In addition, local unions are usually involved with other local organizations, such as the Catholic church, that carry out social service tasks and political solidarity work.

As with many popular environmental groups on other continents, religion plays an important role in Amazonia's social conflicts. Radicalized sectors of the Catholic church, inspired by the "liberation theology" movement—a powerful grass-roots movement in Latin America promoting the interests of the poor as the central practice of Christian faith—began in the early 1970s to work with Amazonian peasants toward organizing "base communities." Stressing self-help and popular resistance against oppressors, these communities have provided a social base for many Amazonian resistance movements. One important organization closely allied to the liberation theology movement is the Catholic Land Commission (CPT). It facilitates the organizing efforts of rural peasants in the Amazon and elsewhere in Brazil. The importance of radical Catholicism is commonly recognized throughout the region. Indeed, "many forest dwellers got their start in active organizing under the Church's auspices," and priests are often targets of reactionary violence, as illustrated by the remark of one rancher: "For every land invasion, a dead priest" (Hecht and Cockburn 1989, 171).

While liberation theology supports the popular movements, reactionary violence against these movements is sometimes justified through appeals to traditional, conservative Catholic beliefs that view the base community movement as subversive and threatening to the church's mission as well as to "sacred" private property rights. Religion further complicates the social landscape as Pentecostal ministers, with their otherworldly form of conservative religion, promote migration to the Amazon as a promised land, while indigenous leaders resist these migrations and prefer a vision of the forest based on primal spirituality and lifeways (see, e.g., Hecht and Cockburn 1989, 213). Social conflicts, and the passions of social actors, are often intensified through ideologies grounding their social objectives in some vision of the sacred. This is one way contending religious ethics play a role in Amazonian social-environmental conflicts.

A final characteristic of the Amazonian social drama worth emphasizing is that most members of the popular classes live at a level of bare subsistence.

Thus the organizations and conflicts they are involved in are all related directly to survival efforts. But the survival strategies of most Amazon groups do not involve sustainable practices. The slash-and-burn methods peasants use, for example, are not even in the short term sustainable practices. Within three or four years after beginning the use of such methods the land is exhausted and will no longer produce. The peasants know this and recognize the irony of risking their lives for land that will soon be unproductive. But they continue both their slash-and-burn farming and their battles for land because both are directly related to survival—at least short-term.

Peasants in Brazil have few options. Many have been forced to the Amazon by structural changes in Brazil, such as the displacement of small farmers due to "the expansion of mechanized agriculture and the flooding of enormous areas of agricultural land" (Hecht and Cockburn 1989, 97, cf. 116). Other peasants, in the wake of the military government's brutal repression of peasant leagues, have seen the Amazon as the only place to hide (Hecht and Cockburn 1989, 104). But it is difficult for relatively recent migrants to practice sustainable lifeways when they often do not have the specialized knowledge of such practices or the necessary tools, as do long-term forest dwellers such as Indians and rubber tappers.[16]

The complex social reality is that sometimes, but not always, Amazonian social conflicts are between those whose objectives include ecologically sustainable practices and those whose do not. And although the Amazon's peoples are directly affected by the consequences of nonsustainable logging, farming, and mining, ecological concerns and sustainability are not usually the central issues for most popular organizations in the Amazon, except where, as with the rubber tappers and Indians, such concerns are simultaneously productive of group survival and self-interest.[17] The reasons for this are clear. People in popular organizations are immersed in a context of conflict and violence, and their first concern is the acquisition of the bare necessities for survival. Nevertheless, ecological concerns are not ignored altogether. Rather, the ecological issues tend to be viewed as part of the larger political and economic context in which these actors are already involved.

Many rural workers in the Amazon, for instance, know that they are often exploited both by powerful individuals and by the economic and political policies of Brazil. It is therefore logical that they would be suspicious of ecological policies, fearing that such policies are just another way to exploit the poor and powerless; and in fact, they often are.[18] Rural workers are also generally perceptive in their understanding of the political dimensions of ecological and environmental questions. They realize that the Amazon cannot be "saved" without addressing the question of land ownership, promoting land reform and, more broadly still, effecting the redistribution of wealth in the country. When peasants own their land and can remain on it, they more easily will be persuaded to adopt sustainable agricultural methods.

Such an integrated view of the ecological questions of the Amazon challenges much thought in the social sciences, which divides issues into discreet parcels in order to enhance the understanding of problems and devise technological solutions to them.[19] But perhaps ironically, the combined insights of current forest dwellers—including rural peasants, rubber tappers and indigenous peoples—regarding the ecological and political problems confronting their region express more faithfully the complexity and interrelatedness of the questions at hand, and also discern more directly what is at stake morally. In the case of the Amazon and the other cases we have been examining, observers interested in promoting ecological sustainability would do well to consider the voices from the various popular movements.

CONCLUSION

The preceding analysis of recent trends and tendencies among environmental movements in less affluent countries is not comprehensive, and it is perhaps dangerous to generalize based on these examples. But in examining such movements globally we can discern certain characteristic tendencies in these movements and in the conflicts they engender. To summarize, there has been a proliferation of such movements during recent years. Conflicts result from efforts to prevent peasant displacement and to gain control over land use and property. Many participants in these movements cling precariously to life and thus survival is often their chief objective. These movements have become increasingly sophisticated about building coalitions both locally and internationally to such an extent that it is now impossible to understand some of these movements without examining the supporting role often played by international environmental organizations funded largely by those in more affluent countries (Pearce 1991, 48–67). Although usually nonviolent, they have often become involved in a brutal dance with the reactionary violence they face. These movements tend to promote or strive to protect land uses which scientists agree are, at the very least, more sustainable than those of their more powerful and wealthy enemies. Women play important and sometimes *the* decisive roles in these movements. Finally, religion is often a critical factor providing inspiration and courage within these movements.

Industrial lifeways—with the consequent deforestation, hydroelectric projects, and mechanized agriculture, all exacerbated by the impact of ever-increasing human numbers—have been clearly linked to global environmental crises such as atmospheric warming, ozone depletion, acid rain, and the accelerating decline of biodiversity. Many conservation biologists now assert that the process of evolution itself has been arrested. Such findings make clear that the importance of these movements goes far beyond specific, contested landscapes. The emerging scientific consensus underscores, we believe, that no political, environmental, and moral task is more important than the rediscovery and development of ecologically sustainable lifeways. Much of what little hope there may be for the development of such lifeways resides in the proliferation of efforts similar to those undertaken by the popular environmental movements discussed in these pages.[20]

NOTES

1. The term "popular" refers to diverse, non-middle-class groups, including workers, peasants, indigenous peoples and participants in the so-called informal economy.

2. For example, A.T. Ariyaratne, founder of Sri Lanka's Sarvodaya self-help movement, recommends that his people "totally de-link from the international economic system" and stop worrying about GNP measures (Ingram 1989, 135). Indigenous Malaysian rain forest activist Martin Chor advocates complete deindustrialization (Pearce 1991, 311). Factionalism among environmental groups often results from disagreements about the merits of industrialism.

3. For a start here, see Callicott and Ames (1989), especially the articles by the editors, LaFleur, Cook, Wei-ming, and Ames.

4. Chidester (1987, pt. 1) shows that religious ethics begins with a human sense of obligation, that it leads to an attempt to harmonize one's actions with the sacred, and that such obligations do not depend on a divine lawgiver.

5. The case of the sacred cow in India can show how the line can be blurred between sacred and secular, and between ecological and economic needs, when part or all of the natural world is seen as sacred. The sacred cow, as mother of prosperity, performs a critical function in the food chain: enriching the soil, providing power requirements for the village, and so forth (Shiva 1988, 165). When Chipko women protest the selling of milk they are denouncing the defilement of the sacred cow through its commodification into a mere milk machine, as well as the economic and social consequences of this commodification. Similarly, when peasants and tribals protest the damming of sacred rivers they are protesting the desecration of sacred sites, as well as the submersion of fertile soils and the displacement of peasants. The lines between the "sacred," the "economic," and the "ecological" cannot be so clearly drawn when the forest is both Aranyanik, goddess of life and fertility, and a resource for survival. See Linenthal (1991) and Sears (1989) on the process of sacred place veneration and defilement.

6. Some observers trace the origin of the Chipko movement to the founding of the Bishnoi sect "in 1485 by the son of a village headman who had a vision in which he saw a period of terrific hardship caused by callous regard for nature." He forbade cutting of green wood and killing of wild animals. But in 1731, a maharaja demand-

ed Bishnoi trees for a palace, and a woman named Amrita Devi hugged a tree in resistance. She was then killed by an axman. Three of her daughters immediately took her place and were killed, and before long 294 men and 69 women died. The maharaja relented and banned logging in Bishnoi areas upon seeing the carnage (Schelling 1991, 17).

7. For discussion of the schism in Earth First!, a radical North American environmental group, see Taylor (1991, 263–65) and Scarce (1990, 57–95).

8. There are now at least three thousand formally structured groups, and a similar number of informally organized social movements in India, many promoting ecological agendas (Berreman 1989, 239).

9. Another guerrilla war fed by resentment about deforestation is led by New People's Army in the Philippines (Pearce 1991, 232).

10. For the Zen Buddhist-inspired spirituality that motivates the founder-activists of these movements, see the unabridged version of Taylor (1991) (author's files) and Seed, Macy, Fleming, and Naess (1988).

11. One exception may be the pygmies, who consider the rain forest to be sacred. Callicott's reflections on such matters will be found in his forthcoming book, *The World's Great Ecological Insights.*

12. Although Kayapo resistance has been especially fierce (Hecht and Cockburn 1989, 143), some of them also are compromised, seeking to profit from and not overturn mining in their areas (Pearce 1991, 135–36).

13. Mendes, for example, was a participant in the Acre region's long tradition of leftist agitation before social forces shifted his priority to ecologically important land-use battles (Hecht and Cockburn 1989, 161–69).

14. This figure is from *Debate,* a church-related magazine published in Rio de Janeiro. It appeared as a supplement of *Contexto Pastoral,* no. 3 (Aug./Sept. 1991).

15. The former estimate is in Ramos's "Frontier Expansion and Indian Peoples in the Brazilian Amazon." More recent estimates suggest that indigenous peoples may now number only 140,000.

16. Wealthy landowners and cattle ranchers also knowingly engage in nonsustainable agriculture in the Amazon, burning forest into pastures in far greater amounts than the peasants. Unlike the peasants, large landowners destroy the bush and forest not for their own survival but for profit.

17. This statement is based on contributor Hadsell's field research, and is not meant to be categorical, since there may be popular organizations whose concerns are primarily ecological. She believes that if there are such popular organizations, however, they are very few in number and very atypical of popular organizations in the region (BT).

18. The control of burning implemented by the Collar government in the last several years is seen by the peasant farmers as one more way to remove them from the land. Recent policy requires farmers to have permits for burning their land before planting. But in order to receive a permit, one must own the land, and few peasants do. Thus they burn at great risk, since one fine can equal more than a season's earnings. Large landowners, of course, can get permits or afford the fines (Hadsell and Evans 1991).

19. Daly and Cobb (1989) well critique such compartmentalized analysis.

20. In a rare, hopeful sign, Colombia recently returned large forest areas to its indigenous peoples to manage, at least for now (Pearce 1991, 262).

REFERENCES

Berreman, Gerald D. 1989. Chipko: A movement to save the Himalayan environment and people. In *Contemporary Indian tradition: Voices on nature and the challenge of change,* ed. Carla Borden, 239–66. Washington/London: Smithsonian Institution Press.

Bondurant, Joan. 1965. *Conquest of violence: The Gandhian philosophy of conflict.* Berkeley: University of California Press.

Callicott, J. Baird, and Roger T. Ames. 1989. *Nature in Asian traditions of thought: Essays in environmental philosophy.* Albany: SUNY Press.

Chidester, David. 1987. *Patterns of action: Religion and ethics in a comparative perspective.* Belmont, Calif.: Wadsworth.

Daly, Herman, and John Cobb. 1989. *For the common good.* Boston: Beacon Press.

Hadsell, Heidi, and Robert Evans. 1991. Is President Collar green? *Christian Century,* November.

Harrison, Paul. 1987. *The greening of Africa: Breaking through in the battle for land and food.* New York: Penguin.

Hecht, Susanna, and Alexander Cockburn. 1989. *The fate of the forest: Developers, destroyers and defenders of the Amazon.* London and New York: Verso.

Holley, David. 1991. China will tame the Yangtze. *Los Angeles Times,* 29 August.

Ingram, Catharine. 1990. *In the footsteps of Gandhi.* Berkeley, Calif.: Parallax.

Kendell, Jeni, and Eddie Buivids. 1987. *Earth first: The struggle to save Australia's rainforest.* Australia: Australian Broadcasting Corporation.

Linenthal, Edward T. 1991. *Sacred ground: Americans and their battlefields.* Urbana and Chicago: University of Illinois Press.

Macy, Joanna. 1983. *Dharma and development: Religion as resource in the Sarvodaya self-help movement.* West Hartford, Conn.: Kumarian Press.

Matthews, Jessica Tuchman. 1991. *Preserving the global environment: The challenge of shared leadership.* New York: W. W. Norton & Co.

Pearce, Fred. 1991. *Green warriors: The people and politics behind the environmental revolution.* London: Bodley Head.

Ramos, Alcida R. 1984. Frontier expansion and Indian peoples in the Brazilian Amazon. In *Frontier expansion in the Amazon,* edited by Marianne Schmink and Charles Wood. Gainesville: University of Florida Press.

Ransdell, Eric. 1991. The rebels, the forest, and the man who watches the stars. *Outside* 16 (5): 88ff.

Sachs, Dana. 1988. *Local heroes. Sierra* 72 (2): 80.

Scarce, Rik. 1990. *Eco-warriors: Understanding the radical environmental movement.* Chicago: Noble.

Sears, John. 1989. *Sacred places: American tourist attractions in the nineteenth century.* New York: Oxford University Press.

Seed, John, Joanna Macy, Pat Flemming, and Arne Naess. 1988. *Thinking like a mountain: Towards a council of all beings.* Philadelphia: New Society.

Schelling, Andrew. 1991. Jataka mind: Cross-species compassion from ancient India to Earth First! activists. *Tricycle* 1 (1): 10–19.

Shiva, Vandana. 1988. *Staying alive: Women, ecology and development.* London: Zed.

Taylor, Bron. 1991. The religion and politics of Earth First! *The Ecologist* 21 (6): 258–66.

Timberlake, Lloyd. 1986. *Africa in crisis: The causes, the cures of environmental bankruptcy.* Philadelphia: New Society.

Weisenthal, Debra Blake. 1990. The forest as a human right. *The Progressive* 54 (April): 14–15.

WuDunn, Sheryl. 1989. In China, dam's delay spares a valley for now. *New York Times*, April 18.

SECTION TWO

The Green Party
Phenomenon

4 The Green Phenomenon in Western Party Systems

HERBERT KITSCHELT

Since the mid-1970s political parties advertising their concern for environmental protection—whether they are called environment, ecology, or Green parties—have emerged in a number of Western democracies. Early innovators, such as the British Ecology party (since 1972) or the various French ecological lists (since 1974) proved not particularly successful at the polls. They were soon overshadowed by Green parties in Belgium, Germany, or Switzerland that entered national parliaments in the first half of the 1980s. Later, Green parties received a significant boost also in Austria, Finland, Italy, and Sweden. By 1990, Green parties existed in most Western democracies, yet received widely varying electoral support.

Three questions have been at the center of the increasingly diverse literature on the Green phenomenon.[1] First, what is the appeal of Green parties? Second, how do we explain their success? Third, how can their internal operation, external outreach, and strategy be accounted for?

In the following three sections, I will briefly sketch major arguments and findings pertaining to each of these questions. Quite naturally, I will attempt to highlight the virtues of the particular line of reasoning I have chosen in my own work on ecology parties (see Kitschelt 1985, 1988a, 1988b, 1989, 1990a and 1990b; Kitschelt and Hellemans 1990a and 1990b). In the fourth and somewhat longer section, I will address frontiers of research on Green parties in the 1990s. Future studies should focus more on the strategic interaction between Green parties and their competitors in the electoral arena. Once the parties have arrived on the political scene, their maintenance or decline does not hinge exclusively on the actions of outside political forces, but on the conscious, calculating strategies of their own voters and politicians. Strategic interaction among competing parties explains the electoral volatility of Green parties that has been evidenced by recent elections in Germany (1990) and Sweden (1991).

THE GREEN POLITICAL APPEAL

What is the range of parties belonging to the Green phenomenon? Is there an internal coherence to Green politics across different countries? These questions have been answered by two contrasting lines of reasoning.

One way to interpret the rise of ecology parties has been to treat them as single-issue parties that are bound to thrive as long as the established parties do not cope with the increased public attention to environmental degradation in contemporary industrial societies. Beyond concern with environmental protection, these new parties were expected to be devoid of distinctive programmatic content. It quickly turned out, however, that ecology parties did adopt a variety of other characteristic political stances, such as strong support for women's emancipation and autonomy, civil rights and minority protection (especially that of foreign migrants and refugees), a comprehensive welfare state, disarmament, and assistance to the less developed countries.

Recent defenses of the view that ecology parties, taken by themselves, represent a genuine cohort of political parties tapping into a unique voter cleavage argue that (1) linkages to other issues such as feminism and pacifism are accidental and that (2) the existence of Green parties lacking strong ties to other protest or leftist causes in France, Sweden, and Switzerland is evidence for the uniqueness of the Green phenomenon (cf. Rüdig 1989). Yet, as I will argue below, whenever Green parties dissociate themselves from the broader elective affinities indicated above, they tend to be electorally unsustainable.

The alternative interpretation of ecology parties treats the Greens as an outgrowth of a broad "postmaterialism" or "new" politics current in contemporary society (cf. Dalton 1988, chap. 8; Inglehart 1990, chap. 8). New politics parties also include many left-socialist parties founded in the late 1950s and in the 1960s and represent a new *cleavage,* not just an issue. Parties represent societal cleavages if they draw on distinct groups in the social structure that have unique political outlooks and dispositions to act (cf. Lipset and Rokkan 1967).[2] With some simplification, the broader category of new politics party satisfies these three conditions. The parties primarily draw on younger, highly educated voters who tend to be employed in the (public) sector of personal services and production of cultural symbols (education, health care, welfare, mass media, arts).[3] Their supporters believe that advanced democracies should devote more effort to increase citizens' autonomy and democratic involvement ("post-materialism") than to improve physical security and material prosperity ("materialism") further. Such electoral constituencies are disposed to endorsing and participating in the so-called "new" social movements of the 1970s and 1980s, such as the environmental, antinuclear, peace, and feminist movements. Of course, there remain differences in the extent to which new politics voters and parties articulate these dispositions. I will offer an explanation for such variations in section 4.[4]

The common denominator of the Green phenomenon is the quest for a new "paradigm" of democratic political action. This paradigm transcends the politics of economic equality concerned with the (re)distribution of privately appropriable goods in favor of a politics concerned with the "quality of life" and highlighting the provision of pure collective goods enjoyed by large groups: institutions that guarantee personal autonomy, enhance effective chances of participation, and protect spheres of life from the intrusion of market exchange or administrative imperatives (Habermas 1982; Offe 1985). With respect to ecology, citizens claim that intangible collective concerns should have priority over imperatives of production: outer nature should be protected (1) *for its own sake,* (2) *for human health considerations that are difficult to value in economic terms (money) or political expediency* and (3) *as an object of aesthetical human enjoyment.*[5]

If the common denominator of the new category of parties is a complex new cleavage, not the concern with the environment by itself, it is possible that some parties not carrying "Green" or "ecology" in their party label belong to that group of parties, while some parties explicitly appealing to ecology in their party name do not. For example, in Germany, there exists a small party, called the *Oekologisch-Demokratische Partei* (ODP), with an authoritarian, statist political agenda. This party hardly represents the same phenomenon as the German Greens. Table 4.1 therefore represents a list of all new politics parties in Western Europe that underwrite the agenda of autonomy and democracy. Green and ecology parties constitute only the younger strand of these parties.

In order to characterize the new category of parties, I wish to go beyond the bland, informative label of "new politics" and focus on the linkage between "old" questions of economic (re)distribution and the "new" politics of autonomy and democracy.[6] The empirical evidence supports the conclusion that the two cleavage dimensions are not entirely independent, but that the notions of "left" and "right" in citizens' self-placement and their perception of the political field encompass both new and old politics. Advocates of citizens' autonomy and democracy and of the internalization of environmental costs implicitly or explicitly call for a containment of private market exchange and for a more egalitarian resource distribution in society. In this sense, Green parties are on the "left." In contrast to the traditional Left, however, they do not wish to replace markets by authoritarian state power, but search for libertarian institutions that enhance personal and small group

Table 4.1. Green and Other Left-Libertarian Parties in Western Europe in the 1970s and 1980s

		Average percentage of support in national parliamentary elections	
		1970-79	1980-89
I. Countries with significant Left-Socialist parties			
DENMARK	Socialist People's party	6.0	12.6
	Left Socialists	2.3	1.9
	Greens	—	0.7
NETHERLANDS	Party of Political Radicals	2.4	
	Pacifist Socialist party	1.3	4.8
	Communist party of Netherlands	3.4	
	Greens	—	0.2
NORWAY	Socialist People's party	7.1*	6.8
	Greens	—	·0.2
SWEDEN	Left party (Communists)	4.9	5.6
	Environment party/Greens	—	2.9
II. Countries with significant Ecology/Green parties			
AUSTRIA	United Greens of Austria	—	4.0
BELGIUM	Agalev and Ecolo	—	6.0
Germany	Greens	—	5.1
SWITZERLAND	Radical Left/Green Alternatives	0.8	3.9
	Green party	0.2	3.9
III. Countries without any significant Left-libertarian parties			
FINLAND	Greens	—	2.7
FRANCE	Unified Socialist party and other Extreme Left	3.3	1.2
	Ecology Lists	1.0	0.9
GREECE	Communist party (Interior)	1.3	1.2
	Ecology Lists	—	0.1
IRELAND	Green Alliance	—	0.1
ITALY	Radical Left/Demoproletarians	1.7	1.6
	Radical Party	1.5	2.4
	Greens	—	1.3
PORTUGAL	Greens (alliance with orthodox Communist party)	—	—
SPAIN	various Green Lists**	—	0.5
UNITED KINGDOM	various Ecology/Green parties	0.1	0.1

* Figure is inflated because it attributes the total vote of the 1973 anti-EC electoral alliance to the Socialist People's party.
** Not incuded are ecologists participating in the United Left in 1986.

autonomy as well as the play of voluntary association and democratic self-governance. For this reason, "left-libertarian politics" captures the spirit of the new party category that appeals to such sentiments.[7]

Of course, there are variations between more moderate and more radical left-libertarian parties (cf. Müller-Rommel 1985), but they may be unrelated to party labels. For example, the German Greens are on most accounts more radical than the Danish Socialist People's party. A certain ideological incoherence of left-libertarian parties is due to the fact that they do not offer simple institutional solutions that fit all social problems. In contrast to the ideologies of the modern age that advocate the supremacy of a single organization principle of society, whether it is the market (liberalism), central organization (socialism) or the community (anarchism), left-libertarian parties realize that in advanced complex societies, the main object is to find a different mix and linkage between markets, formal organization, and community that satisfies the quest for autonomy and participation better than existing institutions (cf. Kitschelt 1989, 90–95; 1992a).

In summary, the voter profiles of Green or left-socialist parties as well as their ideological orientations justifies combining them under the heading of left-libertarian parties. Still, we must account for the fact that left-socialist parties were formed in the late 1950s, while Green left-libertarian parties developed only in the 1970s and 1980s.

THE EMERGENCE OF GREEN PARTIES

The interplay between changing societal demand patterns, political institutions and opportunity structures, and momentous events that serve as catalysts to overcome coordination problems among potential participants and supporters of new parties, explains how left-libertarian parties come about.[8] No doubt, the transition to a "postindustrial" social organization in which a large share of the work force is employed in personal services or manipulates cultural symbols, in which most individuals can satisfy a fairly wide range of economic needs, and in which a large percentage of the work force is protected from economic catastrophe by social insurance systems, is the major precondition for the rise of left-libertarian parties. Only in this climate of security and affluence do individuals begin to broaden their menu of political demands and attribute more salience to social involvement and personal creative growth that surpass the agenda of economic (re)distribution (Inglehart 1990). This argument has recently been confirmed by the formation of East European party systems. Although environmental movements represented prominent, well-publicized avenues of low-level protest under Communist rule in the 1980s, nowhere in Eastern Europe have Green parties been able to attract more than two to three percent of the vote in the founding elections after the collapse of the old regimes. For the time being, Eastern Europe lacks the societal underpinnings that foster left-libertarian parties.

In contrast to this argument, Alber (1985) and Burklin (1987) have suggested that economic uncertainty experienced by dissatisfied intellectuals who lack the skills and resources to become economically successful participants in an advanced economy promotes antisystem politics in Green parties as a "sour grapes" reaction. Such individuals oppose the social order because they cannot reap its benefits. The evidence, however, speaks against this explanation.[9] Left-libertarian predilections often precede and shape the choice of professional careers; moreover, many voters of left-libertarian parties are economically well-protected white collar employees and (higher) civil servants.

The institutions of advanced welfare capitalism, however, do not explain the timing, the label, and the strength of left-libertarian party growth. Beyond economic conditions, the emergence of left-libertarian politics is promoted by political opportunities. Particularly the long-term government incumbency by socialist parties promotes left-libertarian parties. While in opposition, conventional socialist parties up to the 1970s often raised hopes that they would pursue left-libertarian policies, including strict environmental protection, once coming to office. But when that time arrived, socialist parties in the 1970s disappointed such expectations and instead engaged in a technocratic management of the economy that emphasized economic growth. The early group of left socialist parties took off only in countries that had experienced long-term social democratic rule in the 1950s (Denmark, France, Netherlands, Norway). Green parties grew vigorously in the 1980s in those countries in which social democrats had been regular government participants throughout the 1970s (Austria, Belgium, Finland, Germany, Switzerland), and it is in these countries that the older left-socialist parties acquired a strong ecological tinge. Conversely, because in the 1970s French socialists were banned to the opposition benches, electoral opportunities for left-libertarians improved only after almost ten years of socialist rule in the late 1980s (Kitschelt 1990a). In a similar vein, prospects for ecological politics have become brighter in Italy since the second half of the 1980s, when the socialists established themselves as the decisive pillar of a technocratic five-party coalition regime.

More controversial than the influence of socialist party government incumbency on left-libertarian party fortunes is the role of interest representation for left-libertarian party formation. I have argued that centralized, corporatist patterns of labor union organization yielding low national strike rates are closely associated with left-libertarian party strength (Kitschelt

1988a). Corporatist labor unions were firmly linked to governing socialist parties in the 1970s and can also keep in check local radical internal opponents, enabling them to pursue policies of compromise with business that boost economic growth. Such policies are often inherently inimical to left-libertarian demands, as is evidenced by union support for nuclear power programs. Left-libertarian activists must then build their own political organizations, because the conventional Left (unions, parties) is inaccessible to their ideas. Nevertheless, critics of this argument have challenged the association of corporatism with left-libertarian parties, once we hold constant for socialist government incumbency (Wilson 1990, 76–78).

A further controversy surrounds the role of electoral systems in the formation of ecological and left-libertarian parties. No country with a majoritarian electoral system also possesses a strong left-libertarian party. Yet since Britain, New Zealand, Canada and France have experienced the rise of other successful new parties receiving stronger support than the most successful European left-libertarian parties, it remains an open question why other ideological currents and not ecologists could overcome the impediments of majoritarian electoral systems. Greece, Ireland, Spain and Portugal, lack sufficient post-industrialization and show that a favorable electoral system is also no sufficient condition for the rise of left-libertarian parties. Finally, the French shifts from a two-round majoritarian system (1981) to a proportional electoral system (1986) and back to the former (1988) offers a natural experiment to gauge the impact of electoral laws. In 1981, both ecologists and the rightist National Front were marginal electoral forces, yet in 1986, under the new electoral regime, only the latter, not the ecologists, could thrive in voter support. And in 1988, with a majoritarian system in place, the National Front remained strong, whereas the ecologists all but vanished. The electoral system thus cannot account for the failure of French ecologists.

Scholars who believe that ecology parties are a genuine category unrelated to broader left-libertarian issues favor ecological hazards as an explanation for the rise of Green parties. Thus, Affigne (1990) and Affigne and Sjoestroem (1990) argue that while in Sweden (1) the left-libertarian position was already occupied by the Left Communists, a new environmental party was able to establish itself in the 1988 national election (5.6 percent) and (2) this party received greatest support in areas strongly affected by fallout from the Chernobyl nuclear accident in the Soviet Union. Without denying the role of the nuclear controversy as a catalyst of party formation (Kitschelt 1988a), it would be difficult to prove a linkage between ecological deprivation and Green party performance in a cross-national perspective. That the Swedish Greens are a rather unique phenomenon perhaps unrelated to the libertarian Left has been shown by voter studies emphasizing their lack

of ideological identity and influx of former supporters of the Swedish bourgeois parties (Bennulf and Holmberg 1990; Berglund 1989, 187). In other
words, the absence of left-libertarian core voters from the Green party electorate may explain the exceptional volatility of the Swedish Greens. Such
core voters, instead, mostly voted for the Left party, the left-libertarian suc-
cessor organization to the Swedish Communists.

Given the paucity of cases of party formation we are able to compare,
we can never be sure what exactly was decisive in a particular instance. We
probably must be content with identifying configurations and clusters of
variables that in certain circumstances contribute to the rise of left-libertarian
parties.

THE ORGANIZATION OF GREEN PARTIES

The literature on party organization has usually revolved around the question whether the "founding ideology" of a party or imperatives of survival in
a competitive party system ("effectiveness") determine internal party organization in the long run. Panebianco (1988) sensibly argues that parties do
build on ideological foundations, but they "articulate" and "modify" them in
light of systemic conditions. In a similar vein, the mobilization of the left-
libertarian cleavage is the major ideological influence on the organization of
respective parties, but institutional rules and a left-libertarian party's competitive position vis-à-vis its opponents also influence internal structure
(Kitschelt 1989, chap. 2).

The more left-libertarian themes dominate the political agenda and are
boosted by social movements, the more radically will Green parties attempt
to implement a participatory structure of decision making without definite
division of labor, formal rules of exclusion and inclusion in internal debates,
and modes of representation and delegation. This finding has been confirmed in studies of the statutes and the organizational dynamic of left-libertarian parties (Poguntke 1987; Kitschelt 1990b) and even the comparison of
subnational Green party units in West Germany and Belgium (Kitschelt
1989). At the same time, however, institutional conditions, such as the willingness of incumbent political elites in public administration, interest
groups, and other parties to listen to representatives of the new political force
("system openness") or the pivotal position of left-libertarian parties in making or breaking government coalitions (strong competitive position), will
temper this desire for a decentralist grass-roots democracy and provide incentives to build a more traditional professionalized party structure with a hierarchical formal organization. Elite incorporation and the lure of government
participation require that parties can make decisions quickly and present

accountable leaders who can make credible commitments on their behalf. In contrast, broad party democracy is very time-consuming and weakens political leadership.

Even where Green and other left-libertarian parties ignore such systemic imperatives, however, the practice of party activists leads to quite different party structures than the grass-roots democratic ideal often aspired to. Green parties develop organizational routines different from those of traditional European mass apparatus parties with a high concentration of power in the formal parliamentary and party leadership, a dominance of political professionals, and a far-reaching interpenetration with economic interest groups. Yet their actual structure is the unintended and unwanted result of ideological aspirations.[10] The root cause of the gap between democratic intentions and factual outcomes is that Green activists underestimate the complexity of political decision making. A mere equalization of activists' access to decision-making processes does not equalize effective chances to participate in Green parties, because activists have unequal resources, abilities and commitments to invest time and energy in political participation. Grass-roots democracy thus often creates a Hobbesian world of struggle of all against all in which those with the most individual resources (time for politics, cognitive preparation, psychic commitment, informal ties to other activists) dominate the party.

As a consequence, left-libertarian party organizations have been characterized by the following attributes: (1) They attract very few activists compared to the size of their electorate (member/voter ratios of less than 2 percent and activist/voter ratios of less than 0.5 percent) because many sympathizers are discouraged by the time commitment effective participation requires. (2) The parties develop few internal commitment mechanisms (e.g., solidarity), but often produce an extremely hostile, competitive internal climate that leads to high turnover rates. (3) Mechanisms of representation and delegation remain underdeveloped because formal authority, even that of elected representatives, is shunned by the activists; formal leadership is supplanted by informal power cliques including activists with and without formal offices. (4) The parties wish to establish close relations to social movements, but rarely manage to do so because of the limited number of party activists and the party's inability to lay out clear policies. Conversely, social movement organizations usually do not wish to be identified with a single party, for fear of reducing the size of their issue coalition. (5) Green parties are incapable of strategizing, i.e., laying out a premeditated course of action that is pursued over a longer period of time and enhances the public credibility of their policy pronouncements. This renders them unreliable in the eyes of many potential voters and makes them unattractive as potential coalition partners for conventional parties.

In a nutshell, left-libertarian parties tend to develop fragmented, decentralized, informal power structures, promoting the particularistic interests of those individuals and groups that can mobilize the most resources for the intraparty power struggle. In this sense, Green and other left-libertarian parties are neither democracies nor oligarchies, but come close to what Eldersveld (1964) called "stratarchies" in which each stratum and niche of the organization develops its unique power elite. Left-libertarian parties are, in Raschke's (1991) terms, "post-industrial framework parties," and distinct from the professionalized bureaucratic mass apparatus parties so common throughout Europe.

While no scholar believes that left-libertarian party structures are immune to change, it is controversial whether they will succumb to Michels's (1911) "iron law of oligarchy" and become like conventional bureaucratic parties with intermittent efforts to move back to their unique patterns (e.g., Offe 1990). Alternatively, cleavage mobilization, regime openness and electoral competitiveness may be contingent forces that affect party organization without necessarily bringing about a unilinear approximation of traditional party organization.

PARTY COMPETITION, STRATEGY, AND THE FUTURE OF ECOLOGY PARTIES

Particularly social democratic politicians and social scientists with similar sympathies initially expected that ecology parties would be "flash parties"—bound to disappear once activists and voters discovered that parties are compelled to take stances on a wide menu of issues rather than focus on a single policy. The tenacity of ecology and other left-libertarian parties demonstrates that an issue-based explanation is insufficient to account for the rise, let alone the maintenance, of left-libertarian parties. These parties appear to be elements of a far-reaching recentering of cleavage dimensions in Western democracies. The left-right dimension of struggles over distributive issues (taxes, social programs, public regulation of business activity, etc.) does not disappear, but is increasingly linked to a libertarian-authoritarian dimension I have sketched above.

The emergence of a dominant left-libertarian versus right-authoritarian political dimension, however, does not automatically give left-libertarian parties a lease on life. The electoral performance of such parties depends critically on (1) their own strategic position and ability to reach out to relevant voter clienteles and (2) the stances of their closest competitors, primarily that of social democratic and socialist parties. Precisely because the voters of left-libertarian parties tend to be highly educated and politicized, they are especially likely to vote strategically. Strategic voting implies that they are predisposed to reward and punish parties contingent upon their past performance and present strategic stances. As a consequence, a number of left-libertarian parties have experienced *unprecedented volatility in their electoral support*, a problem most recently encountered by the German Greens. Probably the single most important lacuna in the literature about left-libertarian parties is the absence of analysis of the strategic interaction between them and their competitors. In the future, left-libertarian parties will stand and fall with the intelligent choice of parties.[11]

Left-libertarian parties must manage to avoid two pitfalls. On the one hand, they risk becoming so radical and so little inclined to cooperate with other parties in the pursuit of joint policy objectives that they will be abandoned by all but a hard core of committed voters. On the other hand, the parties could moderate their stance to the extent that they become virtually indistinguishable from conventional leftist competitors with slight libertarian concessions in their own programs.[12] In that situation, voters have no incentive to support the left-libertarian party. Staunch left-libertarians will stay home or establish a more radical party; moderates will vote for the social democrats or socialists as the next best option.

The chances for the survival of left-libertarian parties thus depend on their ability to carve out a *market niche* without appearing to be too radical for alliances with other parties. Whereas the conditions for the *emergence* of left-libertarian parties were not chosen by, but imposed on, the parties' future activists, the *maintenance and growth* of such parties, once initially established, is to a considerable extent a matter of activists' own calculations and choices, in interaction with those of their competitors.

The strategic stance that is most favorable for left-libertarian parties varies according to the particular conditions of party competition in a given country at a particular point in time. First, the distribution of voters on the left-libertarian/right-authoritarian dimension varies across time and countries. The greater the proportion of left-libertarians in an electorate ("left-libertarian cleavage mobilization"), the greater is the political incentive to present voters with impeccably left-libertarian strategic stances. For example, there are many more left-libertarians in countries such as The Netherlands or West Germany than in Austria, Belgium or Great Britain. Intermediate to high mobilization prevails in the Scandinavian countries, intermediate to low mobilization in the Mediterranean democracies, including France.

Second, in multiparty systems with at least four serious competitors, vote-maximizing parties have incentives to spread out over the competitive space.[13] Thus, the greater the number of parties located on the main competitive dimension, the more likely the left-libertarian parties will have to confine themselves to a market share at the extreme end of the left-libertarian continuum. Third, the party that is usually the ideological neighbor of left-libertarian parties, the social democratic or socialist party, will, if it is vote maximizing, rationally respond to the "crowding" of party systems and the increase of left-libertarian popular support and displace itself to a position closer to that of left socialist or Green parties. Conversely, in an uncrowded party system with only one or two serious bourgeois competitors and relatively subdued left-libertarian popular support, socialist parties do well to choose moderate stances and leave breathing space for left-libertarian parties to adopt moderate positions themselves.[14]

It can be shown empirically that (1) social democratic and left-libertarian parties managed to gain votes in the 1980s only if they followed this logic, but that (2) not all parties complied with this logic, particularly not all social democratic parties. As a consequence, they often lost votes. Since there is insufficient space here to back this argument by a systematic empirical comparison of West European democracies, I will confine myself to brief sketches on six countries illustrating different strategic configurations and electoral outcomes.

All relevant parties made rational choices in *Belgium,* a country in which the party system is only moderately crowded (competition among a total of five relevant parties is segmented in each linguistic region) and left-libertarian popular mobilization is extremely subdued. In this configuration, the socialists chose a moderate strategy giving relatively little emphasis to left-libertarian issues, and this allowed the two Belgian left-libertarian parties— Ecolo in Wallonia and Agalev in Flanders—to carve out a market niche and to thrive electorally with probably the most moderate positions among all successful left-libertarian parties.[15]

The situation is apparently quite different in *The Netherlands,* where the party system is somewhat more crowded than in Belgium and left-libertarian mobilization has been extremely high since the late 1960s. After initial electoral successes of various left-libertarian parties in the 1960s and early 1970s, the Socialist Labor party adopted quite radical left-libertarian stances in the 1970s and effectively improved its electoral share at the expense of its new competitors in most of the elections between 1977 and 1986 (cf. Wolinetz 1977 and 1988). Unfortunately, its stance also isolated Labor from its bourgeois competitors and confined it to the opposition, with the exception of a brief interlude as coalition partner in 1981–82. In 1989, the party emerged from its isolation after adopting a more moderate position, enabling them to enter a Labor-Christian Democratic government (Tromp 1989). In exchange, however, left-libertarian voters abandoned the party and reinforced the Green Progressive Alliance, a fusion of three left-socialist predecessor parties. The Dutch parties clearly show the strategy-dependence of electoral results.

The same lesson can be learnt from the example of *Denmark*. Here, an extremely fragmented party system and intermediate left-libertarian popular orientation strengthened the prospects of parties with left-libertarian appeals. Also, the social democrats were affected by the centrifugal momentum of this configuration, but long resisted against taking strong left-libertarian stances. As a consequence, the left-libertarian parties—above all the Socialist People's party and, until its internal collapse, the Left Socialists—together garnered around 15 percent of the vote in elections during the 1980s. Given the inability of social democrats to exploit the left-libertarian issues, relatively moderate stances by the genuinely left-libertarian parties maximized their electorate. The social democrats sacrificed votes to the left-libertarian parties in order to contain intraparty divisions that had led to the exit of the Center Democrats in the 1970s and in order to achieve a sometimes pivotal position in the party system that allowed it to shape policy majorities in the Danish parliament, if not coalition governments with the more moderate bourgeois parties. Between 1988 and 1990, however, the Danish social democrats moved toward left-libertarian positions under a new young leader and promptly defeated the Socialist People's party in the 1990 election. Unfortunately, the social democrats' move to the left did not increase their bargaining power vis-à-vis the bourgeois parties and may in fact have weakened the party's position in the quest for policy and cabinet control.

Both in The Netherlands and Denmark, the electoral payoffs of left-libertarian and social democratic parties are strategically interdependent. If the latter choose to compete directly for left-libertarian voters, the former are bound to lose support. The combined share of the left parties often contracts in this event, thus strengthening the hold of bourgeois parties on government. The game between left-libertarians and social democrats tends to be zero sum, if not negative sum.

Whereas in Belgium, The Netherlands, and Denmark left-libertarian parties chose rational positions in the sense that they tended to be as moderate as they could afford to be without losing the independent identity of their parties vis-à-vis social democratic parties[16] and thus made the best out of a difficult competitive situation, in other countries left-libertarian parties tended to violate what rational strategic calculation would have mandated. This was the case particularly in France, Germany, and Sweden, all instances in which left-libertarian parties had to pay a high price for their mistakes.

In *France*, during the 1970s, the socialist party in opposition managed to absorb much of the left-libertarian spectrum, particularly the Unified

Socialist party, and to adopt programmatic stances particularly appealing to women, ethnic minorities, and, to a lesser extent, environmentalists and foes of nuclear power. This made it difficult for ecological lists to find an effective niche in the French political marketplace, which was characterized by a relatively strong bipolarization and only limited left-libertarian mobilization. By choosing a "centrist" position in the 1980s, isolating the ecology issue from other political questions and trying to take a position between the competing left and right party blocs, however, the ecology lists remained unable to attract a substantial electorate in the all-important national legislative and presidential elections, because they could not exploit the opportunity to develop the programmatic of a second, libertarian Left in contrast to the socialists' government practice.[17]

In *Germany*, a party system with little fragmentation and high bipolarity exercised a centripetal pull on Green party positions, particularly when social democrats and Greens combined to control majorities in state legislatures or had a chance to control legislative majorities if small electoral shifts took place. At the same time, the very high left-libertarian popular mobilization in the 1980s pushed the party toward more radical positions. A comparison of state and federal electoral results for the Greens shows nicely that Green electoral success is positively related to (1) moderate Green stances, seeking cooperation with the social democrats, but also (2) social democratic politicians unwilling to put left-libertarian themes at the top of their agenda and thus leaving space for Green politics (Kitschelt 1989, chap. 8). The reverse combination—a radical Green party competing against a social democracy with left-libertarian appeals—has always been electorally disastrous not only for the Greens themselves, but also for the social democrats. This was demonstrated most recently in the December 1990 national election when an internally divided, but often radical, Green party antagonized many of its voters, who proceeded to abstain from voting altogether or cast their vote in support of the social democrats, led by their most prominent advocate of left-libertarian politics, Oskar Lafontaine (cf. Kitschelt 1991).

Just as in Denmark and The Netherlands, direct competition between the conventional and the libertarian left yielded a negative sum game for the combined Left, benefiting only the bourgeois parties.[18] It must be added, however, that both Greens and social democrats have learned their lesson from this experience. In the first half of 1991, an internal power struggle in the Greens resulted in the exit of the most radical faction, while in the social democrats Lafontaine withdrew from national prominence and was replaced by a more moderate leader. As a consequence, both parties have experienced spectacular victories in a string of state elections that have seriously weakened the Christian Democratic federal government.

In *Sweden,* finally, the situation was complicated by a dual representation of left-libertarian politics in the 1988–91 legislature. In an environment of moderately high left-libertarian popular inclinations and extensive party system fragmentation, there was room for both a more radical left-libertarian party—the Left party Communists—and the more moderate environmentalists. The parliamentary representatives of the Greens, however, were unable to sustain this "product differentiation" of left-libertarian politics. They even negotiated with the Left party Communists about a joint electoral platform and generally took positions hostile to both bourgeois and social democratic parties. This strategy antagonized their overwhelmingly bourgeois voters and contributed to the party's decline in the 1991 election. Had the party leadership been electorally rational, it would have been compelled to dissociate itself from left-libertarian themes and to build a "bourgeois" ecology party, a feat unsuccessful in all but one Western party system.[19] This episode in Swedish politics shows that Green parties, divorced from the broader left-libertarian cleavage syndrome, tend to have little staying power.

CONCLUSION

Are Green and other ecology parties here to stay? My analysis has shown that no simple yes or no can answer this question, but that we must take into account a number of contingencies that influence the opportunities for ecology parties. A major precondition of Green success is the continued existence of a left-libertarian sector of popular preferences that combines demands for protection from the logic of the marketplace with calls for the autonomy of individuals and self-organized groups in the governance of important life spheres and a participatory political process. It is unlikely that this syndrome of expectations will disappear as long as economic affluence and modern welfare states are in place.

The existence of a left-libertarian versus right-authoritarian cleavage, by itself, however, is insufficient to give Green parties a lease on life. Several further conditions must be met. First, Green parties must see themselves not as single-issue parties, but in terms of the broader competitive space in which the most promising position is one that combines support for ecology with left-libertarian social and economic policies in order to attract significant shares of the electorate. Second, they are viable only in countries where they do not face an already established left-libertarian party with a left-socialist label, as the Scandinavian experience shows. Finally, Green and other left-libertarian parties can only thrive as long as conventional left parties do not fully embrace their agenda. Although this may occasionally happen, in general, the political costs of such strategies are too high in terms of diminishing the overall electoral strength of the left and of reducing the parties' chances to participate in government office to expect them to become the standard operating procedure of the conventional Left. Thus, Green and other left-libertarian parties may thrive in an environment of increasing "product differentiation" among political parties in parliamentary democracies. On a speculative note, we may conclude that such parties are driving forces precipitating the end of the age of large, "catchall" parties.

NOTES

1. Space limitations prohibit an exhaustive review of this literature. Widely discussed comparative analyses of the emergence of ecology parties include Müller-Rommel (1982, 1989), Rüdig (1985, 1989) and Kitschelt (1988a). There are probably already more than a hundred articles and books on ecology parties in individual countries.

2. For a good discussion of the cleavage concept, compare Bartolini and Mair (1990, 213–20).

3. I will not document this phenomenon here in greater detail because just about every voter analysis of "new politics" party support reaches this conclusion.

4. A detailed comparative analysis of the outlook of left-libertarian party electorates in Austria, Belgium, Denmark, France, Germany, Italy, The Netherlands, Spain and Sweden can be found in Kitschelt (1992, chap. 4). A wide range of useful materials on individual countries has been compiled in Müller-Rommel (1989).

5. Of course, environmentalists often advance arguments for nature protection based on straightforward economic reasoning. Postmaterialist Green politics, however, is concerned with the more radical claim that environmental protection should have priority even when it conflicts with economic considerations.

6. For an empirical analysis with Belgian data, see Kitschelt and Hellemans (1990b).

7. It can be shown empirically that political parties combine "old" left and libertarian positions, yielding a dominant competitive dimension in advanced Western democracies that ranges from left-libertarian to right-authoritarian positions (cf. Kitschelt 1992b, chap. 4).

8. On the general logic of explaining party formation, see Lipset and Rokkan (1967), Hauss and Rayside (1978), and Wilson (1980).

9. For a theoretical and empirical critique, compare Kitschelt (1988a, 1988c) and Goul-Andersen (1990, 103).

10. For a review of organizational studies covering a variety of left-libertarian parties, yet coming to this general conclusion, see Kitschelt (1990b). Detailed studies of the internal politics of the German and Belgian Greens can be found in Kitschelt (1989), Kitschelt and Hellemans (1990) and Raschke (1991), whose findings closely match those of the earlier studies.

11. I have analyzed the interaction between German Greens and social democrats in (Kitschelt 1989, chap. 9). The following paragraphs draw on an exten-

sive empirical analysis of the interaction between left-libertarian and conventional socialist parties in ten countries (Kitschelt 1992b, chap. 4).

12. The fact that social democratic parties have attempted to adopt left-libertarian positions on ecology, feminism, the decentralization of public administration, and minority rights shows that both the "new" and conventional Left compete on the same dimension. In contrast to the expectation of salience theories of party competition (e.g., Budge and Farlie 1983), parties compete over the *same* issues, yet with *different* positions.

13. Proofs of this theorem that had already been presented by Downs (1957) can be found in Cox (1990a, 1990b) and in Shepsle and Cohen (1990).

14. All these propositions presuppose a single-round vote-maximizing strategy. More complex strategies, such as joint vote maximizing of left-libertarian and socialist parties, socialist maximization of the probability of cabinet participation rather than votes, or long-term vote maximization at the expense of short-term losses, are not considered here. These variations are discussed in Kitschelt (1992b).

15. See, for example, Agalev's own ten-year anniversary report reviewing its political stances in the Belgian parliament (Agalev 1991, 24–74).

16. Only in the Danish case, the argument can be made that by 1988, the Socialist People's party had moderated to an extent that it came dangerously close to the positions of the social democrats, and consequently lost votes to the latter party (Smith-Jespersen 1989, 191–92), a problem that became worse in the 1990 election.

17. For a close analysis of French ecology party stances and electoral performance, see Prendiville (1989) and Kitschelt (1990a).

18. This situation was exacerbated by the particular nature of the key campaign issue—German unification. Questions of national identity are difficult to accommodate in the political discourse of both the old and the new Left and the internal divisiveness of this issue in both parties reduced their electoral credibility. For a closer analysis of this development, see Kitschelt (1991a).

19. This exception is Switzerland, where the centrist Green party is slightly stronger (5.1 percent) than the more radical left-libertarian Green Alternatives (4.3 percent). Cf. Ladner (1989).

REFERENCES

Affigne, Anthony D. 1990. Environmental crisis, Green party power: Chernobyl and the Swedish Greens. In *Green politics,* vol. 1., ed. Wolfgang Rüdig, 115–32. Edinburgh: University of Edinburgh Press.

Affigne, Anthony D., and Alf Sjoestroem 1990. Public opinion and the Swedish Greens, 1988–90: Erosion, consolidation and consensus. Paper presented at the Annual Meeting of the American Political Science Association, San Francisco, California.

Agalev. 1991. *Tussen Droom en Daad. Agalev in het parlement.* Brussels: Ploeg.

Alber, Jens. 1985. Modernisierung neuer Spannunglinien und die politischen

Chancen der Grunen. *Politische Vierteljahresschrift*, 26, no. 2:211–26.

Bartolini, Stefano, and Peter Mair. 1990. *Identity, competition, and electoral availability: The stability of european electorates, 1885–1985*. Cambridge: Cambridge University Press.

Bennulf, Martin and Soeren Holmberg. 1990. The Green breakthrough in Sweden. *Scandinavian Political Studies* 13, no. 2:165–84.

Berglund, Sten. 1989. The decline and fall of Swedish Communism? *Journal of Communist Studies* 5, no. 1:83–88.

Budge, Ian and Dennis J. Farlie. 1983. *Explaining and predicting elections: Issue effects and party strategies in twenty-three democracies*. London: Allen and Unwin.

Burklin, Wilhelm P. 1987. Governing left parties frustrating the radical non-established Left: The rise and inevitable decline of the Greens. *European Sociological Review* 3, no. 2:109–26.

Cox, Gary W. 1990a. Multicandidate spatial competition. In *Advances in the spatial theory of voting*, ed. James Enelow and Melvin J. Hinich, 179–98. Cambridge: Cambridge University Press.

———. 1990b. Centripetal and centrifugal incentives in electoral systems. *American Journal of Political Science* 34, no. 4:903–35.

Dalton, Russell J. 1988. *Citizen politics in Western democracies*. Chatham, N.J.: Chatham House.

Downs, Anthony. 1957. *An economic theory of democracy*. New York: Harper and Row.

Eldersveld, Samuel J. 1964. *Political parties. A behavioral analysis*. Chicago: Rand McNally.

Goul-Andersen, Jorgen. 1990. "Environmentalism," "new politics" and industrialism: Some theoretical perspectives. *Scandinavian Political Studies* 13, no. 2:101–18.

Habermas, Jürgen. 1982. *Theorie des kommunikativen Handelns*. Vol. 2. Frankfurt am Main: Suhrkamp.

Hauss, Charles, and David Rayside. 1978. The development of new parties in Western democracies since 1945. In *Political parties: Development and decay*, ed. Louis Maisel and James Cooper, 31–57. Beverly Hills, Calif.: Sage.

Inglehart, Ronald. 1990. *Culture shift*. Princeton: Princeton University Press.

Kitschelt, Herbert. 1985. New social movements in West Germany and the United States. In *Political power and social theory*, vol. 5, ed. Maurice Zeitlin, 273-324. Greenwich, Conn.: JAI Press.

———. 1988a. Left-libertarian parties. Explaining innovation in competitive party systems. *World Politics* 40, no. 2 (January): 194–234.

———. 1988b. Organization and strategy in Belgian and West German ecology parties. A new dynamic of party politics in Western Europe. *Comparative Politics* 20, no. 2 (January): 127–54.

———. 1988c. The life expectancy of left-libertarian parties. Does structural transformation or economic decline explain party innovation? A response to Wilhelm

P. Burklin. *European Sociological Review* 4, no. 2 (September): 155–60.

———. 1989. *The logics of party formation: Structure and strategy of Belgian and West German ecology parties.* Ithaca, N.Y.: Cornell University Press.

———. 1990a. La gauche libertaire et les ecologistes français. *Revue Française de Science Politique* 40, no. 3 (Juin 1990): 339–65.

———. 1990b. New social movements and the decline of party organization. In *Challenging the political order,* ed. Russell J. Dalton and Manfred Keuchler, 179–208. New York: Oxford University Press.

———. 1991. The 1990 German federal election and national unification: A watershed in German electoral history? *West European Politics* 14, no. 4.

———. 1992a. The socialist discourse and party strategy in West European democracies. To appear in *The crisis of socialism in Eastern and Western Europe,* ed. Gary Marks and Christiane Lemke. Durham, N.C.: Duke University Press.

———. 1992b. N.d. *The transformation of European social democracy.* Durham, N.C.: Duke University. Typescript.

Kitschelt, Herbert and Staf Hellemans. 1990a. *Beyond the European Left: Ideology and political action in the Belgian ecology parties.* Durham, N.C.: Duke University Press.

———. 1990b. "The left-right semantics and the new politics cleavage. *Comparative Political Studies* 23, no. 2:210–38.

Ladner, Andreas. 1989. Switzerland: The "Green" and "Alternative" parties. In *New politics in Western Europe: The rise and success of Green parties and alternative lists,* ed. Ferdinand Müller-Rommel, 155–75. Boulder, Colo.: Westview Press.

Lipset, Seymour Martin, and Stein Rokkan. 1967. Cleavage structures, party systems, and voter alignments: An introduction. In *Party systems and voter alignments,* ed. Lipset and Rokkan, 1–64. New York: Free Press.

Michels, Robert. 1911/62. *Political Parties.* English edition. London: Collier-Macmillan.

Müller-Rommel, Ferdinand. 1982. "Parteien neuen Typs" in Westeuropa: Eine vergleichende Analyse. *Zeitschrift für Parlamentsfragen* 13, no. 3:369–90.

———. 1985. The Greens in Western Europe: Similar but different. *International Political Science Review* 6, no. 4:483–99.

———. 1989. *New politics in Western Europe: The rise and success of Green parties and alternative lists.* Boulder, Colo.: Westview Press.

Offe, Claus. 1985. New social movements as a meta-political challenge. *Social Research* 52, no. 4:817–68.

———. 1990. Reflections on the institutional self-transformation of movement politics: A tentative stage model. In *Challenging the political order,* ed. Russell J. Dalton and Manfred Keuchler, 232–50. New York: Oxford University Press.

Panebianco, Angelo. 1988. *Political parties: Organization and power.* Cambridge: Cambridge University Press.

Poguntke, Thomas. 1987. New politics and party systems: The emergence of a new

Herbert Kitschelt

type of party? *West European Politics* 10, no. 1: 76–88.

Prendiville, Brendan. 1989. France. "Les Verts." In *New politics in Western Europe: The rise and success of Green parties and alternative lists,* ed. Ferdinand Müller-Rommel, 87–100. Boulder, Colo.: Westview Press.

Raschke, Joachim. 1991. *Krise der Grunen: Bilanz and Neubeginn.* Marburg: Schueren.

Rüdig, Wolfgang. 1985. The Greens in Europe: Ecological parties and the European elections of 1984. *Parliamentary Affairs* 38, no. 1:56–72.

———. 1989. Explaining Green party development: Reflections on a theoretical framework. Paper presented at the U.K. Political Studies Association Conference, University of Warwick, Coventry, 4–6 April.

Shepsle, Kenneth A., and Ronald N. Cohen. 1990. Multiparty competition, entry, and entry deterrence in spatial models of elections. In *Advances in the spatial theory of voting,* ed. James Enelow and Melvin J. Hinich, 12–45. Cambridge: Cambridge University Press.

Smith-Jespersen, Mary Paul. 1989. A Danish defense dilemma: The election of May 1988. *West European Politics* 12, no. 3:190–95.

Tromp, Bart. 1989. Party strategies and system change in The Netherlands. *West European Politics* 12, no. 4 (Oct.): 82–97.

Wilson, Frank L. 1990. New-corporatism and the rise of new social movements. In *Challenging the political order,* ed. Russell J. Dalton and Manfred Keuchler, 67–83. New York: Oxford University Press.

Wolinetz, Steven. 1977. The Dutch Labour party: A social democratic party in transition. In *Social democratic parties in Western Europe,* ed. William E. Paterson and Alastair H. Thomas, 342–88. New York: St. Martin's Press.

———. 1988. Structure and strategy of the Dutch Socialist party in the 1970s and the 1980s. Paper presented at the Annual Meeting of the American Political Science Association, Washington, D.C.

5 The Ecological Movement and Green Parties in Scandinavia: Problems and Prospects

JAMES P. LESTER
ELFAR LOFTSSON

The purpose of this chapter is to discuss the evolution of the environmental movement and especially the Green party in the Scandinavian region. In doing so, we describe the context in which Green parties developed in Denmark, Norway, and Sweden during the 1970s through the early 1990s. We also discuss the extent to which the Green party in these countries is (or is not) a viable political force in electoral politics at the current time and in the foreseeable future.

Throughout history, the three countries in the Scandinavian region— Denmark, Norway, and Sweden—have in many aspects formed an integrated area.[1] These three countries share a common historical heritage and their languages and cultural traditions are closely related to one another. Furthermore, interactions in the form of trade and immigration have continuously taken place between these countries. Therefore, it is logical that contemporary Scandinavian societies would display many similarities. Politically speaking, all three countries are modern democracies which exhibit considerable similarities in their institutional structures as well as in their political cleavages and the content of their national politics (Petersson 1991).

However, the road to modern democracy has differed between the three countries. In Denmark, for example, the democratization process included a radical breakup of a totalitarian monarchy in the middle of the nineteenth century. In Norway, the democratization process became part of the fight for national liberation from the Swedish-Norwegian union, an alliance that was strongly dominated by Sweden. In Sweden, which is the only one of these countries that has never been occupied by another state, the democratization process evolved more evenly than in the other two countries.

Despite differences in the formation of their modern democracies, the political culture in these Scandinavian countries demonstrates many common features. All three countries have based their political system on the parliamentary model and on proportional representation in their parliaments. Denmark and Sweden have undertaken far-reaching revisions of their constitutions (in 1953 and 1974, respectively) while Norway still bases her political system on the old, so-called "Eidsvold constitution" from 1814. The system of proportional voting in the Scandinavian countries has resulted in multiparty systems with coalition or minority governments as the normal governmental solution. Thus, in the relation between parliament and the executive branch the latter appears, in an international comparison, to be in a weak position (Damgaard 1991).

The political divisions in the Scandinavian countries also display significant similarities. The main structures of the modern party-systems of these countries were established during the period from 1870 to 1920 (Kitschelt 1988). While both the conservative and the liberal parties have roots in the limited franchise of the nineteenth century, the Social Democrats and the agrarian parties were initiated as the franchise was extended to earlier unrepresented social classes. The Social Democrats thus represent the industrial working class and the agrarian parties represent the small farmers and the working people of the rural areas. In Sweden and Norway the latter have broadened their political identity and are now not solely representatives of the agrarian groups; today they have established themselves as parties near the center of the liberal-conservative political scale. However, the dominating group which supports these parties is still the rural population. In Denmark, agrarian interests are mainly represented by the Liberals (Lindblad et al., 1984).[2]

In all three Scandinavian countries, the Social Democrats have been a dominating political force since modern democracy and universal franchise were established in the beginning of this century. The Social Democrats have close connections to the trade unions, to consumer-cooperation groups and to a number of other strongly organized groups. Due to their dominating position in the politics of Scandinavia, the Social Democrats have not only been able to dominate decision making in the three countries' parliaments, but have also been able to dominate substantially the political agenda. Thus, the Scandinavian countries demonstrate a rather uniform political agenda concerning economic matters and the distribution of economic goods in society (Holmberg and Weibull 1989).

However, there are clear signs that the one-dimensional left-right character of Scandinavian politics is breaking up. Until the beginning of the 1980s, political conditions in the Scandinavian countries could be characterized as generally stable. Until this time the main structures of the countries' party systems had remained intact, and to a large extent similar issues had dominated the political agenda. Nevertheless, many studies of social conditions in the Nordic countries have attempted to describe the changes occurring in these societies. In his book on Nordic politics, Olof Petersson (1991) points to two general features of the Scandinavian model of society, i.e., welfare politics and the system of government. According to Petersson, the issue of welfare politics involves several features:

1. The Scandinavian welfare systems are relatively extensive and significantly redistributional.

2. The Scandinavian welfare systems are universal, i.e., they cover the whole population, or in the case of family allowance and old-age pensions, whole groups of people.

3. The welfare systems in Scandinavia have also been described as institutional in the sense that they are primarily based on citizenship, and not only, as in many other European countries, linked to activities on the labor market.

4. Finally, the welfare politics of Scandinavian countries have been characterized by solidarity and a universal aspect. The aims of this policy are to integrate the whole population and to promote equality in society.

The other central aspect of the Scandinavian model of society treated by Petersson has to do with political culture. The fundamental aspects of the Scandinavian political model have been the unification of capitalism, political democracy and the welfare state. This process has provided a constructive solution to the conflicts of interest between the main industrial forces, capital and labor. The strong position of interest-group organizations has led to the Scandinavian societies being characterized as "corporatist." These two features have together furthered the consensual character of Scandinavian politics (Archer and Maxwell 1980).

The similarities between the Scandinavian countries have also been favorable for the cooperation between the countries on the wider international arena. The countries have frequently taken joint stands in United Nations decision-making bodies, and they have built up extended structures for regional cooperation within the Nordic Council and the Nordic Council of Ministers. But, they have also chosen different solutions on some main international issues. Thus, Denmark and Norway joined NATO in 1949, while Sweden held a position of non-alignment and neutrality. And in 1970, Denmark joined the Economic Community, while the other two countries still have not entered the EC.

THE ENVIRONMENTAL MOVEMENT IN SCANDINAVIA

A range of events may have influenced the general public's interest in environmental questions that has emerged in many countries in Europe during the last fifteen or twenty years (Liberatore 1991). The ecological debate had begun earlier in the United States and American influences in the environmental debate in Western Europe were significant forces in the Scandinavian context (Dalton and Kuechler 1990). Further, very visible proofs of the large-scale damage caused by the highly industrial societies as well as the planned economies in Eastern Europe clearly underlined the urgency of a resolute, coherent environmental policy. And at the same time the debates on the arms race and on other large-scale "systemic" issues, particularly the nuclear energy issue, tended to change the focus of politics. While established political parties mainly concentrated on questions of economic growth and the management of the welfare state, public opinion became increasingly worried about the survival and the sustainability of modern society.

In all three Scandinavian countries the energy question in the early 1970s is closely related to the rise of environmental movements (Vedung 1989). In Sweden and Denmark, the energy crisis in 1973–74 focused attention on how the energy supply could be guaranteed in these countries in the future. Both countries had nuclear energy research projects since the early 1950s (Andersen 1990). In Sweden, all the parties of the Riksdag supported the decisions in 1970 and 1971 to build eleven nuclear power plants. This unity was lost in 1973, when the Center party decided to oppose the nuclear buildup program. After that the question of nuclear energy became an issue of significant political controversy in Sweden for many years to come. Finally, the issue was settled by a referendum in 1980 (Holmberg and Asp 1984; Vedung 1988). Three alternatives were presented in the referendum: one strongly in favor of an extended nuclear power program, a second proposing an extended program of twelve power plants and a termination of the program in the year 2010, and finally an alternative for an immediate termination of the nuclear program. The result of the referendum was that the first alternative received 18.9 percent of the vote, alternative two received 39.1 percent of the vote, and alternative three 38.7 percent of the vote (Vedung 1989). Since alternatives one and two gained almost 60 percent of the vote, there was not a clear majority for terminating the nuclear program. Thus, the decision of the Riksdag was in line with the second alternative.

However, the opponents of the nuclear power program had based their campaign on public mobilization and grass-roots participation, while the two other campaigns were strongly financed and administrated by industry and by the organizational establishment. Opinion about nuclear energy in Sweden split along traditional party lines, although the Social Democrats and the Liberal party were severely divided on this issue. The primary opponents of the energy program, who were predominately females and young people, were indeed the groups with rather loose traditional roots in these parties. The experiences from the energy campaign created long-lasting skepticism towards the political establishment among these groups. The result of the referendum was obviously a disappointment for many of the environmental activists who had been deeply engaged in the campaign against nuclear energy.

Soon after the referendum, plans for the establishment of an environmental party took form. Encouraged by the strength and enthusiasm of the earlier antinuclear movement, the Green party in Sweden was established in September 1981 (Weinberg 1983; Vedung 1989). Even in Denmark the energy question was very important in paving the way for the environmental movement. Encouraged by the energy crisis in the early 1970s, a large association of power companies (ELSAM) applied for permission to build nuclear power plants. As a quick response to this application the Organization for Information on Nuclear Power was established in 1974. This organization soon became the main opponent of nuclear energy in Denmark. Obviously influenced by the strong grass-roots opposition to nuclear energy, the Danish parliament (Folketinget) postponed decisions on nuclear power plants. Like those in Sweden, the Social Democrats in Denmark were divided on the issue (Tonsgaard 1989). However, while the proponents of nuclear energy among the Social Democrats in Sweden succeeded with forcing a party decision in favor of modifying the nuclear energy program, their Danish counterparts abstained from fighting internal battles. Instead, the Danish Social Democrats repeatedly postponed any decisions on nuclear energy.

In the beginning of the 1980s, a large parliamentary majority took a stand against a Danish nuclear energy program, and in 1984, the program was also formally canceled. Meanwhile, the disputes on nuclear energy in Denmark had contributed to a renewal of the activities of the Danish Society for the Preservation of National Amenities (*Danmarks Naturfrednings-forening*). This organization, which was founded in 1911, traditionally recruited members among the urban social elite, and it had up to this time mainly focused on the preservation of nature. By the end of the 1970s, the organization started campaigns to recruit new members; these eventually resulted in an increase of memberships from some 50,000 in the 1970s to over 200,000 in 1983. It finally reached some 280,000 members in 1988.

Following this successful membership drive, the organization was the largest nature-preservation organization in Europe (Svold 1989). The rapidly increasing environmental concerns in Denmark during the early 1980s incited an intensive debate in the traditional political parties about environmental questions. The Social Democrats, in particular, had intensive internal debates on these issues. The establishment of the Danish Greens in 1983 was very much a consequence of increasing environmental concern, but it did not make any substantial changes in the Danish party system (Schuttemeyer 1989). Paradoxically, while ecological issues and environmental consciousness have been very strong in Denmark as compared to other countries, the political party taking these questions as their main programmatic platform, the Greens, was from the beginning only a marginal political force in Danish politics (Andersen 1990).

In stark contrast to Denmark and Sweden, the nuclear energy issue has

117

never been important in Norway. The reason is obviously that the country has very little need for nuclear energy due to its rich access to hydroelectric power and oil reserves in the North Sea. Despite this favorable energy situation, the energy issue has been very polarized and controversial in Norway. The development of hydroelectric power gave rise to strong protests and a range of demonstrations in the period from 1970 to 1980. When the construction of the Alta Dam in northern Finland was begun in 1980, some violent confrontations took place between sit-down demonstrators and the police.

So, whereas the object of protest differed between Norway on the one hand and Denmark and Sweden on the other, the political effects seem to have been similar. All three countries experienced a growing, mobilized grass-roots movement and protests against large-scale energy projects aiming to provide for future industrial needs and economic growth. To many of the opponents of these programs, the programs represented a merged interest of large-scale industry and the political establishment.

THE GREENS IN SCANDINAVIA

As in many other European countries, the main ideological structures in Scandinavia have their roots in the nineteenth century. The changing preconditions for subsistence, industrialization and the urbanization connected with the modernization process in these countries were followed by new ideas in politics. The dominating ideology in this process was liberalism, which later confronted critics both from the old establishment in society and from the new classes generated by the modernization process. Conservative opposition to liberalism expressed itself both as a general mistrust of liberal concepts of individual freedom and sovereignty, and of liberalism's instrumental notion of the state and other central institutions of the society. The early trade unions and other organizations of the industrial workers were initially influenced by Marxist theory, but soon the labor movement separated from many of the obviously unrealistic ideas of Marx and formulated a reformist program of socialism, characterized by liberal democracy, equality and a pragmatic view of capitalism.[3] Basically, two ideological dimensions of Scandinavian politics can be distinguished. On the one hand, there is a dimension concerning production, preservation and the distribution of values (mainly material values), and on the other hand there is a dimension regarding the subject of politics, i.e., whether the focus of politics should be a) individuals, b) social classes, or c) the state as a carrier of the common and long-term interest of the whole nation. Table 5.1 details the scope of this ideology.

Table 5.1. The Scope of Classical Ideologies

Focus on	*Main Objective of Politics*		
	production of values	*distribution of values*	*preservation of values*
Individuals	classical liberalism	social liberalism	neo-liberalism
Social Classes	Marxism	classical social democracy	
The State		modern social democracy	classical conservatism

Source: Compiled by the authors

At the initial stage of the Green movement, proponents of its ideas emphasized that their ideology was not compatible with the ideas of the established political parties, and they particularly stressed the irrelevance of the left-right political dimension. Instead, the "Green ideology" focused on a quality-of-life approach rather than the material approach of traditional political parties (Miljopartiet de Grona under 10 ar 1991). Furthermore, Green movement ideologues stressed the responsibility of politics for the whole of nature—not just for human beings. Obviously, the first part of this argument can be related to the values formerly introduced.

Classical ideologies were concerned about both material and nonmaterial values. The other aspect of the Green argument, that of being concerned with the whole of nature, clearly represented a widening of the scope of the established ideologies. Simplifying table 5.1 above and extending the dimension for central focus we get a generalized picture of the modern ideological scope in table 5.2.

Table 5.2. The Scope of Modern Ideologies

	Main Objective of Politics	
	production and distribution of values	*preservation of values*
anthropocenteric focus	liberalism social democracy Marxism modern conservatism	classical conservatism
biocentric focus	the new left	the Green ideology

Source: Compiled by the authors.

119

James P. Lester and Elfar Loftsson

The Green parties in Scandinavia fit well into the pattern discussed above. The introduction of the 1989 party program of the Danish Green party, from 1989, may serve as a good illustration:

> We consider ourselves as an alternative to the established parties. We are a society of free people reluctant to [show] obedience to hierarchical party structures . . . A change of attitudes away from short-sighted, economical thinking is necessary. It is wrong to think that the present, high-consuming society makes people more happy. On the contrary, it makes people more stressed and unfree. Not until we strive to liberate ourselves from overrating our material needs and recognize the limits set by nature, will we be able to develop the fantasy that is needed for a life in harmony with our environment and with each other. (De Gronne 1989, 4)

In all the Scandinavian countries the Green parties have been a marginal phenomenon in politics if the criteria they are judged by is only the size of their results in parliamentary elections. With its 3.2 percent of the vote in the 1991 elections, the Swedish Green party is still the largest. Since its establishment the Swedish Green party has taken part in four parliamentary elections. After two unsuccessful attempts to be represented in Parliament in 1982 and in 1985, which left the party far from the 4 percent threshold for parliamentary representation, the party had great success in the 1988 elections, when it won 5.6 percent of the votes and gained twenty seats in parliament (Vedung 1989; Gilljam and Holmberg 1990). However, in the 1991 elections, the Swedish Green party only obtained 3.2 percent of the vote, thus losing its seats in the new parliament (Rexed 1991).

Both the Danish and the Norwegian ecological parties were established later than their Swedish counterpart and up to now these parties have only gained a marginal part of the electoral vote. The percentage of the Green vote in elections since their establishment is shown in table 5.3.

Table 5.3. Election Results of Green Parties in Scandinavia, 1982–91 (in percentages).

	1982	1985	1987	1988	1989	1990	1991
Countries:							
Denmark		2.8*	1.5	1.4		0.8	
Norway			0.4*		0.4		0.4
Sweden	1.7	1.5		5.6			3.2

*Municipal elections only.

Source: Authors' elaboration based on election studies for Sweden, Norway and Denmark.

Apart from the short period of representation of the Swedish party in Parliament from 1988 to 1991, none of the Scandinavian Green parties has been well represented in the national parliaments. The provisions for representation in national and local elections differ, and the Greens have been able to get representation in some municipal councils in all the countries.[4] It would, however, be superficial to restrict the analysis of the Green movement's political influence to parliamentary results. Many studies indicate that the Green movement has been much more influential in all the Scandinavian countries than voter figures reveal (Rüdig 1991).

As already mentioned, the growth of environmental consciousness in Denmark caused a number of policy disputes in the traditional parties. A similar phenomenon has occurred in all the other Scandinavian countries. In Denmark, the appearance of the Green movement mainly affected the left side of the political spectrum. As a result, the Left Socialists and the Social Democrats have responded to the challenge of the environmental movement by increasingly emphasizing environmental questions both in their programs and in their parliamentary activity. For the parties to the right on the political spectrum, the adoption of environmental values has been much less notable. While the environmental dimension in Danish politics has to a large extent followed the left-right continuum, a somewhat different picture is found in Sweden and Norway. The agrarian-dominated Liberal party in Denmark has a rather low environmental profile; however, the agrarian center parties in both Sweden and Norway have been stressing the importance of decentralization, ecological balance in the development of society, and other core environmentalist values for a number of years. Yet, similar to Denmark, the Social Democrats and the Left Socialists have promptly adopted many of the positions of the environmentalist party.

In Norway, the very limited size of the Green party obviously does not reflect the preeminence of environmental questions among the public. A number of election studies have shown that the Norwegian voter gives a high priority to environmental issues. In the Norwegian election study of 1989, the respondents were confronted with the statement, "In order to provide economic growth we need industrial expansion, even if this may conflict with protection of the environment." The results were illustrative of the Norwegian emphasis on environmental protection. Forty-two percent of the respondents disagreed with the statement, while 40 percent agreed with it and 18 percent were neutral or answered "don't know" (Aardal 1990). In the Norwegian case, it has been shown that among the established parties environmental concerns have been particularly strong within the Liberal party and the Socialist Left. Table 5.4 illustrates this phenomenon.

121

Table 5.4. Environmental Concern by Party, 1989

	Socialist Left	Labor	Liberal	Christian Democrats	Center	Conservative	Progressive
Environment most important issue	75% (212)	30 (502)	92 (74)	29 (138)	40 (96)	22 (340)	21 (176)
Supporting Environmental Protection	62% (221)	39 (598)	76 (75)	43 (150)	37 (108)	36 (397)	40 (201)

Reprinted from Bernt Aardal, "Green Politics: A Norwegian Experience," *Scandinavian Political Studies* 13, no. 2 (1990): 155.

The general picture, then, for all the Scandinavian countries, is that the Green parties have effectively been neutralized as political competitors by the traditional political parties, which to a significant extent have adopted vital parts of the "new politics" of the Greens. This development, indeed, seems to fit well with the changing cleavages in the multiparty systems assumed by Ronald Inglehart. In Inglehart's schema, the concept of affluence is central (Inglehart 1984). The continuous economic and technological growth in the Western world has, according to Inglehart, made it possible for the citizens to direct attention from primary needs (e.g., food, housing, economy, etc.) that call forth materialist values, to a higher order related to secondary needs or "postmaterialist" values. In an attempt to characterize the Swedish party system in accordance with Inglehart's conception, Holmberg and Bennulf (1990) analyzed the relation between party choice and stand on certain issues. Table 5.5 shows their data.

Table 5.5. Party Voted for in 1988 Election and Inglehart Value Types in Sweden

	Postmaterialists	Mixed	Materialists	Total	Difference p–m*
Party Choice					
Communists/Left party	37%	42	21	100	+16
Social Democrats	16	56	28	100	−12
Center party	13	54	33	100	−20
Liberals	18	60	22	100	−4
Conservatives	11	68	21	100	−10
Christian Democrats	8	48	44	100	−36
Green party	33	45	22	100	+11
Total	17	57	26	100	−9

*Postmaterialists minus Materialists.
Source: Martin Bennulf and Soren Holmberg, "The Green Breakthrough in Sweden," *Scandinavian Political Studies* 13, no. 2 (1990): 173.

The results presented in table 5.5 point to a strong postmaterialist profile for the Communists and the Greens, while the Christian Democrats demonstrate the most clearly materialist profile.[5] Because of the difficulty of measuring the so-called "postmaterialist" values, the small number of these responses, and the small number of respondents for the small parties, these conclusions must be somewhat tentative.

THE GREEN VOTER

The success of the Greens in the Swedish elections in 1988 incited great interest among students about the characteristics of the Green sympathizers. A summary of some of the findings from the Swedish election studies is presented in table 5.6.

Table 5.6. Some Social Characteristics of the Green Party Voters in Sweden

	Overrepresentation	Underrepresentation
Gender	women	men
Age	20–40	60+
Occupation	middle white collar professionals/managers	industrial workers farmers
Occupational sector	public	private
Education	high	low
Place of residence	countryside	big cities

Source: Table adapted from Bennulf and Holmberg, "The Green Breakthrough in Sweden," *Scandinavian Political Studies* 13, no. 2 (1990): 165–73.

It is clear from the table that Green party members in Sweden are largely female, younger, middle-income, well-educated professionals who work in the public sector and live in the rural towns. To a substantial degree the social characteristics of the Green voters in Sweden seem to be valid for the Greens in Denmark as well (Schuttemeyer 1989).[6] However, a key characteristic of Green voters in Sweden is that they are very volatile—they exhibit very low levels of party loyalty (Holmberg and Gilljam 1987).

ORGANIZATION AND STRATEGY

A main idea among the Greens has been to establish an alternative to the established political parties. This has been reflected in the wider scope of political ideology of the party, but it has also been demonstrated in the ambition to form an organization that is resistant to centralization, professionalism and specialization. The argument for this has been that the old

123

parties, by their concentration on strategy, professionalism and coordinated actions, have developed a gap between, the top of the party and the party members and sympathizers. In order to avoid this the Green parties have developed some specific organizational features of which the Swedish part is an illustrative case. First, the party has refrained from appointing a party leader. Instead, the leadership has been shared by a group of three people (*Spakror*). Second, the party has adopted a "rotation principle" which limits the tenure potential for elected members in the various committees of the party and in Parliament. Third, while the continuous work in the established political parties in Sweden rests in the hands of an executive committee, the Greens have established four functional committees (political, administrative, organizational and publishing committees). By this division of the central powers of the party, by limiting coordination functions and by prohibiting double terms, the ambition of the Greens has been to avoid centralized power and to maintain smooth working relationships between the grass-roots level and the functionaries and representatives (Lundgren 1991).

By the twofold strategy of decentralized party organization and an anti-establishment, environmentalist mobilization, the Greens in Sweden produced a very successful election campaign in 1988. However, during the electoral period 1988–91, this strategy proved to be difficult. The parliamentary representatives were unprepared for the great amount of paper work in the various committees, and they were poorly supported by their organization in this new role. During this period the Greens presented a large number of bills concerning environmental issues, but many of them were voted down without much discussion. At the same time, the party had substantial difficulties in mobilizing their sympathizers in the elections in 1991.

CONCLUSIONS

The Greens in Scandinavia have played an important role in the development of the contemporary political agenda. They have also been able to mobilize substantial popular support for their ideas. But they have been much less successful playing the political game, as important parts of their ideas have been absorbed by the competing political parties (Rüdig 1991). Neither have they been able to capture the environmentally concerned part of the electorate. Three important factors help to account for this failure to mobilize voters effectively. The first such factor is political organization. In all the Scandinavian countries the Green parties have grown out of a Green movement based on popular mobilization which has felt deeply about the creation of alternatives to the life-style of modern Western societies. Retention of the mass-movement character has been an important question when establishing the parties. The reluctance toward professionalism and specialization, together with the tendency to discuss all issues openly and extensively among the party members, has contributed to the lack of a united image and generated lengthy debates when prompt decisions have been needed (Rüdig 1990). The unwillingness to accept principles of modern organization has also made it difficult to design political campaigns suited for winning the lasting attention of the media (Vedung 1989).

Ideology has also hampered the success of Green parties in Scandinavia. As noted earlier in this chapter, the Greens have contributed toward an extension of the ideological scope of political life in the Scandinavian countries. However, the deep emphasis on environmental questions has, on many occasions, conveyed a picture of the parties as single-issue parties. In addition, there have been substantial controversies within the parties on social, economic, international, and other traditional political issues. This has given the opponents of the Greens among the established parties rich opportunities to point out inconsistencies and controversies among the Greens.

The third such factor is the "greening" of the established parties; that is, the established parties have incorporated much of the platforms of the Green parties. Paradoxically, at the very time that public interest in environmental questions has increased substantially in the Scandinavian countries, the Green parties have had great difficulties in establishing themselves as political institutions. The most important factor is the capacity of the "old" parties to incorporate the new environmental positions. The parties to the left of the traditional left-right continuum have been the most effective in that respect, but also the liberal parties and the center parties have included many environmental issues in their programs and involved themselves in environmental questions. The new emphasis on environmental issues among the established parties has, to a large extent, neutralized the Greens. By taking over many of their core issues, the political choice from the citizens' point of view has turned on the issue of credibility. And, when it comes to credibility, the traditional parties have a distinct advantage over the Greens. The central question for the future, then, is whether the Greens can survive in the 1990s as the more traditional parties "do their best to adopt their own green policies and thus present an environmentally friendly image to the electorate" (Rüdig 1991).

NOTES

1. Our analysis includes Denmark, Norway and Sweden, which are often referred to as the "Scandinavian countries." Strictly speaking, only Norway and Sweden are situated on the Scandinavian peninsula. The three countries, however, in

many respects represent the most integrated block of the Nordic countries, to which also two other independent states, Finland and Iceland, belong.

2. The Danish name is *Venstre* and the party was established in 1870 as a liberal party. However, after a party split in 1905 the party has had the farmers as a core group.

3. An interesting comparative study on changing structures of political values and citizen politics in the U.S., Great Britain, West Germany and France is provided in Dalton (1988).

4. To be eligible for seats in the Swedish Parliament, political parties must obtain at least 4 percent of the total national vote. On this point, see Vedung (1988).

5. The formal party name was *Vansterpartiet Kommunisterna* (the Left party Communists) until 1990, when the name was changed to *Vansterpartiet* (the Left party).

6. According to a survey from 1985 in Denmark very similar results were found regarding age, gender, education, and so on; see Tonsgaard (1989a). "Miljopolitisk enighed?" in J. Elklit and O. Tonsgaard, eds., to folketingsvalg (Aarhus: Politica, 1989).

REFERENCES

Aardal, B. 1990. Green politics: A Norwegian experience. *Scandinavian Political Studies* 13:147–64.

Andersen, J. G. 1990. Denmark: Environmental conflict and the greening of the Labour movement. *Scandinavian Political Studies* 13, no. 2: 185–210.

Archer, Clive, and Stephan Maxwell. 1980. *The Nordic model: Studies in political innovation.* Gower: Westmead.

Bennulf, M., and S. Holmberg. 1990. The Green breakthrough in Sweden. *Scandinavian Political Studies* 13:165–84.

Dalton, R. J. 1988. *Citizen politics in Western democracies: Public opinion and political parties in the United States, Great Britain, West Germany and France.* Chatham, N.J.: Chatham House.

Dalton, R. J., and M. Kuechler, eds. 1990. *Challenging the political order: New social and political movements in Western democracies.* London: Policy Press; New York: Oxford University Press.

Damgaard, Erik, ed. 1990. *Parlamentarisk forandring i Norden.* Oslo: Universitetsforlaget.

De Gronne. 1989. *Program.* Kopenhagen.

Gilljam, M., and S. Holmberg. 1990. *Rott blatt gront: En bok om 1988 ars Riksdagsval,* Stockholm, Bonniers.

Holmberg, S., and K. Asp, 1984. *Kampen om karnkraften: En bok om valjare, massmedier och folkomrostningen, 1980,* Stockholm: Liber.

Holmberg, S., and Lennart Weibull, eds. 1989. *Attiotal, Svensk opinion i empirisk belysning.* SOM-rapport 4. Stockholm: Gothenburg.

Inglehart, R. 1984. The changing structure of political cleavages in Western society. In *Electoral change in advanced industrial democracies: Realignment or dealignment?* ed. R. J. Dalton, S. C. Flangan, and P. A. Beck, 25–69. Princeton: Princeton University Press.

Jamison, Andrew, Ron Eyerman, Jacqueline Cramer, and Jeppé Laessøe. 1990. *The making of the new environmental consciousness.* Edinburgh: Edinburgh University Press.

Kitschelt, Herbert P. 1988. Left-libertarian parties: Explaining innovation in competitive party systems. *World Politics* 40 (January): 194–234.

Liberatore, Angela. 1991. Problems of transnational policymaking: Environmental policy in the European Community. *European Journal of Political Research* 19, nos. 2–3: 281-305.

Lindblad, I., C. E. Stalvant, K. Wahlback, and C. Wiklund. 1984. *Politik i Norden, en jamforande oversikt.* Stockholm: Liber.

Lundgren, Aasa. 1991. Miljopartiet—en alternativ partiorganisation. *Statsventenskaplig Tidskrift,* no. 1.

Miljopartiet de grona under 10 ar. 1991. *En ny ideologisk dimension i politiken.* Stockholm: The Green party.

Müller-Rommel, Ferdinand. 1989. *New politics in Western Europe: The rise and success of Green parties and alternative lists.* Boulder, Colo. Westview Press.

Parkin, S. 1989. *Green parties: An international guide.* London: Heretic Press.

Petersson, Olof. 1991. *Nordisk politik.* Stockholm: Allmanna forlaget.

Rexed, Knut. 1991. *Swedish labor during the 1990s.* New York: Swedish Information Service.

Rüdig, Wolfgang, ed. 1990. *Green politics I: 1990.* Carbondale: University of Southern Illinois Press.

———. 1991. Green party politics around the world. *Environment* 33 (October): 6–9 and 25–31.

Rüdig, Wolfgang, and P. Lowe. N.d. *The Green wave: A comparative analysis of ecological parties.* Cambridge: Polity Press. Forthcoming.

Schuttemeyer, S. 1989. Denmark: De gronne. In *New politics in Western Europe,* ed. F. Müller-Rommel. Boulder, Colo.: Westview Press.

Svold, C. 1989. Danmarks Naturfrednings forening. Fra paen forening til aggressiv miljoorganisation. Aarhus: PLS consult.

Tonsgaard, O. 1989. Hojre og venstre i dansk politik. In *To folketingsvalg,* ed. J. Elklit and O. Tonsgaard, 157–75. Aarhus: Politica.

———. 1989a. Miljopolitisk enighed? In *To folketingsvalg,* ed. J. Elklit. Aarhus: Politia.

Vedung, Evert. 1989. Sweden: The miljopartiet de Grona. In *New politics in Western Europe,* ed. F. Müller-Rommel. Boulder, Colo.: Westview Press, 1989.

James P. Lester and Elfar Loftsson

————. 1988. The Swedish five-party syndrome and the environmentalists. In *When parties fail: Emerging alternative organizations,* ed. Kay Lawson and Peter H. Merkl. Princeton: Princeton University Press.

Weinberg, Gunnar. 1983. Hur miljopartiet vaxte fram. In *Nu kommer miljopartiet.* Stockholm: Timo, 1983.

SECTION THREE

International Organizations and International Law

6 International Nongovernmental Organizations: Prospects for a Global Environmental Movement

JOHN McCORMICK

Of all the changes that have taken place in global politics and economics since World War II, one in particular stands out: that politics and economics have taken on an international flavor of unprecedented and probably irreversible proportions. Many policy decisions are now being taken not by national governments working in isolation, but as a result of international negotiation and compromise. Many of these decisions come either as a result of bilateral or multilateral negotiation, or of discussion through international governmental organizations (such as the United Nations system and the General Agreement on Tariffs and Trade [GATT]). With the European Community, the West Europeans have gone further by creating a (so far) unique form of supranational government, submitting themselves to a new level of international legal authority that may provide a model for other regions of the world.

In the environmental arena, there has been a parallel growth in international cooperation, notably through the work of agencies such as the United Nations Environment Programme (UNEP) and through the agreement on a growing body of international laws and conventions on the environment. There has also been a globalization of scientific research, which has in turn made it abundantly clear that many of our most pressing environmental problems (e.g., acid rain, global warming, threats to the ozone layer, and trade in wildlife) are transnational in nature, and so can be addressed only at the international level.

Against this background, however, the development of effective environmental policies has suffered from a lack of political leadership. Almost without exception, national governments have proved slow, unwilling or unable to take the initiative in developing effective bodies of law on environmental protection, to initiate rational and comprehensive environmental policies, or to create administrative departments with adequate funding and powers; the prevailing approach of most governments and political leaders has been reactive rather than proactive. The reasons for this are various, but they include concerns that environmental protection will be expensive and retard short-term economic growth, and a simple lack of understanding about the causes and consequences of environmental problems and their long-term costs.

In the absence of such leadership, environmental interest groups have taken it upon themselves to exert pressure on governments for change, particularly in liberal democracies. They have also promoted research and public education, and have often taken direct action, such as purchasing and managing areas of ecological value. The influence of national groups on national governments has been well documented (see, for example, Fox 1981, Lowe and Goyder 1983, and McCormick 1991); less well appreciated have been the existence and the work of international environmental interest groups, which have both helped globalize the environmental debate and helped emphasize the global dimensions of many issues.

This chapter sets out to ask how and why these international nongovernmental organizations (INGOs) have evolved, to assess the work and the accomplishments of the major INGOs, to discuss the handicaps they face, and to comment on their role in the future.

THE INGO COMMUNITY

Despite the breadth of the literature on interest groups, there is little agreement on the definition of the terms "interest group" or "non-governmental organization" (NGO). Most of the disagreements are little more than quibbles. For present purposes, the terms "nongovernmental organization" and "interest group" will be considered interchangeable, and both are defined simply as private (i.e., nongovernmental) bodies organized for the purpose of directly or indirectly influencing public policy either on behalf of their members or on behalf of what they perceive to be the broader public interest.

An international NGO works in more than one country, and directs its appeals either to more than one national government or to international bodies. INGOs should not be confused with quasi-governmental organizations (such as the U.S.-Canadian International Joint Commission, set up in 1909 to monitor management of the Great Lakes), nor with national NGOs with international interests (such as the World Resources Institute or the Worldwatch Institute in the United States, or the Fauna and Flora Preservation Society in Britain).

In the absence of reliable national directories of groups, it is difficult to put an exact figure on just how many environmental NGOs and INGOs exist. The United Nations has a very broad notion of what constitutes an NGO, if the list of bodies enjoying consultative status with the UN Economic and Social Council is any indication. Among those groups are professional, corporate and intergovernmental bodies, many with very limited goals and small constituencies. This definition upsets some of the more "traditional" NGOs, which would prefer the UN to recognize as

NGOs only nonprofit, voluntary, "people's" organizations (IIED 1991). Using this latter definition, a 1982 estimate put the number of national NGOs at more than fifteen thousand, of which more than 85 percent were based in Europe and North America (UNEP 1982). Given developments in the last decade, it may now be possible to inflate that figure by at least 25 percent.

Assuming that INGOs are defined as international, nonprofit, voluntary organizations, there are probably no more than one hundred INGOs currently active (mainly or exclusively) on issues of environmental concern. Just as there are different kinds of national NGOs, using different methods, pursuing different goals, and appealing to different constituencies, so there are different kinds of INGOs. Broadly, though, they mainly fall into one of two categories: international organizations, and international coalitions or umbrella bodies.

INTERNATIONAL ORGANIZATIONS

The most obvious form of INGO is a group set up specifically as an international organization. There are many examples of these, most of which have emerged out of the postwar era of international cooperation. A prime example is the International Union for Conservation of Nature and Natural Resources (IUCN). A hybrid of governmental and nongovernmental bodies that is almost unique, IUCN was founded in 1948 as the International Union for the Protection of Nature (IUPN). As such, it set out to promote the preservation of wildlife and the natural environment, largely through public education and scientific research. Its lobbying activities at that time were very limited. Headquartered at first in Brussels, it subsequently moved to Switzerland, and is now based in Gland, near Geneva.

IUPN was not the product of a popular movement, but the creation of a few enthusiasts (McCormick 1989). The most influential among these was Julian Huxley, the first director-general of UNESCO (founded two years before in 1946), who used his influence to try to win access for IUPN to UNESCO. IUPN began life as a small, financially impoverished organization run—in the words of one of its founders—by "emotionally inspired missionary individuals and groups" (Nicholson 1981). It was a small and exclusive body with little organizational ability and financial support, few national bodies or committees with which it could work, and very little hard scientific evidence upon which to base an agenda and design policies. For all these reasons, there were some who felt it had been created prematurely (Nicholson 1981).

Above all, IUPN had a narrow range of interests, being concerned mainly with wildlife and nature rather than broader environmental issues. Its interests broadened, however, as reflected in its decision in 1956 to change its name (on American insistence) to the International Union for the Conservation of Nature and Natural Resources (IUCN). Its second basic problem—a lack of money—was addressed in 1962 with the creation in London of the World Wide Fund for Nature (WWF, formerly the World Wildlife Fund). WWF today has semi-autonomous national offices in twenty-seven countries, and it has funded conservation, research and education projects in most countries of the world.

The *Environmentalist* (1, no. 1 [1981]: 65–74) points out that while WWF was ostensibly founded as the fund-raising wing of IUCN, it rapidly set off on a parallel rather than an auxiliary course to IUCN. This was to cause problems over the next twenty years, with IUCN constantly in deficit and WWF consistently performing well financially, and eventually outgrowing IUCN. By the mid-1980s, the artificiality of many of the divisions between the two organizations led to an attempt to mold their shared Swiss headquarters into a "World Conservation Center." Operating largely in tandem, IUCN/WWF carry out scientific research (notably compiling the Red Data Lists of endangered species), fund environmental protection programs throughout the world (including the protection of natural areas), promote conservation education, and directly lobby governments. At the international level, IUCN has either helped draft—or provided a secretariat for—several key conventions, such as the Convention on International Trade in Endangered Species (CITES) and the World Heritage Convention.

The most concerted attempt by IUCN/WWF to influence environmental policy began in 1980 with the publication of the World Conservation Strategy, an attempt to encourage national governments to publish conservation programs aimed at promoting sustainable development. Several national strategies have since been published, but their quality is variable, and there is as yet little sign that they have resulted in tangible changes in national policies.

Four other organizations provide a taste of the kind of work being undertaken by INGOs. The International Council for Bird Preservation (ICBP) and its offshoot, the International Waterfowl Research Bureau (IWRB), primarily undertake research on bird-life habitats. IWRB is a research organization, but has also been involved in strengthening international law; for example, IWRB convened a series of conferences and technical meetings in the 1960s which resulted in the signing of the 1971 Convention on Wetlands of International Importance (the Ramsar Convention) (Lyster 1985).

The International Institute for Environment and Development (IIED) was founded in the wake of the 1972 UN Conference on the Human Environment (held in Stockholm). Headquartered in London, it undertakes research on sustainable development, and works with other NGOs and INGOs on reports for national governments and the private sector. During

1990–91, IIED promoted the preparation of a series of national NGO reports for the 1992 UN Conference on Environment and Development (UNCED) held in Rio de Janeiro. The goal was to make sure that governments published their official national reports for the conference only after a series of open discussions with the NGO sector in their respective countries (IIED 1991).

The World Information Service on Energy (WISE) works primarily as an international information exchange network on behalf of the antinuclear movement. It was founded following the nongovernmental Conference on a Non-Nuclear Future, held alongside an International Atomic Energy Agency conference in Salzburg, Austria, in May 1977. It subsequently derived its funding from licensing arrangements on the copyrighted symbol of the movement: a bright red smiling cartoon sun on a yellow background, surrounded by the slogan "Nuclear Power? No thanks." By 1983 the symbol was available in forty languages (Patterson 1983); its success seemed to indicate the growing presence of a new and more activist environmental movement unconstrained by national frontiers.

The Institute for European Environmental Policy (IEEP) works—in its own words—"to raise the level of debate about environmental policy-making in Europe" (Haigh 1990). IEEP has offices in Britain, Germany, France, Belgium, and the Netherlands, publishes authoritative reports on policy issues in the European Community, convenes conferences and technical meetings on these issues, and maintains a network of NGO contacts throughout the Community.

The seven groups described here are representative of the work of a growing environmental INGO community made up of groups working in almost every country of the world. Given the lack of many effective international governmental organizations, those INGOs whose activities include lobbying tend to work mainly with individual national governments. Given that most are based in Europe and North America, they also tend to use the kind of lobbying methods normal in their home countries; such methods, however, may not always be appropriate to local circumstances in other countries. In general, INGOs have achieved the most when they have carried out research, education, and conservation projects, and have focused their attention on local communities.

INTERNATIONAL COALITIONS

As national NGOs have become more aware of the international and global nature of environmental problems, they have deliberately worked more closely with each other. Cooperation and coalition-building among interest groups are often difficult to track, because they are often informal, ad hoc and unpublicized. They may even be as simple as several NGOs sharing the same building and staff.

If groups agree that by pooling their resources and staff they can exert greater influence, more formal coalitions and umbrella groups may be formed. In their study of interest groups in the United States, Schlozman and Tierney (1986) note that coalition-building is often necessitated by the complexity of the issue being addressed, and that coalitions can play a central role in influencing how much public attention is given to an issue. Cooperation may take place at different stages in the policy process, and will often be determined by the nature of the issue being addressed. Given the breadth and complexity of international or global environmental issues, the motives for coalescing have been compelling.

Coalitions vary both in the number of groups involved and in their duration (Loomis 1986). As well as limited, *ad hoc* cooperation, environmental groups have also established formal coalitions with specific, long-term objectives. Organizations such as the Centre for Our Common Future, founded in Geneva in 1988, are primarily umbrella bodies; the Centre was created to encourage and oversee activities following up on the recommendations of the 1987 report of the World Commission on Environment and Development (the Brundtland Commission) (WCED 1987). The Centre has a network of NGOs, individuals, and other groups in sixty-five countries. As well as arranging meetings between environmental NGOs, industry, professions, and citizens groups, the Centre also coordinated various NGO activities during preparations for the UN Conference on Environment and Development in Rio de Janeiro in 1992.

A coalition group with different objectives is the Environment Liaison Centre (ELC). Based in Nairobi, the ELC provides material and information on UNEP activities to national NGOs, and acts as a point of contact for groups lobbying UNEP. While the ELC may sound useful in theory, its efficacy is limited by the weaknesses of UNEP. Since its creation in 1973, UNEP has suffered three fundamental problems: a lack of funding, poor internal management and—above all—a lack of power. It is not a full agency of the UN, and it has very little power beyond that of simply watching over the activities of other UN agencies and commenting wherever appropriate. UNEP successes, such as its Regional Seas Programme and its role in encouraging international agreement on reductions in chlorofluorocarbons (CFCs), have been all too rare. It has little power to compel other UN agencies—or national governments—to take action. Thus UNEP's record in influencing national government policies has been mixed at best. Against this background, the ELC has only limited power, influence, or value to NGOs or INGOs.

A coalition group with potentially more power is the European Environmental Bureau (EEB), an umbrella body for national NGOs operating in the twelve European Community countries. The EEB was founded in 1974 with the active encouragement of the European Commission (Daltrop 1986), the major policy-making and bureaucratic arm of the EC. The EEB acts as a conduit for the representation of environmental interest groups to the Community, particularly the European Commission. It has more potential power than the ELC simply because the European Community has far more legal power over its member states than UNEP has over its members. The European Community (EC) is unique in the sense that it is the only international organization in the world with the power to make environmental policies binding on its member states. It has been at the heart of the most concerted program being undertaken anywhere in the world to replace national environmental controls with international regulation (McCormick 1991). Since the mid-1970s, the EC has formulated several directives (pieces of legislation binding on EC member states) on the environment, including those on lead in gasoline and air, sulfur dioxide and suspended particulates, and emission of pollutants from industrial plants.

As well as playing a crucial role in changing the policies of its member states on problems such as acid rain and protection of the ozone layer, the EC has also provided new opportunities for interest groups. First, it has actively encouraged interest-group activity at the Community level. At the planning stage of new legislation, the European Commission solicits the help of interested groups in drafting proposals. It asks the groups for factual and statistical information, and seeks their opinion on potential support for—or opposition to—its proposals. Daltrop (1986) argues that this process has developed to the point where consultation has actually become an integral part of the legislative process. Interested groups are given the opportunity to comment on draft legislation at almost every stage in the process. This may slow down the process of decision making, but it also encourages active lobbying. The input of groups has even reached the point where some policy-makers have begun arguing that the more powerful interest groups are becoming too influential, and that access and consultation need greater control and regulation in order to prevent the wealthier and more powerful groups from exerting too much influence.

Second, Community membership has given groups new outlets for lobbying, mainly in the form of the European Commission, the European Parliament, and the European Court of Justice. The Commission is the key point of access for the lobbyist, so interest groups try to win representation on Commission consultative committees and to establish long-term contacts with Commission departments (Daltrop 1986). Particularly since the institution of direct elections, the European Parliament in Strasbourg has become increasingly important as a point of access, mainly because of its powers to amend or delay Commission proposals. As well as lobbying and influencing the design of new EC legislation, groups have also fulfilled an increasingly active watchdog role, reporting national governments to the EC for failing to respect or implement EC laws.

Although more groups have been more involved in recent years in lobbying the European Community, this is still a relatively new development. The result is that few groups have really begun to appreciate the potential of the Community as a policy-making body. This is mainly because their home constituencies are not constructed in a way that would make European law obviously relevant. Among those groups that have turned their attention to the Community, however, there has been an increasingly systematic approach to Euro-lobbying, and a clear trend towards seeing domestic environmental problems as part of Community-wide problems.

While this may not necessarily have promoted the creation of new European INGOs, it has encouraged domestic NGOs to work more closely together and to form transnational coalitions. A number of national groups have also recently opened offices in Brussels. Until 1985, only the EEB operated in Brussels. Since then, offices have been opened there by Friends of the Earth, Greenpeace, and the World Wide Fund for Nature. Other groups, such as Britain's Royal Society for the Protection of Birds, have not opened full-time Brussels offices, but have employed full-time lobbyists. Baldock (1989) notes that while the opening of offices by other groups has tended to undermine the ability of the EEB to speak on behalf of Community environmental groups, the Bureau is still important as an umbrella group. Haigh (1990) feels that its value lies in its work as an umbrella body for those EC interest groups that operate mainly at the domestic level. Generally, Baldock (1989) sees a long-term tendency towards the creation of more European networks of organizations at both the voluntary and statutory levels.

A variation on the theme of coalition groups can be found in the international offices of groups operating mainly at the national level, e.g., Friends of the Earth (FoE) and Greenpeace. While essentially national NGOs, FoE and Greenpeace have developed multinational coalitions as the opportunities for lobbying international organizations have grown. FoE was founded in the United States in 1969 following a disagreement between one of the oldest and most influential of the traditional American NGOs—the Sierra Club— and its executive director, David Brower. Brower had been executive director of the Club since 1952, and had set out to involve the Club in critical public issues, such as support for the 1964 Wilderness Act. Although authorized to carry out as much political lobbying as the tax-exempt status of the Club allowed, Brower's campaigning against plans to build two dams in the Grand Canyon was instrumental in the loss of the Club's tax-exempt status. He was therefore removed from office in 1969.

Upon his removal, Brower founded Friends of the Earth, whose philosophy was that the solution to environmental problems lay not in temporary remedies but in fundamental social change. It adopted vigorous campaigning methods aimed at achieving maximum publicity and drawing attention to activities and ventures that threatened the environment. It subsequently drew its support from young, well-educated, middle-class malcontents (Cotgrove and Duff 1980). It was conceived from the outset both as an organization that would be legislatively active and as an international organization (Brower 1984; Burke 1982). The FoE "formula," according to Brower, was "to find people in other countries who [shared FoE's] own ideas about the limits to growth . . . and who [had] a respect for biological diversity. Then these people become the Board of Directors for their own country. They run their own show" (Brower 1984).

The first FoE office was opened in San Francisco in 1969, followed in 1970 by offices in Paris and London. Initially, Brower simply appointed friends as his overseas representatives, but the recruitment process was subsequently formalized. Two meetings in 1971 resulted in the establishment of an international institution nominally headquartered in San Francisco. Autonomous groups were subsequently set up in most West European countries and further afield (e.g., Malaysia and South Africa). The methods and patterns of organization were often different, but all pursued the aim of promoting more rational use of natural resources. FoE now has offices in thirty-five countries, and its multinational operations are overseen by Friends of the Earth International (Frisch 1990).

It was pollution—specifically that created by fallout from atmospheric nuclear tests—which led to the creation of Greenpeace, the most overt of the direct action groups. American plans to explode a nuclear device on Amchitka Island (off the coast of Alaska) in 1971 encouraged a group of American environmentalists to protest by sailing a fishing boat into the area, thereby contributing to the postponement of the test and the eventual cancellation of all tests on Amchitka (Morgan and Whitaker 1986). Similar tactics were subsequently used by the group, which ultimately named itself Greenpeace, to protest French nuclear tests in the Pacific.

Greenpeace has also campaigned against whaling, sealing, nuclear power and radioactive waste disposal. In many cases it has adopted the same tactics of direct action, such as attempting to obstruct the disposal at sea of nuclear waste, or sealing in the Arctic. The key to its activities is the generation of graphic and visually effective media publicity. As Greenpeace grew,

139

autonomous groups rejecting the control of the original headquarters in Vancouver were set up in Britain, France, and The Netherlands. There are now Greenpeace offices in fifteen countries, coordinated by a Greenpeace international office in England.

CURRENT PROBLEMS

The activities of NGOs (environmental or other) are circumscribed by the nature of the institutions they lobby and the constituencies they represent. National groups in liberal democracies often have the advantages of'member-ships that identify closely with them and provide them with political power. They also have identifiable (and politically significant) lobbying targets (in the form of national and local government institutions), bodies of law that can be exploited to effect change, and mass media that can provide publicity. National NGOs have enjoyed variable levels of influence, depending on a combination of these factors.

INGOs, by contrast, face much greater problems. The first and most fundamental of these is the paucity of effective and powerful international bodies that they can lobby. This is a particular problem for environmental INGOs, because UNEP—the only truly global environmental agency—has such limited power and influence. Other parts of the UN system, particularly the Food and Agriculture Organization (FAO) and the UN Educational, Scientific and Cultural Organization (UNESCO), are also active in areas relating to environmental management, and are subject to INGO lobbying and consultation. The UN system, however, is regarded among INGOs as having only limited influence and power, mainly because its decisions are not binding on member states, but partly because of funding and personnel problems. In other words, they tend to see the UN as less than wholly efficient.

The second problem faced by INGOs relates to the weaknesses inherent in international law. Bodies of domestic environmental law have grown slowly and fitfully over the last century (and particularly in the last two decades), often only with the encouragement of national interest groups. Despite the patchy nature of national law, most liberal democracies have seen the advent of bodies of law that interest groups have been able to use to good effect. Groups also have the benefit of established governmental and judicial institutions they can lobby. At the international level, however, the situation is very different. While there has unquestionably been a growth in the number of international conventions and laws concerning issues as varied as trade in wildlife, air pollution, water pollution, transportation of toxic wastes, and whaling, the application of such laws has been variable. Unlike national NGOs, INGOs lack the benefits of a strong system of enforcement that can be used to support their attempts to see international law implemented.

The third problem experienced by INGOs has been the lack of a constituency that can provide them with political power. A compelling argument that might be put forward by national interest groups open to public membership is that their members are also voters, and as such may consider the environmental policies of governments in making choices at elections. Domestic environmental constituencies amount to substantial voter blocs; for example, approximately 4.5 million Britons (8 percent of the population) and approximately 7 million Americans (3 percent of the population) are estimated to be members of environmental groups (McCormick 1991; Rosenbaum 1991). INGOs, however, can make no such claims. While some—such as Greenpeace and WWF—may have substantial memberships when all the national memberships are added together, these memberships work mainly at the domestic level; at the global level such numbers do not translate into political power. The European Community is so far the only example of a substantial supranational authority that need pay any heed to voters; this has been especially true since the institution in 1979 of direct elections to the European Parliament.

The fourth problem experienced by INGOs and many of their domestic counterparts is financial. National NGOs have the opportunity of raising money through membership dues, national appeals, and merchandising. INGOs, lacking a distinct constituency, find it difficult to make such appeals, and must often rely on corporations, large private benefactors, or (in the case of coalitions) dues from member organizations. One constitutional problem relating to funding is the debate among national groups about whether they should lobby international organizations directly or delegate that responsibility to an appropriate INGO. In regard to the EEB, for example, Haigh (1990) notes the problem of whether the Bureau should serve the needs of its members or carry out independent lobbying. The level of utility of INGOs to national NGOs is directly related to the funding support those INGOs can expect.

A fifth problem facing INGOs is of a cultural nature. Lobbying and other forms of interest-group activity are essentially Western concepts, and although there are effective and vocal national NGOs in many non-Western countries, they are not always relevant or appropriate in terms of understanding how policy is influenced and made in those countries. Since INGOs really operate only out of countries with a significant national NGO presence, most of the best known and most active environmental INGOs are based in Europe and North America, from which they also derive most of their support and influence. They may direct much of their lobbying activity towards African, Asian and Latin American governments, but to some extent they are handicapped by a perception among those governments that they represent Western interests rather than the interests of non-Western countries.

CONCLUSION

Given that the fundamental objective of an NGO is to influence public policy from outside the formal structure of elected government, the effectiveness of NGOs and INGOs alike depends on two basic factors:

1. their political influence (as measured by the level of public support they enjoy, and their ability to use political structures effectively);

2. the importance of having clearly defined constituencies and clearly defined avenues through which to make their appeals and to influence government.

National governments and political parties throughout the world have proved slow to respond to the needs of the environment as a political and economic issue. While the body of national laws has grown in recent decades, and more of that legislation is being applied, it is arguable that few governments would have taken any action without public pressure, particularly that emanating from environmental interest groups. It might be argued that, in the absence of leadership and initiative from national governments, these groups have undertaken much of the research, monitoring, and practical action needed to manage the environment.

The same could be said in the sphere of international environmental policy, but to a lesser extent. Handicapped as they are by the lack of effective lobbying targets and supporting constituencies, INGOs have been able to achieve only as much as the influence of international governmental bodies will allow. Consultation and cooperation between national governments, however, is increasingly common and effective. The end of the cold war may also mean that at least part of the "peace dividend" will be directed at environmental management and protection on a global scale. As this happens, and as scientific research provides us with more certainty about the causes and consequences of environmental mismanagement, the role of INGOs in lobbying and working with governments can only continue to improve and grow.

REFERENCES

Baldock, David. 1989. Institute for European Environmental Policy. Personal communication.

Brower, David. 1984. Friends of the Earth. Personal communication.

Burke, Tom. 1982. Friends of the Earth and the conservation of resources. In *Pressure groups in the global system,* edited by Peter Willetts. London: Francis Pinter.

Cotgrove, Stephan, and Andrew Duff. 1980. Environmentalism, middle-class radicalism and politics. *Sociological Review* 32:92–110.

Daltrop, Anne. 1986. *Politics and the European Community.* Harlow: Longman.

Fox, Stephen. 1981. *John Muir and his legacy.* Boston: Little, Brown.

Frisch, Monica. 1990. *Directory for the environment.* London: Green Print.

Haigh, Nigel. 1990. Institute for European Environmental Policy. Personal communication.

International Institute for Environment and Development. 1991. *United Nations Conference on Environment and Development: A user's guide no. 1.* London: IIED.

Loomis, Burdett A. 1986. Coalitions of interests: Building bridges in the balkanized state. In *Interest group politics,* edited by Allan J. Cigler and Burdett A. Loomis. Washington, D.C.: CQ Press.

Lowe, Philip and Jane Goyder. 1983. *Environmental groups in politics.* London: George Allen & Unwin.

Lyster, Simon. 1985. *International wildlife law.* Cambridge: Grotius Publications.

McCormick, John. 1989. *Reclaiming paradise: The global environmental movement.* Bloomington: Indiana University Press.

———. 1991. *British politics and the environment.* London: Earthscan Publications.

Morgan, Robin, and Brian Whitaker. 1986. *Rainbow warrior.* London: Arrow Books.

Nicholson, Max. 1981. *The first world conservation lecture.* London: World Wildlife Fund.

Patterson, Walter. 1983. *Nuclear power.* Harmondsworth: Penguin

Rosenbaum, Walter. 1991. *Environmental politics and policy,* 2d ed., Washington, D.C.: CQ Press.

Schlozman, Kay Lehman, and John T. Tierney. 1986. *Organized interests and American democracy.* New York: Harper & Row.

United Nations Environment Programme. 1982. Review of major achievements in the implementation of the Action Plan for the Human Environment. UNEP Doc. Na. 82-0006-1142C. (26 January). Nairobi: UNEP.

World Commission on Environment and Development. 1987. *Our common future.* Oxford: Oxford University Press.

7 International Organizations and International Institutions: Lessons Learned from Environmental Regimes

ORAN R. YOUNG

Any effort to understand the place of intergovernmental organizations (IGOs) in international environmental negotiations must begin with the observation that negotiations of this type ordinarily focus on the (re)formation of institutional arrangements or regimes intended to regulate the behavior of members of international society (including that of individuals and firms operating under their jurisdiction) which would otherwise produce harmful environmental impacts extending beyond their jurisdictional boundaries. To comprehend the role of international organizations in these negotiations, therefore, we must direct our attention toward institutional bargaining. This is bargaining of the type that occurs when several autonomous parties seek to reach agreement on the terms of networks of rights and rules expected to govern their subsequent interactions in a given issue area; it stands in contrast to bargaining over single-shot or self-contained issues, which is the type envisioned in most formal models of bargaining.[1]

To set the stage for a consideration of the place of international organizations in institutional bargaining relating to the (re)formation of environmental regimes, some preliminary definitions and illustrations are in order. Regimes are constellations of agreed-upon principles, norms, rules and decision-making procedures that govern the interactions of actors in specific issue areas. As such, they provide the rules of the game that define the character of recognized social practices.[2] While they vary greatly in terms of membership, functional scope, geographical domain, complexity, degree of formalization, and stage of development, all regimes are properly understood as social institutions. Organizations, by contrast, are material entities possessing offices, personnel, equipment, budgets, and legal personality. They play important roles in implementing and administering the provisions of many, though by no means all, international regimes. Studies of the interplay of institutions and organizations constitute a central concern of those interested in governance at the international level.[3]

The United Nations Environment Programme (UNEP) is an organization; the environmental protection arrangements for the Mediterranean

Basin set forth in the 1976 Barcelona Convention for the Protection of the Mediterranean Sea Against Pollution and Its Related Protocols—as well as those for stratospheric ozone that were formalized in the 1985 Vienna Convention for the Protection of the Ozone Layer, together with the 1987 Montreal Protocol on Substances That Deplete the Ozone Layer (as amended in 1990)—are international regimes. The Economic Commission for Europe (ECE) is an organization; the 1979 Geneva Convention on Long-Range Transboundary Air Pollution, coupled with its 1985, 1988, and 1991 protocols on sulphur emissions, nitrogen oxide emissions, and volatile organic compounds, lays out the terms of an international regime. Similar observations are in order about the relationship between the International Commission for the Protection of the Rhine Against Pollution (ICPR) and the Rhine River regime articulated in the provisions of the 1976 Bonn Conventions on the protection of the Rhine River against chemical pollution and against chloride pollution and articulated in the terms of the 1987 Rhine Action Programme.

International organizations figure prominently in international environmental negotiations in two distinct capacities. Organizations like UNEP, the ECE, and the ICPR can and often do become instruments of regime formation in the sense that they play significant roles in the institutional bargaining processes which produce constitutional contracts giving rise to environmental regimes.[4] Those engaged in institutional bargaining, by contrast, often foresee a need for organizations to implement and administer the provisions of the international regimes they create, so that the character of the organizations to be established in connection with environmental regimes regularly becomes a prominent agenda item in institutional bargaining processes. Some organizations—UNEP is a striking example—figure in both capacities, serving initially as instruments of regime formation and subsequently assuming roles in the administration of the regimes they help to form. For purposes of this analysis, I shall label these considerations "international organizations as instruments" and "international organizations as objects," respectively, and take them up in turn in the substantive sections that follow.

INTERNATIONAL ORGANIZATIONS AS INSTRUMENTS

We live in an era marked by rapid growth in the number and variety of intergovernmental organizations.[5] Partly, this is a reflection of rising levels of interdependence in international affairs and the resultant need for organizations to manage complex webs of interdependencies linking the members of international society.[6] In part, it is a product of the emergence during the postwar period of a worldview which highlights benefits expected to accrue to individual members of international society from intensive interactions with others while, at the same time, it deemphasizes the dangers of foreign entanglements and the attractions of autarky. There is, under the circumstances, no shortage of international organizations capable of playing active roles in international environmental negotiations.

A choice of organizations

A variety of international organizations can and do become actively involved in environmental negotiations. Multipurpose organizations, like the ECE and the Organization for Economic Cooperation and Development (OECD), assume leading roles in some environmental negotiations; organizations whose mandate is limited to environmental issues, like UNEP, take on these roles in other cases. Even among environmental organizations, there is an important distinction between those focused on a single issue area and those whose concerns extend to a broad spectrum of environmental issues. Whereas the ICPR has played a key role in devising the terms of the Rhine River regime, for example, UNEP has emerged as an important player in the development of regimes to control regional pollution, protect the ozone layer, regulate transboundary shipments of hazardous wastes, and, most recently, preserve biological diversity.

Nor is there any presumption that participation in negotiations concerning specific environmental issues will be limited to a single international organization. A number of organizations, including UNEP, the Food and Agriculture Organization (FAO), the International Maritime Consultative Organization (now simply the International Maritime Organization or IMO), the International Atomic Energy Agency (IAEA), the World Meteorological Organization (WMO), and the World Health Organization (WHO), joined forces to develop the Mediterranean Action Plan in the 1970s. Similarly, in the ongoing effort to form an international regime to cope with climate change, UNEP and WMO have worked together to structure and facilitate the course of institutional bargaining, which is actually taking place under the auspices of yet another organization, the Intergovernmental Negotiating Committee on Climate Change established by the U.N. General Assembly specifically to work on the development of a climate regime. Among other things, these alliances can give rise to new organizational arrangements, such as the Joint Group of Experts on the Scientific Aspects of Marine Pollution (GESAMP) in the Mediterranean case and the joint UNEP/WMO Intergovernmental Panel on Climate Change (IPCC) in the climate change case.

What accounts for the choice of international organizations to become involved in environmental negotiations? Some organizations are endowed with legal or constitutional mandates giving them strong claims to participate in any negotiations taking place in a more or less well-defined issue area. It would be awkward, for instance, to proceed with negotiations relating to high seas fisheries issues without the participation of FAO or with negotiations dealing with atomic energy in the absence of IAEA as a significant player. In other cases, the choice is determined more by suitability or, in other words, by the fit between an organization's membership, functional scope, or geographic reach and the shape of the issues under consideration. This accounts for example, for the choice of the ECE in contrast to the European Community (EC), the OECD, or the Conference on Security and Cooperation in Europe (CSCE) as the organizer of the negotiations leading to the 1979 Geneva Convention on transboundary air pollution. The membership of the EC was too narrow and that of the OECD too broad, while the CSCE had not emerged as an effectual organization at the time. Similar remarks are in order about the choice of UNEP over the OECD in the negotiations leading to the 1989 Basel Convention on the Control of Transboundary Movements of Hazardous Wastes. Because relations between developed and developing countries became a central issue in these negotiations, UNEP was better situated than the OECD to operate as an instrument of regime formation in this issue area.

Frequently, however, the choice of organization to become active players in environmental negotiations involves political considerations as well. Prior to 1986, for example, the United States and some of it allies preferred the OECD's Nuclear Energy Agency over the IAEA as an arena for negotiations relating to nuclear security, not only because of its technical sophistication but also because of the political compatibility of the countries participating in the work of this agency. Though the members of the Antarctic club have long maintained that the Antarctic Treaty Consultative Meetings (ATCMs) are more suitable than various United Nations organs as a forum for efforts to work out additional elements of the Antarctic Treaty System, it is no secret that the Antarctic Treaty Consultative Parties have a strong preference for the ATCMs in part, at least, because this forum maximizes their control over the negotiating process and blunts efforts to apply the doctrine of the common heritage of mankind to Antarctic activities. Much the same could be said about the roles of the United Nations Conference on Trade and Development (UNCTAD), the World Bank, and the United Nations Development Program (UNDP). Whereas many developing countries prefer UNCTAD because it tends to mirror their views on North/South issues, the developed countries are far more comfortable with the World Bank, where their influence is greater. These conflicting preferences have strengthened the role of UNDP in some environmental negotiations because this organization has endeavored, with some success in the eyes of many observers, to steer a middle course between the preferences of the developing countries and those of the developed countries.[7]

One of the more striking developments of the last two decades in the realm of international environmental affairs is the emergence of UNEP as a prominent and effectual player in international environmental negotiations. Given the modest political and material resources at its disposal, the success of UNEP in launching the Regional Seas Programme, promoting the ozone protection regime, and sponsoring the negotiations on transboundary movements of hazardous wastes is remarkable. What accounts for this success? It seems clear that a combination of endogenous factors and exogenous factors has facilitated the work of UNEP. The organization itself has achieved a reputation not only for technical competence but also for strong leadership. At the same time, UNEP's strategy of bringing science to bear and stressing the technical aspects of issues like marine pollution, ozone depletion and hazardous wastes has served it well, in part at least because the countries involved in these negotiations have found it expedient to downplay the political dimensions of the issues at stake.

Will UNEP be able to play an equally central role as we focus increasing attention on efforts to come to terms with global environmental issues like climate change and the loss of biological diversity? There can be no doubt about UNEP's technical competence to participate in negotiations regarding these matters.[8] Yet it will be much harder to deemphasize the underlying socioeconomic and political issues at stake in negotiations over climate change and biological diversity.[9] Coping with climate change may require drastic alterations in our thinking about economic growth; coming to terms with the loss of biological diversity is apt to necessitate actions that seem highly intrusive to countries, like Brazil, possessing large tracts of moist tropical forests. In both cases, negotiators will come face to face with profound questions relating to the links between environment and development and to relations between developing countries and advanced industrial countries. Under the circumstances, the relatively apolitical approach UNEP has adopted successfully in dealing with regional seas, hazardous wastes, and even ozone depletion is not likely to prove tenable as a way of handling issues like climate change and biological diversity. This is surely one of the lessons to be drawn from the controversy surrounding Resolution 44/228, which the United Nations General Assembly passed in December 1989 and which set forth the terms of reference for the 1992 United Nations Conference on Environment and Development (UNCED). Similar concerns undoubtedly account for the decision of the General Assembly (articulated in Resolution 45/212 of December 1990) to establish a separate entity (the INC) to handle the climate change negotiations. This is not to say that UNEP's role in international environmental negotiations will now evaporate; the organization has emerged, for instance, as the principal negotiating forum for the effort to devise a regime dealing with biological diversity. But it does seem clear that we are entering a new phase in the effort to establish and implement international environmental regimes.

Roles for international organizations

What specific roles do international organizations play when they become involved in institutional bargaining dealing with environmental issues? It is customary in many quarters to stress the technocratic or apolitical nature of these roles. This is certainly understandable as a form of deference to states which have long been regarded as the primary, if not exclusive, members of international society and which exhibit a pronounced tendency to react negatively to perceived encroachments on their primacy in international affairs. Nonetheless, as we move further into an era of complex interdependence, it is increasingly apparent that international organizations cannot and will not confine themselves to narrowly technical roles. Nowhere is this more evident than in the realm of international environmental affairs.

International organizations (together with nongovernmental organizations in many instances) frequently play a catalytic role with respect to environmental negotiations, influencing the way in which the issues are conceptualized or framed and acting to propel them toward the top of the international policy agenda. Capitalizing on the momentum generated by the 1972 United NationsConference on the Human Environment (UNCHE), for example, UNEP has had remarkable success in advancing one issue after another to the top of the international agenda. In cases like the Regional Seas Programme, moreover, the organization has contributed substantially to the fund of intellectual capital (for example, by developing the concept of an ecological region) available to those engaged in environmental negotiations. On a related note, international organizations can and often do keep international environmental issues alive during periods when one or more of the major states have reasons to deemphasize them. The role the IPCC (a joint enterprise of UNEP and WMO) has played in countering efforts on the part of some states (including the United States) to slow the pace of international negotiations pertaining to climate change on grounds of scientific uncertainty is particularly instructive in this regard.[10]

Increasingly, international organizations have also assumed a coordinating role in environmental negotiations. Because environmental issues cut across many other concerns, efforts to form environmental regimes typically touch on the interests of a number of functionally oriented agencies. At the international level alone, for example, those agencies concerned with Mediterranean pollution during the 1960s and 1970s included IMCO, FAO, UNESCO, WMO, WHO, IAEA, and (following its establishment in 1973) UNEP. Under the circumstances, it is easy to grasp the significance of GESAMP's role as a coordinating mechanism. And part of the genius of UNEP's effort in the period immediately preceding the signing of the 1976 Barcelona Convention surely lies in the organization's success in coordinating the activities of an array of interested agencies.

More and more, international organizations have become a source of leadership in environmental negotiations, a development that makes it appropriate to speak of them as architects of the institutional arrangements emerging from these negotiations.[11] Partly, this is a matter of developing negotiating texts on key issues. While there is nothing new about this source of influence, international organizations are now increasingly active in formulating negotiating texts, often during the period prior to the initiation of formal negotiations. What this means is that organizations like UNEP can exercise considerable influence over the course of environmental negotiations, even when they are not key players during the negotiation phase itself. To this we must add the fact that individuals acting in the name of international organizations, such as Maurice Strong and Mostafa Tolba at UNEP, Janos Stanovnik at the ECE, or Hans Blix at IAEA, have become influential leaders in environmental negotiations. And the nature of the roles these leaders play is by no means limited to purely technical considerations.[12] Whether observers regard the results as good, bad, or indifferent, then, it is hard to avoid the conclusion that international organizations now find themselves in the thick of environmental negotiations; no account of specific negotiations is likely to make sense today unless it considers the roles these organizations play.

On the other hand, international organizations, like states, may emerge on occasion as obstacles to the negotiation and implementation of environmental regimes. Institutional arrangements espoused by some actors may either impinge on the interests of particular organizations or require an assessment of the principal forces at work that conflicts with the premises on which existing organizations operate. It is sometimes said, for instance, that the World Bank has been part of the problem rather than part of the solution in efforts to reconcile the demands of development and environmental protection in the Third World, because it has relied on a theory of economic development that fails to account properly for the value of standing stocks of natural resources and that does not accord adequate weight to environmental externalities, like the loss of biological diversity arising from the destruction of moist tropical forests.[13] Whatever the merits of this case, there is no reason to assume that the influence of international organizations on environmental negotiations will always be constructive. Like states, these organizations have interests that may or may not provide them with incentives to occupy a place in the vanguard when it comes to coping with specific transboundary environmental issues.

Some observers have suggested as well that international organizations loom larger in some phases of the negotiating process than in others. Specifically, the idea has surfaced that international organizations are more central to the preparatory or prenegotiation phase and to the implementation phase than they are to the actual bargaining phase.[14] There is some merit to this idea. The experience of UNEP leaves little doubt that international organizations can and often do exercise considerable influence over the formulation of environmental issues before negotiations actually get under way. And depending upon the character of the regimes formed, organizations may be critical to the implementation or administration of the mechanisms established (more on this subject later). Even so, it would be a mistake to overlook the growing importance of international organizations during the course of institutional bargaining over the provisions of environmental regimes per se (for example, the current efforts to reach agreement on the terms for regimes to control climate change and protect biological diversity). As I have implied in the preceding paragraphs, we have reached the stage where it seems fair to conclude that if international organizations were not available to participate in institutional bargaining, we would have to invent them.

The effectiveness of international organizations

How effective are international organizations as instruments of regime formation with regard to environmental issues? Not surprisingly, a review of the record in this area yields a mixed picture. UNEP has been, for the most part, a success story. Much the same can be said of the role of the ECE with regard to transboundary air pollution, the International Maritime Organization (IMO) in the case of the regime established under the terms of the 1973/1978 Convention for the Prevention of Pollution from Ships (MARPOL), and the International Union for the Conservation of Nature and Natural Resources (IUCN)—a hybrid that is a cross between a nongovernmental organization and an intergovernmental organization—in connection with biological regimes, like the arrangements for trade in endangered species set up under the 1973 Washington Convention on

International Trade in Endangered Species of Fauna and Flora (CITES). In other cases, international organizations have been less successful. The OECD encountered significant limits in dealing both with nuclear security and with transboundary movements of hazardous wastes. The IAEA may well have set its sights too low in pushing, in the immediate aftermath of the Chernobyl accident, for the adoption of the 1986 Vienna Conventions on notification and assistance in the event of a nuclear accident. The FAO has had a hand in establishing a number of international regimes dealing with fisheries, but the regimes themselves have not proven particularly effective once in place. Somewhat similar observations are in order regarding the role of UNCTAD in establishing commodity regimes to regulate international trade in primary products, like tin, coffee, sugar, and wheat.[15] Beyond this, there are hints in some recent cases that international organizations can become overactive participants in environmental negotiations, exacerbating the collective-action problems associated with such negotiations rather than helping to solve them or pushing for arrangements that seem attractive on paper but that are unlikely to prove workable in practice. While the evidence is far from clear-cut, such problems seem to have occurred in the negotiation of some of the contemporary regimes dealing with the conservation of species and ecosystems.

What accounts for the variation in the effectiveness of international organizations as players in environmental negotiations? The answer to this question undoubtedly turns on a combination of exogenous and endogenous factors. In the case of ozone depletion, for example, UNEP benefited from strong public interest, the development of a relatively high degree of consensus among scientists regarding the issue, and the emergence of the necessary political will among the participating states. Yet it is undeniable that UNEP was also able to capitalize on the reputation for efficacy it had developed through prior activities (for example, the Regional Seas Programme) and that Mostafa Tolba, UNEP's executive director, played a highly skillful leadership role, particularly in the crucial negotiations eventuating in the 1987 Montreal Protocol on Substances That Deplete the Ozone Layer. Similar observations appear to be in order regarding the regime for transboundary movements of hazardous wastes articulated in the 1989 Basel Convention. What is needed, in effect, is a convergence of exogenous and endogenous factors that combine to maximize the effectiveness of international organizations in environmental negotiations.

Are convergences of this type likely to occur regularly in the future and, in particular, can we expect them to occur in conjunction with emerging issues of global environmental change, like climate change and biological diversity? There is, in my judgment, no basis for taking it for granted that such convergences will occur. As the 1989 United Nations debate on UNCED and the 1990 decision to establish the INC as a separate entity suggest, these issues may become too important and too politicized to be left to an organization like UNEP, no matter how competent it seems in technical terms. It may be that issues like the responsibility of states for environmental destruction occurring within their own jurisdictions or the obligations of developed countries to assist developing countries in dealing with their environmental problems can only be resolved at the highest political levels. Yet it would be inappropriate to arrive at bleak conclusions about the probable roles of international organizations as instruments of environmental regime formation during the near future. Just as the 1972 United Nations Conference on the Human Environment set in motion a train of events that facilitated the work of UNEP during the 1970s and 1980s, UNCED may propel organizations like UNEP, WMO, or other international agencies to the forefront in coming to terms with issues of global environmental change during the 1990s. What this suggests is that the roles international organizations play in specific environmental negotiations are closely linked to broader political developments. To the extent that these larger trends are favorable, therefore, international organizations may emerge as key players in a variety of environmental negotiations during the next decade.

International organizations as objects

So far, I have been examining roles international organizations play in negotiations that give rise to environmental regimes, without paying much attention to the nature of the specific issues at stake. But it is appropriate, now, to shift gears in order to address some questions relating to efforts during the course of environmental negotiations to design international organizations intended to implement or administer the provisions of environmental regimes. In other words, it is time to move from a discussion of organizations as instruments to an examination of organizations as objects. As it happens, the cases referred to in the preceding discussion also suggest a number of interesting observations about how international organizations, created as products of institutional bargaining, eventuate in the formation of environmental regimes.

The demand for organizations

When are organizations needed to implement or administer the provisions of international regimes dealing with environmental matters? While this is a complex subject, it is clear at the outset both that some regimes are capable of operating successfully with little or no assistance from organizations and that there is considerable variation among regimes in these terms. The core regime for Antarctica established under the terms of the Antarctic Treaty of 1959 has no administrative apparatus; the complementary regime for living resources created under the terms of the 1980 Convention on the Conservation of Antarctic Marine Living Resources (CCAMLR) is administered by a commission assisted by a scientific committee and backstopped by a secretariat. Though the regime for whales set up under the 1946 International Convention for the Regulation of Whaling features standing organizations of some significance, the international regime for the conservation of polar bears relies entirely on administrative mechanisms operating with the range states. Similar observations are in order regarding the regime for the protection of stratospheric ozone. Whereas it made perfect sense to rely on national governments to administer the provisions of the 1987 Montreal Protocol, the administration of the compensation fund established under the 1990 London amendments has been entrusted to an international organizational mechanism known as the Executive Committee.

This said, an examination of actual practice at the international level suggests the value of differentiating between a number of functions that may justify the creation of organizations to administer the provisions of environmental regimes. The need to gather and disseminate information, a category that encompasses (but is not restricted to) research, seems to many to constitute an undeniable, albeit circumscribed, basis on which to build the case for establishing organizations in conjunction with international regimes. How could the International Whaling Commission set quotas for harvest or establish moratoria, the World Heritage Committee make decisions about sites to be included on the World Heritage List, or the biennial CITES conferences reach conclusions regarding the placement of species on Appendices I and II without a ready source of credible information? But even this argument is not ironclad. The core Antarctic Treaty regime has functioned well without an apparatus of its own for gathering and disseminating information.[16] Much the same is true of the polar bear regime and the regime for North Pacific fur seals (though the latter arrangement collapsed in the 1980s for other reasons).

Similar comments are in order about other functions that seem to require an administrative apparatus, like authoritative decision making, raising and disbursing revenues, handling transfer payments (including technology transfers), managing buffer stocks, eliciting compliance, resolving disputes, and evaluating outcomes. Given the way the regimes in question are structured, it seems natural to turn to organizations to handle tasks like deciding whether Antarctic marine living resources are sufficiently abundant to allow commercial harvests. It seems natural to turn to them to handle economic returns and rents accruing from deep seabed mining, to manage the compensation fund for developing countries endeavoring to phase out their use of chlorofluorocarbons (CFCs), to certify compliance with the terms of rules pertaining to the peaceful uses of atomic energy, and so forth. But it is worth noting that imaginative negotiators can and often do succeed in devising ways to perform these tasks that eliminate or minimize the need to create new international organizations. To illustrate, the across-the-board reductions in the production and consumption of CFCs mandated under the terms of the Montreal Protocol are being carried out under the supervision of national administrative agencies operating with the participating countries. National administrators can take responsibility for implementing common rules within their own jurisdictions, as in the case of rules regarding polar bears, without any need for an international organization to oversee the administration of a regime. And the mutual inspection provisions of the 1959 Antarctic Treaty offer an ingenious device for ensuring compliance without creating a specialized organization to handle this function.

What can we conclude from these observations? While the establishment of organizations is certainly justifiable in connection with some international environmental regimes, it is worth emphasizing the extent to which ingenious negotiators can devise institutional arrangements that operate effectively in the absence of organizations to administer their provisions. There is a sense, moreover, in which the burden of proof rests on those who advocate the creation of international organizations in conjunction with environmental regimes. All organizations are costly to operate, whether we measure these costs in straightforward monetary terms or in terms of more intangible consequences like opportunities lost as a result of bureaucratization or the inefficiencies arising from cooptation by special interests. It follows that where it is possible to eliminate or minimize reliance on organizations without sacrificing effectiveness, the case against the creation of new international organizations is compelling. In the more typical case in which there are trade-offs between the usefulness of organizations in the pursuit of effectiveness, on the one hand, and the costs associated with the operation of these organizations, on the other hand, there is a need for clear-sighted analysis to make appropriate decisions. In some instances, the parties engaged in institutional bargaining regarding international environmental regimes will have conflicting preferences regarding these trade-offs. But in many cases, the problem is more to arrive at well-reasoned conclusions about the character of suitable organizations than of bargaining to resolve conflicts of interest.

Types of organization

A conclusion that some sort of organization is needed to implement or administer the provisions of an international regime does not resolve the issues at stake. On the contrary, such a decision is a gateway to several additional sets of considerations. There is, to begin with, the question of whether to create an independent organization to administer a new regime, whether to piggyback on an existing organization created initially for some other purpose, or whether to form a coalition with others for the purpose of sharing administrative mechanisms between several distinct regimes. The CITES regime, for instance, delegates many of the relevant administrative chores to UNEP, which has handed them over in turn to IUCN and the World Wildlife Fund (WWF). For many years, the Bureau of Whaling Statistics, which antedated the 1946 convention on whaling and was never formally a component of the international whaling regime, was able to handle a number of tasks relating to the collection and dissemination of information about whaling. Similar comments are in order about the role of the IAEA, an organization created some time ago for other reasons, in administering the provisions of the 1986 conventions dealing with notification and assistance in the event of nuclear accidents.

Though we live in an era marked by a rapid growth in the ranks of international organizations, there is much to be said for taking seriously the ideas of piggybacking on existing organizations or sharing organizational arrangements between regimes. The downside of this approach is that the resultant arrangements cannot be tailor made to fit the needs of particular regimes. In some cases, this may seem a significant drawback. But those negotiating the terms of environmental regimes are well aware of the fact that it is difficult in today's world to fund international organizations in a secure fashion and that a diversified portfolio of functions may contribute to the financial stability of any organizations they establish. Here, again, there may be conflicts of interest among the participants in institutional bargaining relating to the formation of international environmental regimes. More often than not, however, this issue is likely to become a topic for joint problem solving, as the participants seek to devise administrative mechanisms capable of handling tasks effectively, while minimizing the financial burden placed on the members of the resultant regimes.[17]

It is apparent as well that the nature of the organizations needed will be closely tied to the character of the regimes or institutional arrangements they are intended to serve. Any regime calling for authoritative decisions about catch quotas or harvesting limits, the inclusion of species on protected lists, measures to protect migration routes, and the like will require a sophisticated capability for making scientific judgments about the population dynamics of individual species (not to mention other species with which they interact) and for monitoring the results of these decisions over time. A regime that relies on command-and-control regulations, like the arrangements governing sulphur and nitrogen oxide emissions under the 1979 Geneva Convention, calls for different administrative capabilities than that of a regime that makes use of incentive systems, like transferable fishing permits or permits for the emission of various pollutants. Regimes that contemplate the raising or distribution of revenues, like the ozone compensation fund or the revenue-generating provisions of the now defunct Convention for the Regulation of Antarctic Mineral Resource Activities (CRAMRA), require administrative mechanisms that are not needed where there are no issues pertaining to revenues (other than the costs of administration per se). Even more dramatically, the Enterprise, envisioned as an operating authority under the deep seabed mining provisions set forth in Part 11 of the 1982 Law of the Sea Convention, would differ profoundly from the International Seabed Authority (ISA), envisioned as an agency with regulatory authority but no capacity to engage in mining operations in its own right.

It is easy to imagine the emergence of conflicts of interest regarding the nature of the organizations to be established in conjunction with environmental regimes. This follows directly from the fact that such matters are closely tied to the underlying character of the regimes themselves. Given the clash between the United States and the Group of 77 over the fundamental character of a regime for deep seabed mining, for example, it is hardly surprising that it was ultimately impossible to reach agreement on organizational details pertaining to the International Seabed Authority and the Enterprise. Much the same can be said of the sharp differences between environmentalists and others that surfaced regarding the administrative machinery envisioned in CRAMRA. Because organizations are material entities that are relatively easy to think about in concrete terms, it is to be expected that those participating in negotiations aimed at creating environmental regimes will bargain particularly hard over the character of the organizations set up to implement and administer the institutional arrangements they create.

Avoiding perennial problems

Though the establishment of organizations may make perfectly good sense under the circumstances at hand, any move in the direction of setting up new organizations triggers concern about a number of classic problems that are just as relevant to international environmental regimes as they are to any other social institutions. These problems include paralysis, underfunding, cooptation, intrusiveness, and bureaucratization. There are no magic solutions to these problems. But those engaged in institutional bargaining at the international level would do well to foresee the relevance of such matters to the specific situations they are confronting and to take steps in advance to mitigate their impact.

The problems of paralysis and underfunding are twin dangers that emerge again and again in connection with international organizations. Paralysis typically occurs when those setting up an organization insist on a decision-making procedure requiring unanimity, so that they are assured the power to veto actions they dislike even after the organization is up and running. Interestingly, there are examples of imaginative ways to alleviate this problem. One constructive device is to rely on a majoritarian decision rule with a provision for a limited veto, as in the case of CRAMRA, or with a provision allowing individual members to opt out of specific decisions, as in the cases of the whaling regime and CITES. Another is to combine a majoritarian rule with some form of weighted voting, as in the case of the International Monetary Fund (IMF). In some instances, the problem of underfunding is at least as serious as the danger of paralysis in limiting the effectiveness of international organizations. The common tendency of member states to refuse to grant international organizations a means of generating their own revenues and, therefore, to compel them to rely exclusively on dues or voluntary contributions from individual members have proven particularly debilitating in this regard. Yet the development of environmental regimes offers some particularly attractive options for mitigating this problem. The idea of allowing organizations, acting in the name of the common heritage of mankind, to collect economic royalties or rents, as envisioned in the cases of the International Seabed Authority and the commission called for under CRAMRA, is an interesting one. So is the idea of allowing organizations to collect revenues through the sale of permits for the harvest of renewable resources or the emission of various effluents.

The danger of cooptation or the capture of administrative agencies by special interests is just as relevant, though perhaps less familiar, at the international level as it is in domestic society. The developing countries have long complained about the capacity of affluent countries in general and the United States in particular to control IMF decisions. For its part, the United States has taken a similar view of the role of the Group of 77 in UNCTAD and the potential role of this group in the activities of the ISA. The Antarctic Treaty Consultative Parties claim that any move to bring the Antarctic Treaty System under the umbrella of the United Nations would play into the hands of the special interests of the developing countries. And many environmentalists have asserted that mining interests would be able to exercise undue influence over the behavior of the organizational mechanisms (especially the regulatory committees) envisioned under CRAMRA. No doubt there is an element of truth to some of these charges; few organizations are immune to pressure from special interests. But the danger here is that steps taken to minimize the problem of cooptation, like insisting on unanimity as a decision rule, run the risk of exacerbating other classic problems, like paralysis.

Intrusiveness and bureaucratization, also, are problems well known to those who have studied the behavior of administrative agencies in domestic society. The administration of complex regimes requires the promulgation of implementing regulations. Regulations in turn are apt to become bones of contention. Some would say that they are not being implemented in a manner consonant with the intent of a regime's creators; others would say that the resultant red tape constitutes an unjust burden on actors whose activities they regulate. While there is no final solution to such problems, experience in the domestic realm does suggest lessons that are worth considering in creating organizations to administer international environmental regimes. Systems relying on transferable use rights in contrast to command-and-control regulations, for example, leave more room for discretionary action on the part of subjects and encourage efficiency by allowing subjects to meet requirements in the least expensive manner. Similarly, devices designed to maximize transparency as a means of ensuring compliance have the virtue of reducing the need for intrusive monitoring and avoiding inconclusive arguments regarding the extent to which subjects have or have not complied with applicable rules in specific situations.[18]

It is to be hoped that those responsible for negotiating the terms of international environmental regimes will give systematic thought to alleviating these perennial problems. There is no guarantee that the resultant negotiations will be trouble-free; it is not difficult to foresee conflicts of interest regarding such matters. Those who fear cooptation are likely to push for unanimity as the applicable decision rule, while those more concerned about paralysis will favor some form of majoritarian rule. Negotiators hailing from capitalist countries are apt to be more resistant to arrangements based on command-and-control regulation than those who come from socialist countries. Those concerned about the deadening effects of bureaucratic red tape are likely to resist efforts to provide international organizations with sizable revenue sources that they can control on their own. There will always be differences of opinion regarding matters of this sort. Negotiations about them are therefore apt to take on the mixed-motive character long familiar to students of bargaining.[19] Yet we should not conclude from this that the search for solutions to these perennial problems of administration offers no opportunities for imaginative and mutually beneficial problem solving. In fact, there is much to be said for the proposition that this is an area where there is considerable scope for inventiveness on the part of those who think about questions of institutional design; it also requires leadership efforts on the part of those who participate directly in institutional bargaining concerning international environmental regimes.[20]

Conclusion

We live in an era of rising international interdependencies that give rise to growing needs for institutions to manage human activities that would otherwise lead to harmful impacts on others. Nowhere is this more apparent than in the realm of issues relating to natural resources and the environment. In this connection, the anarchical character of international society will strike many as an obstacle to progress. But this is not the only perspective from which to approach issues relating to the management of environmental interdependencies. The absence of a central government at the international level does not rule out the prospect of creating international environmental regimes and the organizations needed to implement and administer them. Equally important, the absence of a central government makes it possible to avoid parochial opposition on the part of interests entrenched in the existing organization. A review of recent experience makes it abundantly clear that the resultant opportunities have given rise to considerable ferment with regard to the development of international environmental regimes. While recent initiatives in this realm vary greatly in terms of their effectiveness and desirability on other grounds, there are good reasons for a sense of cautious optimism among students of international environmental affairs.[21]

At the same time, new challenges are arising that may soon make the issues of the recent past seem elementary by comparison. The advent of an era of global environmental changes is particularly striking in this regard. Some of these changes, like the climate-altering potential of the greenhouse effect, may well require fundamental revisions in the way we think about economic growth and force us to confront seriously North/South issues as they arise in discussions of environment and development in forums such as UNCED.[22] Others, like the loss of biological diversity, will raise complex questions regarding the international stake in activities occurring largely inside the borders of individual states and the justifiability of various forms of intervention on the part of outsiders claiming to act in the name of the international community. While the potential for conflicts of interest over such matters is great, there are also opportunities for international cooperation that could provide a basis for the establishment of important new international institutions and the organizations needed to implement and administer them. To the extent that such opportunities come into focus during the foreseeable future, it will be essential to draw lessons from the experiences of the recent past about what works and what does not work when it comes to institutions and organizations capable of solving large-scale environmental problems. Only through the conduct of such analyses can we learn from our experiences and prepare ourselves to deal constructively with the challenges that lie ahead.

NOTES

1. For an extended account of institutional bargaining, see Oran R. Young, "The Politics of International Regime Formation: Managing Natural Resources and the Environment," *International Organization* 43 (Summer 1989): 349–75. On formal models of bargaining, consult Oran R. Young, ed., *Bargaining: Formal Models of Negotiation* (Urbana: University of Illinois Press, 1975).

2. This definition follows the formula devised at a meeting of directors of major research projects on regimes held at Dartmouth in November 1991. The report of this "Regimes Summit" is available from the Institute of Arctic Studies at Dartmouth. For a variety of analytical perspectives on international regimes, consult Stephen D. Krasner, ed., *International Regimes* (Ithaca, N.Y.: Cornell University Press, 1983); Oran R. Young, *International Cooperation: Building Regimes for Natural Resources and the Environment* (Ithaca, N.Y.: Cornell University Press, 1989); and Robert O. Keohane, *International Institutions and State Power: Essays in International Relations Theory* (Boulder, Colo.: Westview Press, 1989).

3. For an extended discussion of the relationships between institutions and organizations, see Young, *International Cooperation*, chap. 2. For a range of perspectives on international governance, see James N. Rosenau, ed., *Governance without Government: Change and Order in World Politics* (New York: Cambridge University Press, 1992).

4. While we often associate constitutional contracts with formal statements of the provisions of regimes in treaties or conventions, the concept applies as well to informal practices centered on unwritten networks of rights and rules. Many regimes encompass both formal and informal elements. See James M. Buchanan, *The Limits of Liberty: Between Anarchy and Leviathan* (Chicago: University of Chicago Press, 1975), esp. chap. 4.

5. Clive Archer, *International Organizations* (London: George Allen and Unwin, 1983).

6. Robert O. Keohane and Joseph S. Nye, *Power and Interdependence*, 2d ed. (Glenview, Ill.: Scott, Foresman and Company, 1989).

7. This is not to say that UNDP has been particularly well managed or effective in its major undertakings. There is, in fact, considerable controversy regarding UNDP's performance.

8. This does not mean that UNEP's internal management has been particularly efficient. There are those who maintain that UNEP has succeeded in a number of its undertakings despite weak or inefficient management.

9. For a sophisticated account that reaches somewhat different conclusions, see Richard Elliot Benedick, *Ozone Diplomacy: New Directions in Safeguarding the Planet* (Cambridge: Harvard University Press, 1991).

10. On the politics of regime formation in the case of climate change, see Eugene B. Skolnikoff, "The Policy Gridlock on Global Warming," *Foreign Policy* 79 (Summer 1990): 79–93 and James K. Sebenius, "Negotiating a Regime to Control Global Warming," in World Resources Institute, *Greenhouse Warming: Negotiating a Global Regime* (Washington, D.C.: World Resources Institute, 1991): 69–98.

11. For a study that focuses on the concept of architecture in this context, see Alan K. Henrickson, *Negotiating World Order: The Artisanship and Architecture of Global Diplomacy* (Wilmington, Del.: Scholarly Resources, 1986).

12. For a general account of the roles that individual leaders play in institutional bargaining, see Oran R. Young, "Political Leadership and Regime Formation: On the Development of Institutions in International Society," *International Organization* 45 (Summer 1991): 281–308.

13. On the need for an accounting system that incorporates the value of standing stocks of natural resources, see Robert Repetto, "Balance-Sheet Erosion—How to Account for the Loss of Natural Resources," *International Environmental Affairs* 1 (Spring 1989): 103–37.

14. On the concept of prenegotiation, see Janice Gross Stein, ed., *Getting to the Table: The Process of International Prenegotiation* (Baltimore: Johns Hopkins University Press, 1989).

15. Jock A. Finlayson and Mark W. Zacher, *Managing International Markets: Developing Countries and the Commodity Regime* (New York: Columbia University Press, 1988).

16. This situation has undoubtedly contributed to the development of a significant role for the Scientific Committee on Antarctic Research (SCAR), a nongovernmental organization which belongs to the International Council of Scientific Unions (ICSU) and has no formal link to the Antarctic Treaty System.

17. For a helpful account of problem solving or integrative bargaining in contrast to distributive bargaining, see Richard E. Walton and Robert B. McKersie, *A Behavioral Theory of Negotiations: An Analysis of a Social Interaction System* (New York: McGraw-Hill, chaps. 4 and 5).

18. Abram Chayes and Antonia H. Chayes, "Adjustment and Compliance Processes in International Regulatory Regimes," in Jessica Tuchman Mathews, ed., *Preserving the Global Environment: The Challenge of Shared Leadership* (New York: Norton, 1991): 309–23.

19. For a seminal account of bargaining as a form of mixed-motive interaction, see Thomas C. Schelling, *The Strategy of Conflict* (Cambridge: Harvard University Press, 1960).

20. On leadership in the context of institutional bargaining, see Young, "Political Leadership and Regime Formation." See note 12.

Oran R. Young

21. For a sophisticated assessment of recent experience in this realm, see Peter H. Sand, *Lessons Learned in Global Environmental Governance* (Washington, D.C.: World Resources Institute, 1990).

22. See Michael Grubb, *The Greenhouse Effect: Negotiating Targets* (London: Royal Institute of International Affairs, 1989) and the review of this work provided in James K. Sebenius, "Report on Reports," *Environment* 32 (November 1990): 25–30.

8 Transboundary Problems in International Law

LETTIE WENNER

Most environmental problems have major international implications. Pollutants recognize no national boundaries. Effluents and emissions created in one nation state soon find their way into another's jurisdiction. There is no incentive to prevent pollution at the source because the ill effects can be so easily transported to the territory of others. Cumulative impacts from the common behavior of all nations, such as excessive production of carbon dioxide, sulfur oxides, and other pollutants, create global problems for all humankind. Therefore, it would appear only reasonable that the solutions to such problems should be sought in the international arena. Transnational problems merit international solutions.

One major obstacle exists to holistic solutions to those problems—the same obstacle that has prevented solutions to other international problems: the sovereignty of nation states. No country is willing to give up any of its freedom of decision making in order to obtain security from common threats, such as global climate change or destruction of the ozone layer. Even the 1972 Stockholm Conference on the Human Environment concluded by reiterating the primary principle of sovereignty before mentioning the major concern that had brought the nations together. Principle 21 states:

> States have, in accordance with the Charter of the United Nations and the principles of international law, *the sovereign right to exploit their own resources pursuant to their own environmental policies* and the responsibility to ensure that activities within their jurisdiction or control do not cause damage to the environment of other States or of areas beyond the limits of national jurisdiction. (Springer 1988, 20; emphasis added)

Despite this major caveat, some nation states have been tentatively edging toward international solutions to transnational environmental problems for several decades. This movement culminated in the 1972 meeting in Stockholm which created the United Nations Environmental Program, now headquartered in Nairobi. This program includes concern for every type of environmental problem, from depletion of tropical rain forests and elimination of endangered species to hazardous waste dumping on the international market.

165

A variety of mechanisms exist by which programs to protect the environment can be carried out. The most theoretically draconian would be to give an international body the authority to regulate individual behavior that affects more than one nation state or the entire globe. This is obviously the most threatening to nation states, as it would infringe on the sovereign authority of individual nation states to control the behavior of their own nationals. The least intrusive control is for nation states to negotiate bilaterally their claims against each other after damage has allegedly been done by nationals in one state to the welfare of nationals of another. There are various intermediate points between the two extremes, including adjudication and arbitration of grievances, and regional agreements administered through representatives of two or more governments that meet to decide a specified agenda of questions.

The history of international environmental controls shows very gradual movement away from bilateral diplomatic negotiation about damages that have already occurred to a more multinational attempt to prevent harm before it occurs. This history tracks that of air and water pollution control in the United States and other industrialized nations in the 1960s and 1970s. Originally, the only recourse for individuals who felt they had been harmed by pollution created by others was to take the issue to court under the common law of nuisance and to hope the responsible parties would be held liable for damages beyond their property lines. Gradually, however, laws were passed which made it an offense to pollute communal natural resources such as water and air. Administrative agencies were created to set standards, issue permits to discharge, and monitor the amounts of harmful pollutants emitted by multiple sources. A system of compensation after the fact was replaced by one that attempts to prevent harm.

This chapter analyzes transboundary issues relevant to the abatement of air and water pollution. Examples of each process—bilateral negotiation, arbitration, regional agreements, and international institutions—are discussed briefly. Then one problem, the pollution of the high seas by oil tankers, is considered at some length. In this issue area, an effort has been made to move from bilateral negotiations to an international organization with authority to prevent pollution. Yet here, too, efforts have been only partially successful.

Throughout the chapter, particular attention is paid to the important role that national sovereignty has played in slowing attempts to control pollution through international law. The unwillingness of nation states to give up any of their sovereignty continues to prevent a move from bilateral diplomacy and arbitration to regional and international institutions in order to solve these problems. The chapter concludes with a discussion of the need to make this move in order to prevent water and air pollution rather than merely compensate for it after the fact.

BILATERAL DIPLOMATIC SOLUTIONS
TO WATER PROBLEMS

One recurring environmental problem between nation states has been the need to share water resources when a river or other body of surface water extends between states and/or creates the international boundary between nations. At first this problem was seen primarily as one of quantity of water to be shared, since the upper riparian state could, theoretically, use up the entire flow of water before it reached the downstream nation. In 1895 U.S. Attorney General Judson Harmon said that the United States could divert as much of the water of the Rio Grande River as it wished before it reached Mexico (Utton 1988). The Harmon Doctrine exemplifies the principle of national sovereignty by stating specifically that an upper riparian owner can lay claim to all the water in a river simply by virtue of the fact that the water passes through its territory first. Despite the fact that no nation state has ever denied its right to act in such a selfish manner, in practice there has been considerable modification of this doctrine. This has always been accomplished through diplomatic negotiation and bilateral decision making. In 1944, for example, Mexico and the U.S. signed treaties distributing the waters of the Rio Grande River and the Colorado River between the U.S. and Mexico.

Beyond the mere willingness to share quantities of water with neighbors, there is also the issue of the quality of water that reaches the lower riparian owner. By the 1940s the quality of water reaching Mexico from the Colorado River had become degraded because of the repeated use of the same water in several states. Irrigating multiple crops produces very saline water because each time water passes through soil it leaches salts from it. Mexico argued the water was unusable on its entry into Mexico. This controversy continued until 1973, when the U.S. agreed to treat the water to reduce its salinity (Lammers 1984, 262). In so doing, the United States made it clear it was not relinquishing any of its sovereign powers, nor recognizing any international obligation to act in a responsible manner concerning the quality of water it allowed to pass over its borders to the next riparian state. Nevertheless, it agreed to treat the water because it recognized the burden it was placing on the Mexican economy as well as the fact that the U.S. also receives water from other nations.

Mexico and the U.S. have also argued about the separate responsibilities of border towns such as Ciudad Juarez and El Paso, Texas, to treat sewage before releasing it to the international waters of the Rio Grande. Both countries have complained about the other's pollution of shared waterways. The most recent manifestation of this dispute came in the 1991 discussion of a free-trade zone between Mexico and the United States. Local authorities in

Texas argued that location of additional industry in Mexican border towns will only add to the pollution problem, since Mexico has more lax standards for the treatment of sewage than the U.S. Bilateral diplomatic negotiation remains the method by which the two governments attempt to resolve their differences over the quantity and quality of water shared by them.

AIR POLLUTION CONTROL THROUGH INTERNATIONAL ARBITRATION

One case that illustrates the unwillingness of nation states to rely on international organizations because of the latter's encroachment on national sovereignty involved air pollution between two neighbors whose history of amicable relations should have enabled them to settle their differences with a minimum of posturing. During the 1920s agricultural interests in the State of Washington complained about sulfurous fumes coming from a Canadian copper smelter in Trail, British Columbia, which, they said, caused damage to their crops and timber industry. In 1927 the issue was turned over to an international joint commission (IJC) established earlier by Canada and the United States to handle water disputes (see below). In 1931 the IJC assessed the amount of damage in the U.S. to be worth $350,000. However, as the international commission had no means of enforcement, the decision proved a pyrrhic victory. Canada regulated the smelter to a degree, but no compensation was paid, and the U.S. government remained dissatisfied.

In 1933 the U.S. government took up the issue again with the Canadian government, and this time both governments agreed to form an arbitral tribunal in 1935, consisting of one member each from Canada and the U.S., and one from Belgium (Lammers 1984, 518). In 1937 the tribunal found that indeed the Trail Smelter had caused $350,000 of compensable damage before 1932 and additional damage in the form of reduced crop yields worth $78,000 since then. The tribunal dismissed other claims from the U.S. for damages due to pollution of the Columbia River and damage to livestock (Lammers 1984, 522). By the terms of the settlement, Canada also agreed to impose a smoke abatement system on the smelter, but the settlement fell short of eliminating the pollution because neither country involved wished to establish a precedent that would impose excessive costs on industry on either side of the international border.

Because there were no international precedents to use, this decision was based almost entirely on precedents from the U.S. Supreme Court concerning disputes between states within the United States about air pollution. The decision established the principle that:

no state has the right to use or permit the use of its territory in such a manner as to cause injury by fumes in or to the territory of another or the properties or persons therein, when the case is of serious consequence and the injury is established by clear and convincing evidence. (Trail Smelter Arbitral Tribunal 1972)

This was the beginning of the concept that even a sovereign nation owes neighboring states some preventive protection from pollution by industry within its jurisdiction. This was the principle acknowledged in the 1972 Stockholm Conference, but always with the understanding that national decision makers will determine how this obligation will be carried out.

In order to have this principle interpreted by an arbitral tribunal, it is necessary that the state suffering the injury obtain the consent of the nation where the pollution originates. That seems unlikely to occur until the latter agrees that there has indeed been an injury. When residents in Ciudad Juarez, Mexico complained about noxious fumes coming from stockyards in El Paso, Texas, in 1961, the U.S. State Department regretted any "inconvenience or discomfort" the activities caused, but argued that there was no economic damage done and hence no compensable injury (Springer 1988, 69). Obviously, the same nation (in these cases, the United States) will play the role of both accuser and accused from time to time, and its attitude about responsibility will vary depending on the situation in which it finds itself.

REGIONAL COMPACTS FOR AIR AND WATER POLLUTION CONTROL

In addition to bilateral treaties the U.S. has also helped to form continuing bilateral organizations to deal with transboundary water quantity and quality problems. The 1909 Boundary Waters Treaty between Canada and the United States was designed to avoid diversion of water by one nation without notifying the other and obtaining its agreement. But it also stipulated that waters flowing across the boundary "should not be polluted on either side to the injury of health or property of the other" (Ruster and Simma, 1909, vol. 10).

Obviously, this understanding has not prevented significant degradation since 1909 of all the Great Lakes as well as the rivers shared by Canada and the United States. Industry and municipalities on both sides of the international border have contributed to the pollution problem, which has kept both nations from insisting that the letter of the law be enforced.

The Boundary Waters Treaty of 1909 created the U.S./Canada International Joint Commission (IJC), which was designed to become an international judicial institution for settling disputes (Springer 1988). Either of the two signatories can send problems to the IJC and it can report on facts and circumstances surrounding pollution problems, but these are not decisions. Article 10 allows the IJC to issue binding decisions on issues the parties mutually agree to send to it (Ruster and Simma 1909). The U.S. originally referred the Trail Smelter dispute to the IJC. Although the IJC made a decision, this was never carried out and the issue had to be resolved through arbitration, as described above.

The IJC can take no action on its own, for neither Canada nor the U.S. has relinquished any of its national sovereignty. This arrangement is simply a recognition of political reality, because both countries would have to agree to any decision reached by the IJC in order to bring it into force. IJC remains a useful institution for bringing experts from both countries together to discuss common problems of both air and water pollution. Each nation often refers to the general principle of responsibility of the other state to avoid polluting its environment—a responsibility laid out both in the Trail Smelter case and in principle 21 of the Stockholm Conference Declaration. Nevertheless, both seem to expect to use international diplomatic channels to resolve any real disputes that arise between them about pollution of their shared waterways.

The Trail Smelter case was not the last word in the dispute between Canada and the U.S. over air pollution, however. The impact of sulfur dioxide is not limited to the immediate fallout on lands close to the source of the pollutant. In recent decades scientists have made policymakers aware that acid deposition from the atmosphere may have deleterious effects on lakes, crops, wildlife, and forests far from the sources of the pollutants. These effects range from decreased tree growth to acidification of lakes and reduction of fish populations in them. Acid rain is particularly dangerous for some areas of the world—for example, the eastern provinces of Canada—because their soil is naturally acidic and cannot buffer plants and animals from further acidification as alkaline soil can. In addition, the prevailing winds in the North American continent tend to move in a northeasterly direction, placing most of Canada's eastern provinces downwind from the major coal and oil-burning utility plants in the U.S. midwest. Since the U.S. is more industrialized and populous than Canada, it sends a great deal more sulfur dioxide into Canada than it presently receives from Canada.

INSTITUTIONAL MECHANISMS FOR ENFORCING POLLUTION CONTROLS

Multinational organizations have also tried their hands at settling environmental problems. Because of its situation, Canada was one of the most enthusiastic supporters of the Long-Range Transboundary Air Pollution

Convention (LRTAPC) held in Geneva in November 1979. There some thirty-four Western industrialized nations met to discuss reducing their annual emissions of sulfur dioxide. In 1984 in Ottawa and again in Munich some eighteen countries, including Canada and the Scandinavian countries downwind of many pollution sources in western Europe, formed the Thirty Percent Club. They agreed to reduce their sulfur oxides emissions 30 percent from the base they were producing in 1980 (Bjorkbom 1988). Notably absent from this group were the United Kingdom and the United States, both of which argued they had already reduced their sulfur oxides in the 1970s before the other states became interested in the problem (McMahon 1988). The U.S. was reluctant to do more than the Clean Air Act of 1977 required because, it argued, Canada was planning to reduce not real emissions but allowable ones that it had avoided by switching to nuclear and hydroelectric power.

Regardless of how many nations have or have not joined the Thirty Percent Club, there is no mechanism to implement what amounts to an essentially voluntary unilateral decision by each of the signatories to reduce their country's emissions. Indeed, there is no way to determine whether any of the promised actions have taken place before 1993, the deadline agreed upon for reaching the 30 percent reduction goal (Fouere 1988). At that time it seems likely there will be another meeting where national representatives will argue about the degree to which they have and others have not responded to the acid rain crisis.

An alternative to more diplomacy and additional international agreements would be to turn the whole issue of compliance over to the International Court of Justice (ICJ) at The Hague. This institution was created after World War II for adjudication of grievances that one country has against others. However, the ICJ has failed to live up to the role that its creators planned for it. Generally, it is incapable of calling major sovereign powers to account for such obvious acts of aggression as the United States's mining of Nicaraguan ports. Very rarely do countries with grievances against their neighbors take them to the ICJ rather than negotiate bilaterally, because there have been so few successful adjudications.

There has been only one case involving an environmental problem adjudicated in the ICJ, and its result was at best indecisive. In the 1960s a partial nuclear test ban treaty was negotiated between the nuclear powers to ban tests above ground, but both France and China refused to sign. In 1974 Australia and New Zealand sued to halt France's planned tests of nuclear weapons in French Polynesia in the Pacific Ocean, claiming that they would receive harmful radioactive fallout. Using the Trail Smelter case as precedent, the members of the ICJ voted eight to six to protect Australia and New

Zealand against such tests. Although France refused to recognize ICJ authority in the case, in 1974 France announced that it would conduct all future tests underground, as other nuclear powers were then doing. Pressure from world public opinion about the case may have contributed to this decision (Schneider 1979). Subsequently, the ICJ decided that the case had become moot and dropped it from its agenda (Australia v. France, 57 ILR 350–600; ICJ Reports 1974, 253). In so doing the ICJ did little to increase its own authority, prestige, and potential for influence in future cases.

INTERNATIONAL ORGANIZATIONAL
APPROACH TO OIL POLLUTION OF THE SEAS

In addition to the kinds of transboundary issues that have been discussed above, there is the problem of how to protect the quality of commonly held natural resources, such as the high seas, that are the property of no nation, but the concern of all. This cannot be easily relegated to diplomatic negotiations between two or more powers. It concerns the well-being of all nations and demands some mechanism for continuing international attention to the problems inherent in the abuse and overuse of commonly held resources.

In 1967 a dramatic oil spill alerted the world to the dangers of oil pollution in international waters. The tanker *Torrey Canyon,* owned by a subsidiary of the Union Oil Company of California, went aground off the coast of Cornwall in Britain, spilling 29 million gallons of crude oil. At the time, it was customary for no one to touch a ship or cargo that had run aground until the flag state could attempt to salvage it. Nevertheless, in the *Torrey Canyon* disaster, the British government ordered the Royal Air Force to bomb the listing tanker and ignite the oil cargo to prevent its drifting to the Cornish beaches. Despite this attempt to prevent harm, the leaking oil fouled that shore, much of the English Channel, and the coast of Normandy in France as well.

After this disaster there were many others that caught the attention of the world press, including that of the *Argo Merchant,* which in 1976 spilled 7.7 million gallons near the Georges Bank fisheries off the coast of Maine; the *Amoco Cadiz,* which spilled 55 million gallons off Brittany in 1978; the *Exxon Valdez,* which released 11 million gallons in Prince William Sound, Alaska, in March 1989, and finally the *Braer,* which broke up near the Shetland Islands and released 26 millions of light crude oil in January 1993. Despite the drama of these incidents, the major problem of oil pollution of the high seas and coastal areas does not come from such spectacular accidents, but rather from operational discharges of oily ballast from oil tankers and other types of seagoing vessels. Although all vessels empty their ballast tanks regularly, oil tankers create the largest amounts of pollution because they do not have separate cargo and ballast tanks. Sea water is used to provide ballast when moving an empty tanker after it deposits its cargo; it is also used to wash out the tanks while en route. The ballast was traditionally dumped when the tanker reached the port where it would pick up more oil.

For three decades a subsidiary of the United Nations has attempted to grapple with these problems. The International Maritime Consultative Organization (IMCO) was founded in 1948 not as an environmental regulatory force, but as an organization of the maritime states formed to advance their economic interests. The maritime industry originally objected to any authority by an international body over its economic well-being. This industry concern and the traditional reluctance of nations to relinquish any sovereignty managed to delay IMCO's coming into force for ten years. By 1958 twenty-one nations had ratified the agreement, including most of the major seafaring nations of the world, such as Great Britain, Japan, and Norway. IMCO's name was subsequently changed to the International Maritime Organization (IMO), but it has continued to acknowledge the practical reality that unless the major maritime powers are willing to accept a program, it is useless to attempt to create one.

In the years since its inception, IMO's organization and membership have greatly changed. It now has a council, assembly, maritime safety committee, oil pollution subcommittee, and marine environmental protection committee. Developing states were originally underrepresented on the council, but that has changed somewhat. The great maritime nations still must ratify important changes in IMO policy, and this has resulted in incremental changes. But poorer nations have not been as eager to adopt strenuous standards for tankers as their status as nonmaritime powers might lead one to expect. This is because of their need for cheap energy and reliance on oil for development. They feel that the industrialized world developed during a period when pollution was rampant and uncontrolled. To increase international regulation now would only force less-developed countries to pay more for their development than industrialized nations did earlier.

Even before the creation of IMO, some countries had expressed concern about oily discharges spoiling their shores. In 1926 the first international conference to discuss the problem had proposed a ban on oily discharges consisting of more than one hundred ppm. of oil to water in a zone extending fifty miles from every coast. Although never ratified by any state, ships that voluntarily complied simply emptied their ballasts just before approaching their destination. In 1954 the International Convention for the Prevention of Pollution of the Sea by Oil met and agreed to forbid oil tankers from dumping oily waste of more than one hundred ppm. concentration within fifty miles of land. In 1969 a new conference extended this ban to one hundred miles.

Many experts argued that the only way to prevent ships from discharging more than one hundred ppm. of oil to water was to design new tankers over twenty thousand tons deadweight with separate tanks for ballast and cargo and to provide for on-land waste disposal facilities at ports. Industry representatives joined the conference in 1962 and suggested an alternative method to achieve the one hundred ppm. limit: the so-called Load on Top (LOT) method. Oily wastes and ballast are kept in slop tanks and, since oil floats on water, most of the sea water can be decanted by emptying it from the bottom of the tank. A new cargo of crude oil is loaded on top of the water/oil mixture in the bottom of the tank. It is alleged this method prevents 90 percent of the oil previously dumped from being discharged into the sea, but it seems likelier that it is approximately 50 percent effective. IMO accepted LOT in 1969 with the additional stipulations that tankers not discharge more than sixty liters per mile and that the total volume of oil discharged should not exceed 1/15,000th of a given tanker's cargo-carrying capacity (McGonigle and Zacher 1979). These changes to the international agreements did not take effect until 1978, when the requisite number of states had ratified them.

Some states such as the United States continued to urge separation of ballast and cargo on tankers because they feel that it is impossible to enforce the discharge limits. In 1978 another meeting of IMO reached a compromise. All tankers built after 1979 were to have segregated ballast tanks. However, another modification in operations was designed to obviate the need to retrofit older tanks. This latest method, Crude Oil Washing (COW) was designed originally by the oil industry to reduce loss of product, but was sold to IMO as a pollution prevention measure. COW is a technique to wash out tankers with crude oil rather than seawater and cuts down on the loss of oil.

It is difficult for an objective observer to discern how much oil is dumped from ships traveling on the open sea. Therefore, the limits set by IMO are for practical purposes unenforceable, as they depend upon self-reporting by the ship's crew. Members of IMO originally agreed to take any disputes to the International Court of Justice, but to date none has done so, and in subsequent years this was included only as an optional protocol (Springer 1988, 157). The real key to impact lies not in what the nations of IMO have agreed to, but what the individual nation states are willing to enforce in regard to their own citizens. The principle of the sovereignty of nations prevents anyone other than the state whose flag flies over a given vessel from controlling its behavior by taking it to court or fining it. Coastal states have authority only over activities in their territorial waters. The state that has to absorb the costs of pollution, therefore, has no authority to enforce the discharge regulations, while the state that benefits from having its ships minimize their costs is charged with enforcement. Hence, although coastal states frequently report what they consider to be clear violations of the prohibition against discharge in the hundred-mile limit, few of these are pursued in the courts of the countries to whom they are reported.

At the time of the *Torrey Canyon* disaster the 1958 Convention on the Limitation of Liability allowed for recovery for damages of only $67 per ton of the ships' tonnage, about 40 percent of its deadweight carrying capacity. This formula would have amounted to less than $5 million in damages for France and Britain, much less than the actual damages. The law of the sea at that time allowed for a wealthy multinational corporation, such as the Union Oil Company, to hide behind the legal fiction that only the shipowner is responsible for accidents. This obvious injustice resulted in a meeting of the IMO Council to raise the limit. In 1971 IMO agreed to extend the maximum amount of liability to $35 million an incident. Any payments beyond the traditional limits are made from an international fund that is collected from the entire oil industry based on need in any given year (McGonigle and Zacher 1979, 171).

Change has been incremental regarding controls on pollution of the high seas from oil. There is an obvious built-in conflict between coastal states and flagship (maritime) powers, even though some of the latter, such as the United Kingdom, have themselves suffered the effects of some of the worst disasters. Most powers refuse to acknowledge the severity of oil pollution because of their own dependence on oil. Any advances that have occurred have followed major catastrophes and have depended on an advancement in technology. This only occurs when industry is forced to search for new techniques by a major power, like the U.S., threatening to take unilateral action. Only slowly has industry accepted LOT and then COW. It still resists separate ballast tanks and double-hulled tankers. Oil and insurance industries dominate Western Europe, which has most of the maritime states on which IMO depends. The fleet of tankers owned by U.S. interests are mostly registered in Liberia and Panama to avoid U.S. regulations, and they too agree with oil corporations' demands. IMO can only act when the majority of the U.S./West European bloc agree.

CONCLUSIONS

In many ways the situation regarding international environmental problems is analogous to the situation that prevailed in the United States in the 1960s.

Numerous polluted waterways existed and were recognized as a problem by all those living near them. Under the terms of the 1956 Federal Water Pollution Control Act, conferences were held among states and municipalities contributing to a common water pollution problem. Since each unit was autonomous, in order to make any progress each jurisdiction had to take independent action, and each tended to wait for other jurisdictions to do the job for them. Not until the 1970s, when the federal government obtained authority to issue permits, take administrative actions, and sue polluters independently of state laws, did any real progress take place.

Four different mechanisms have been used to deal with transboundary pollution problems: bilateral negotiation, international arbitration, regional compacts, and multinational organizations from the ICJ to the newer United Nations Economic Program and IMO for pollution of the high seas. Each has been used from time to time to settle international disputes arising over shared water and air resources. However, because of the reluctance of all nation states to see their sovereignty diminished, most settlements have come through the first or second mechanism: diplomatic negotiation or international arbitration. Before any real progress can be made, however, it is necessary for countries to learn to rely more on the latter two mechanisms, which have the potential to prevent harm rather than compensate for it after the fact.

At the present time, organizations such IMO have the authority to meet and discuss mutual problems which the technical staff can identify. However, to have an impact any agreement must be ratified by the major maritime powers, and each state that agrees must then pass national legislation to implement it. Many nations continue to prefer a unilateral approach, not wanting to give up any independence of action. Most settlements come in the form of compensation for damages that have already occurred. There have been few preventive measures taken to date. This is primarily due to all nation-states' reluctance to reduce their cherished national sovereignty.

The history of international environmental controls continues to be one of incremental movement from bilateral diplomatic negotiation about damage that has already occurred to multinational attempts to prevent harm before it occurs. International law faces the difficult challenge of moving from a system of after-the-fact compensation to one of prevention. This can be accomplished to some degree by getting each nation state to agree to force industries within its borders to reduce their pollution before damage across the border occurs. However, in cases like pollution of the high seas improvement can be achieved only through international law and effective organizations to enforce that law. It appears that the unwillingness of sovereign nations to surrender any of their closely held independence must be overcome before any international agency can enforce a mechanism for genuine pollution prevention. Given the resurgence of nationalistic fervor in the 1990s, prospects for such a change seem remote.

REFERENCES

Benedick, Richard E. 1985. Transboundary air pollution. Current policy series no. 723 (July). Washington, D.C.: U.S. Department of State, Bureau of Public Affairs.

Birnie, Patricia. 1988. International law and solving conflicts. In *International environmental diplomacy,* ed. John C. Carroll, 95–121. Cambridge: Cambridge University Press.

Bjorkbom, Lars. 1988. Resolution of environmental problems: The use of diplomacy. In *International environmental diplomacy,* ed. John C. Carroll, 123–37. Cambridge: Cambridge University Press.

Caldwell, Lynton K. 1988. Beyond environmental diplomacy: The changing institutional structure of international cooperation. In *International environmental diplomacy,* ed. John C. Carroll, 13–27. Cambridge: Cambridge University Press.

Carroll, John C. 1988. The acid rain issue in Canadian-American relations. In *International environmental diplomacy,* ed. John C. Carroll, 141–71. Cambridge: Cambridge University Press.

Caponera, Dante A. 1985. Patterns of cooperation in international water law: Principles and institutions. *Natural Resources Journal* 25:564–87.

Dahlberg, Kenneth A., Marvin S. Soroos, Anne Thompson Feraru, James E. Harf, and B. Thomas Trout. 1985. *Environment and the global arena.* Durham, N.C.: Duke University Press.

Edwards, David. 1988. Review of status of implementation and development of regional arrangements on cooperation in combating marine pollution. In *International environmental diplomacy,* ed. John C. Carroll, 239–72. Cambridge: Cambridge University Press.

Favre, David S. 1989. *International trade in endangered species.* Dordrecht, The Netherlands: Martinus Nijhoff.

Fouere, Erwan. 1988. Emerging trends in international agreements. In *International environmental diplomacy,* ed. John C. Carroll. Cambridge: Cambridge University Press.

Kiss, Alexandre. 1985. The protection of the Rhine against pollution. *Natural Resources Journal* 25:613–37.

Lammers, J. G. 1984. *Pollution of international watercourses.* The Hague: Martinus Nijhoff.

McGonigle, R. Michael, and Mark W. Zacher. 1979. *Pollution, politics and international law.* Berkeley: University of California Press.

McCrossen, Ann Macon. 1985. Is there a future for proposed water uses in equitable apportionment suits? *Natural Resources Journal* 25:791–812.

McMahon, Michael S. 1988. Balancing the interests Canada-American. In *International environmental diplomacy,* ed. John C. Carroll, 147–71. Cambridge: Cambridge University Press.

Organization for Economic Cooperation and Development. 1985. *Transfrontier movements of hazardous wastes.* Paris.

Park, Chris C., ed. 1986. *Environmental politics.* London: Croom Helm.

Rodgers, Ann Berkley, and Albert E. Utton. 1985. The Ixtapa draft agreement relating to the use of transboundary groundwaters. *Natural Resources Journal* 25:713–72.

Rosencranz, Armin. 1988. The acid rain controversy in Europe and N. America. In *International environmental diplomacy,* ed. John C. Carroll, 173–85. Cambridge: Cambridge University Press.

Ruster and Simma, 1909. Vol. 10 of *U.S. and Canada: Convention Concerning the Boundary Waters,* Article IV 2, pp. 5158–66, Washington, D.C.

Springer, Allen L. 1988. U.S. environmental policy and international law. In *International environmental diplomacy,* ed. John C. Carroll, 45–65. Cambridge: Cambridge University Press.

Teclaff, Ludwik A., and Albert E. Utton. 1981. *International groundwater law.* London: Oceana Publications.

Teclaff, Ludwig A., and Eileen Teclaff. 1985. Transboundary toxic pollution and the drainage basin concept. *Natural Resources Journal* 25: 581–612.

"Trail Smelter Arbitral Tribunal." 1972. *American Journal of International Law* 35 (Spring): 219.

Utton, Albert E. 1988. Problems and successes in international water agreements: The example of U.S. and Mexico. In *International environmental diplomacy,* ed. John C. Carroll, 67–83. Cambridge: Cambridge University Press.

SECTION FOUR

Comparative Politics and Public Policy

9 Environmental Policy in the European Community

DAVID VOGEL

This essay examines the environmental policies of the European Community. It consists of three parts. The first part traces the development of Community environmental policy from the 1960s through the mid-1980s. Part 2 discusses environmental regulation since the adoption of the Single European Act in 1987. The remainder of the essay presents a case study of EC regulation of automotive emissions.

The European Community was established in 1957 by six European nations, primarily as an economic union. Since 1973, six additional nations have joined. The EC's twelve member nations have a total population of 325 million people, encompassing nine-tenths of the population of Western Europe. During the last three decades, the scope of the Community's powers has broadened considerably and now includes a wide range of social, industrial and regulatory policies. In 1987, the member states of the EC approved the Single European Act (SEA) in order to accelerate the pace of economic integration. At a major conference on the future of the EC held in Maastricht, The Netherlands in December 1991, the heads of the Community agreed to move toward the creation of a common currency and to cooperate more closely on foreign policy.

The EC consists of a number of different institutions. The Council of Ministers, which is comprised of cabinet ministers from each member state, is responsible for approving Community legislation. Its membership varies according to the policy area under consideration. Thus environmental policy is decided by a council consisting of the environmental ministers from each member state. The European Commission is responsible for proposing legislation to the council and implementing legislation after it is approved. It consists of twenty-three directorates, each with responsibility for a particular dimension of EC policy. Directorate (DG) XI is responsible for "environment, consumer protection and nuclear safety." Each directorate is headed by an EC commissioner chosen from among the member states on a rotating basis. The European Court of Justice is responsible for interpreting Community law: it interprets disputes between member states and Community institutions. Finally, the European Parliament is directly elected by voters in each member state. Elections are held every five years.

David Vogel

ENVIRONMENTAL REGULATION UNDER
THE TREATY OF ROME

The word "environment" does not appear in the 1957 Treaty of Rome that established the European Community. Nevertheless, during the mid-1960s the Community began to recognize that the creation of a common market also required the eventual enactment of common environmental regulations. In 1967, the EC adopted its first environmental directive. It established standards for classifying, packaging and labeling dangerous substances. Three years later the Council approved a directive on automotive emissions. In 1972, the EC heads of state pledged that future economic expansion would take into account the need to protect the environment. At the same time, the European Commission was authorized to establish a separate administrative body or directorate with responsibility for environmental protection.

The following year, the Council of Ministers adopted the EC's first official environmental program. Based on article 2 of the Treaty of Rome, which stated that the Community's objective was to promote "a harmonious development of economic activities," the EC's "action plan" stated that "major aspects of environmental policy in individual countries must no longer be planned or implemented in isolation . . . and national policies should be harmonized within the community" (O'Riordan 1979, 249).

The plan specified three main objectives or principles to guide EC environmental regulations (Briggs 1986, 110–11). The first was to reduce and prevent pollution both by "developing protective measures" and by requiring that the "polluter pay." The second was that both national and Community regulations should seek to protect the environment as well as improve the quality of life. Third, the Community pledged its support for "international initiatives" to address those environmental problems which could not be adequately addressed on either a regional or national basis.

The Community's Second Environmental Action Program, which was adopted in 1977, restated and extended these aims. It also stressed the need for additional research and data collection on the environment and expressed the EC's intention of developing a system of environmental impact assessment. The Community's Third Program, which was approved in 1983, reflected the growth of concern about unemployment and resource depletion: it emphasized the role of environmental regulation in both preserving scarce resources for future use and "creating employment by developing environmentally compatible industries and technologies" (Briggs 1986, 110–11). It also shifted the Community's priorities from pollution reduction to pollution prevention.

Each of these three action plans was accompanied by a steady expansion in the scope of Community environmental regulations. Between the early 1970s and the mid-1980s, the Community issued 120 regulations and directives. (A regulation is directly applicable to all member states and thus automatically becomes a part of national law. By contrast, a directive establishes a framework for national policies; it only becomes effective after member states have enacted legislation implementing it. Directives generally specify the result to be achieved, leaving it up to national authorities to determine the means and mechanisms of implementation. Most EC environmental rules take the form of directives.)

The EC's environmental policies enacted during this period covered a wide range of areas, from the regulation of air, water and noise pollution to waste disposal, the prevention of accidents, safety requirements for chemicals, environmental impact assessment and wildlife and habitat protection. By the mid-1980s, virtually all aspects of national environmental policy had been addressed, in one form or other, at the Community level (Haigh and Baldock 1989). In many policy areas, the locus of environmental policy making in Western Europe had shifted from the nation-state to Brussels.

The growth of EC environmental regulation during the 1970s was due to a number of factors. Political developments in Europe played an important role. The EC was responding to the increase in public concern about environmental issues that took place in virtually all industrialized nations during the late 1960s and early 1970s. A survey taken in the (then) nine EC member states in 1973 found that "pollution was cited as the most important problem, ahead of inflation, poverty and unemployment" (Liberatore 1991, 289). About this time, environmental organizations became more politically active in a number of European countries, and most national governments significantly expanded and strengthened the scope of their own regulatory controls over industry.

In order to preserve their own legitimacy, EC institutions attempted to respond to these new political forces and public pressures by enacting environmental regulations as well. EC environmental policy can thus be seen as a way for Community officials to address the "democratic deficit": the gap between the Community's power and its lack of accountability to the electorate of its member states. In addition, environmental policy-making provided a way for officials in Brussels to preserve the momentum of European integration, which in other policy areas appeared to have stagnated during the 1970s.

Economic considerations also played an important role in the growth of EC environmental policy. The expansion of national environmental regulation posed a serious economic threat to both the creation and maintenance

David Vogel

of a common market. If nations were allowed to adopt their own product standards, such as for the safety of chemicals or emissions from vehicles, the free flow of goods within the EC would be reduced, since nations with strict environmental standards would then seek to "protect" their citizens by excluding goods produced in member states with weaker regulatory requirements. In the case of production standards, nations that had adopted more stringent pollution controls than other member states would find their industries placed at a competitive disadvantage. In addition, free trade within the EC increased the exposure of member states to the import of environmental pollutants, such as toxic and hazardous wastes, from other nations within the EC.

A third motivation for EC environmental policy was geographic. The twelve nations of the EC comprise a large land-area—roughly 1.6 million square kilometers. They encompass a considerable diversity of climate and topography; while the environmental problems of Greece and The Netherlands may have little in common, most member states are physically close to one another. Consequently, the quality of their physical environment, as well as the health of their populations, is significantly affected by the environmental policies of their neighbors.

For example, the Rhine flows west through three EC member states, namely, Germany, France and The Netherlands; accordingly, the quality of Dutch water is significantly affected by the stringency of German and French pollution controls. Because winds in Europe travel from west to east, the air quality in northern Europe is affected by industrial emissions from Britain. As one journalist observed, "Environmental regulations are among the world's toughest in . . . West Germany and The Netherlands. But that does little good when winds waft Britain's loosely regulated power-plant fumes and their product, acid rain, eastward" (Diehl 1988, 9). Moreover, industrial accidents are unlikely to respect national boundaries. And since many wild birds tend to migrate across national borders, the effectiveness of the efforts of any one member state to protect them is limited.

A number of important EC environmental initiatives reflect the high degree of physical interdependence of the Community. For example, the "Seveso Directive" was adopted in 1982 following a major industrial accident in Italy that unleashed into the atmosphere large quantities of the chemical dioxin. The directive addressed the issue of accident prevention and required industries to prepare safety reports and emergency response plans. The EC's Directive on the Conservation of Wild Birds, adopted in 1979, required member states "to preserve, maintain or reestablish a sufficient diversity and area of habitats for birds" (Haigh 1989, 288). And following the disclosure that forty-one drums of waste from Seveso that had been lost in transit had been found in the French countryside, a directive was approved that established a system for controlling and regulating the collection and disposal of hazardous wastes moving across frontiers from collection to disposal.

For all these reasons—political, economic and geographic—the Community attempted to harmonize a wide range of national environmental regulations. However, this effort led to considerable conflict between those nations which favored stricter environmental standards and those which did not. The former, most notably Germany, Denmark and The Netherlands, tended to be relatively affluent and have strong domestic environmental movements. Other nations, such as Great Britain, France and Italy, had weaker environmental pressure-groups and their industries were less willing or able to absorb the costs of stricter environmental controls. Still others, such as Greece and Spain, were even less interested in Community air quality and water quality standards. Not only were they relatively poor, but they were physically distant from the "core" of the EC.

Since all EC environmental directives and regulations had to be approved unanimously by the Council of Ministers, the result was frequently a compromise that reflected the competing economic and political interests of the member states rather than the needs of the environment. And those nations which favored stronger environmental controls for their own citizens and industry frequently found themselves frustrated when the EC limited their ability to impose standards stricter than those approved by the Council of Ministers.

The form of pollution control also led to disputes among the member states. Most nations favored uniform emission standards for industrial processes, since that would impose roughly similar costs on firms throughout the EC. The British, however, argued that since their rapidly flowing rivers could absorb relatively large amounts of pollution without impairing water quality, uniform emission standards were inappropriate; they instead favored water quality standards. Once again the result was a compromise: highly hazardous substances would be regulated by uniform emission standards, while less dangerous substances would be regulated by water quality standards.

Notwithstanding the steady growth of regulation, the legal basis of EC environmental policy remained somewhat tenuous. Most regulations could be justified under Article 100 of the treaty, which authorized the harmonization of all national regulations that directly affected the functioning or establishment of a common market. Others appeared to make sense because of the physical proximity of EC members; indeed, in a number of cases, non-EC states in Europe agreed to adopt Community standards for precisely this reason. But a number of EC directives meet neither of these criteria. For

185

example, what was the legal or physical basis for establishing EC standards for drinking or bathing water quality or for designating specific areas as nature reserves? Why should regulations in these areas be made at the Community rather than the national level (Close 1978, 461–81)?

Furthermore, the Treaty of Rome, by not explicitly mentioning environmental protection, provided EC policymakers with no framework for balancing environmental protection with other EC goals, the most important of which was obviously the creation of the common market itself. For virtually any level of environmental regulation was compatible with increased economic integration, providing that it was uniform throughout the Community. Many observers argued that the requirements of many EC directives tended to reflect the "least common denominator" and that therefore the Community had, in effect, subordinated environmental goals to economic ones.

THE SINGLE EUROPEAN ACT

The Single European Act (SEA), which went into effect on 1 July 1987, revised the Treaty of Rome. While its most important purpose was to facilitate the creation of a single European market, it also introduced a number of important changes into Community environmental policy and policy-making procedures.

Most importantly, Article 100A of the SEA explicitly recognized the improvement of environmental quality as a legitimate Community objective in its own right, meaning that EC environmental policies would no longer have to be justified in terms of their contribution to economic integration. Thus the EC now had a firm constitutional basis for regulating any aspect of the environment. The SEA also stated that in harmonizing national regulations, "the Commission . . . will take as a base a high level of [environment] protection," thus explicitly linking harmonization to the strengthening of environmental regulation (Office of Official Publications on the European Communities, 20). Article 130R further declared that "environmental protection requirements shall be a component of the Community's other policies" (Kramer 1987, 651). This provision accorded environmental protection an unusually high priority among the Community's objectives, since no other EC goal was accorded a commensurate provision. In practical terms, it strengthened the hands of the commission's environmental directorate in its conflicts with those directorates whose focus was essentially economic.

The Single European Act also facilitated the adoption of environmental regulations by the council. Prior to 1987, all environmental legislation had to be approved unanimously. However, the SEA permitted directives approved under Article 100A—which provides for the approximation of laws concerned with the functioning of the common market—to be approved by a "qualified majority," defined as fifty-four of seventy-six votes. Under this voting system nations with larger populations have more votes and smaller states are deprived of the power to veto Community directives.

The Single European Act expanded the role of the European Parliament—which has generally been more supportive of stricter environmental standards than the council—in shaping Community legislation. For ten articles of the EC treaty, the SEA established a "cooperation procedure" under which Parliament has the right to propose amendments to legislation approved by the Council of Ministers. If the commission chooses to retain these amendments, the council must then either reject them unanimously or adopt them by a qualified majority.

The Single European Act also altered the relationship between national and harmonized standards. To reassure those member states which feared that harmonization would require them to relax existing national regulations, individual member states were granted the right, under certain circumstances, to enforce national regulations that were stricter than those approved by Brussels. These regulations, however, were subject to one important limitation: they could not constitute a form of "hidden protectionism" (Kramer 1987, 681). The determination as to whether a national regulation that affected the completion of the internal market created an open or disguised barrier to trade was left up to judgment of the European Court of Justice (Vandermeersch 1987, 407–29; Kramer 1987, 559–88).

The SEA also contributed to the strengthening of EC environmental policy in another, more indirect way. A primary purpose of the new Community treaty was to accelerate the move toward the creation of a single internal market—a goal which had been formally outlined in a commission white paper issued a few years earlier. However, Community officials recognized that the removal of all barriers to intra-Community trade by the end of 1992 was also likely to exacerbate Europe's environmental problems. A report entitled *"1992" the Environmental Dimension,* released in 1989, examined some of the adverse environmental consequences of the completion of the internal market. The most important of these was a dramatic increase in transportation, which would significantly increase emissions of both sulfur dioxide and nitrogen oxides. Thus the Community's commitment to increased economic integration made the strengthening of EC environmental standards even more urgent.

The strengthening of environmental protection within the Community's constitution both reflected and reinforced a major heightening of public concern with environmental issues that took place throughout

David Vogel

Europe during the latter part of the 1980s. Provoked in part by the Soviets' Chernobyl disaster and a massive spill of toxins into the Rhine River that destroyed a half-million fish in four countries—both accidents occurred in 1986—environmental issues moved rapidly to a prominent position on the political agenda in a number of EC member states. The *Washington Post* observed:

> Dead seals in the North Sea, a chemical fire on the Loire, killer algae off the coast of Sweden, contaminated drinking water in Cornwall (England). A drumbeat of emergencies has intensified the environmental debate this year in Europe, where public concern about pollution has never been higher. (Herman 1988, 19)

A poll taken in December 1986 reported that 52 percent of the German electorate regarded environment quality as the most important issue facing their nation (Kirkland 1988, 118). In 1987, the German Green party received 8.3 percent of the votes cast for the Bundestag and increased their number of seats in the legislative body of the Federal Republic of Germany to forty-two. More significantly, in the elections to the European Parliament held in June 1989, Europe's Green parties captured an additional seventeen seats, bringing their total representation to thirty-seven and making them among the biggest "winners" of the first "European" election held after the enactment of the SEA.

An EC official publication observed in 1990,

> Major disasters (and) global problems like ozone depletion and the greenhouse effect, and quality of life issues such as drinking water and air pollution have all contributed in recent years to a "greening" of European public opinion, to a widening consensus in favour of "cleaner" and more sustainable economic growth. (Office of Official Publications on the European Community 1990, 5)

A survey published by the EC in 1989 revealed "strong support for a common EC-wide approach to environmental protection" (Office of Official Publications on the European Community 1990, 15).

Since the SEA, the EC has come to play a more active and aggressive role in the making of environmental policy both in Europe and throughout the world. One of the EC's most important policy initiatives strengthened regulations designed to protect the ozone layer. In 1987, thirty-one nations signed the Montreal Protocol, in which they pledged to reduce the production of chlorofluorocarbons by 50 percent by the end of the century. However, in March 1989, the EC went a step further: it announced that its member states had agreed to cut production of this chemical by 85 percent as soon as possible and to eliminate production entirely by the year 2000. In addition, after five years of negotiations, the EC approved a large combustion plant directive that set nitrogen and sulfur emission standards for large power plants, thus reducing a major cause of acid rain in much of northern Europe.

In 1987, the EC approved its Fourth Environmental Action Program. It established four priorities: the preservation of the ozone layer, mitigation of the greenhouse effect, comprehensive regulation of hazardous wastes and fighting tropical deforestation. Two years later, the European Council voted to create the European Environmental Agency. It is intended to serve as a central information clearinghouse and a coordinator for national centers of environmental monitoring and evaluation.

In 1988, the European Court issued a far-reaching decision concerning the right of national governments to enforce stricter regulations than those mandated by the Community (see the *Journal of Environmental Law* 2, no. 1 [1990]: 89–107). In 1986, the Commission had brought Denmark before the European Court of Justice on the grounds that a 1981 Danish law that required beer and soft drinks to be sold in returnable bottles with a mandatory deposit constituted a trade barrier, thus violating Article 30 of the Treaty of Rome.

While noting that Denmark's requirements applied to both domestic and imported products alike, the commission argued that the Danish collection system put imported products at an unfair disadvantage due to the higher costs involved in the long-distance transport of empty containers. In addition, the commission contended that "the adverse impact of the collection system on trade was disproportionate to the objective of protecting the environment" (Nolan 1990, 10). The commission's position "clearly signaled its fear that member states would take refuge behind the environmental banner to avoid opening their markets to imports" (Nolan 1990, 10).

The Danish government replied that its legislation was justified by a genuine desire to reduce the amount of waste and denied that its regulations were a disguised form of protectionism. The European Court upheld the position of Denmark, although it did require some modifications in the Danish regulation so as to make it easier for non-Danish bottlers to comply with it. In its decision, the court stated that protecting the environment was "one of the Community's essential objectives" and that therefore environmental regulations could be allowed to limit free trade—a view which it found confirmed in the Single European Act (Nolan 1990, 10). The court acknowledged that such regulations must be both proportionate to their objective and designed in such a way as to interfere with free trade as little as possible. It concluded that the Danish regulation met these tests, "since a deposit and return system was . . . indispensable for recycling containers (Nolan 1990, 10).

This ruling represented the first time that a trade barrier had been sanctioned on environmental grounds, although the court had previously sustained a number of trade barriers for health and safety reasons. While "it will take further cases to show exactly where the European Court draws the line between greenery and trade," the court's decision constituted a major victory for the environmental directorate over DG 111—the directorate responsible for the creation and completion of the internal market, which had insisted on taking Denmark to court in the first place (*Economist,* 14 October 1989, 22). However, as the scope of Community regulations has grown, the problem of enforcing them has become more acute. The increased number of Community regulations not only makes the monitoring of their enforcement more difficult, but also more urgent, since significant variations in national compliance threaten to place the industries in some EC member states at a competitive disadvantage. The Community itself has no police or enforcement powers. It only knows of a violation if someone complains about it. If it finds the complaint is justified, its final legal recourse is to bring the member state to the European Court. This, however, is a time-consuming procedure; an average of fifty months elapses between the arrival of a complaint and a ruling from the court. The problem of enforcement is further complicated by the fact that while EC directives are intended to bind national governments, in many countries it is local governmental officials who are responsible for enforcing them.

As of May 1991, the EC had a backlog of 372 cases of noncompliance with environmental directives and regulations (*Economist,* 20 July 1991, 52). Three-quarters of its disciplinary proceedings concerned four areas of environmental law: birds, bathing water, drinking water, and environmental impact assessments. While the commission received more complaints about Britain than any other country, this reflected not so much the relative lack of British compliance as the eagerness of British environmental groups to complain to Brussels. In some of the Latin countries, public distrust of government bureaucracies discouraged people from complaining in the first place. Spain and Italy had the poorest record of compliance with the decisions of the European Court; the former does not even have a ministry of the environment.

In February 1990, the EC commissioner in charge of environmental protection publicly complained about unsatisfactory member state implementation of the Community's environmental directives (Wagerbaum 1990, 465). In June 1990, the European Council acknowledged the extent of the enforcement problem by adopting the "Declaration on the Environmental

Imperative," which stated that "Community environmental legislation will only be effective if it is fully implemented and enforced by the Member States" (Wagerbaum 1990, 455). The following month, 130 members of the European Parliament proposed the establishment of a committee on the transposition and application of Community environmental legislation.

A number of suggestions have been advanced for improving national compliance with Community directives. One is to allow citizens to sue their own governments in national courts; presently the ability of citizens to file such suits is determined by national rather than EC laws. Another is to provide the newly established European Environment Agency with the resources to monitor national compliance, thus freeing the commission from having to rely upon citizen complaints to determine if its directives are being enforced. A third is to create a Community "ombudsman." To date, none of these proposals has been adopted, but this may well change in the near future.

AUTOMOBILE EMISSIONS

One of the most important and contentious EC environmental policy disputes has been over automotive emission standards. The Community's nearly twenty-year effort to develop common standards for both automobile emissions and fuel content illustrates some of the complexities and difficulties of harmonizing environmental regulations among twelve different nations.

By the late 1960s, there was considerable evidence that airborne lead—a significant proportion of which came from motor vehicles—threatened children's mental development. As a result, a number of member states had begun to restrict the lead content of gasoline sold within their borders. However, the disparity in national rules and regulations regarding fuel content presented an "obstacle to the free movement of both fuel and motor vehicles within the Community" (Johnson and Corcelle 1989, 124). For if the lead content of gasoline sold in the various member states varied significantly, it would become very difficult to design automobiles that could be sold in every member state. Moreover, oil companies would not be able to sell the same gasoline throughout the Community. Accordingly, the Community attempted to harmonize the lead content of fuel.

In 1973, the commission forwarded to the council a directive designed to standardize national rules for the lead content of gasoline. But it proved extremely difficult for the council to agree on a common standard for leaded gasoline. Some nations, notably Germany, had already substantially limited the lead content of fuel, and they were reluctant to weaken their standards in order to remove an obstacle to intracommunity trade. Other nations, such as

Great Britain, had also reduced the level of lead permitted in gasoline, but by not as much. As a result, it was not until 1978 that the European Council was able to adopt a directive on the lead content of gasoline.

Because agreement on a common standard proved impossible, the 1978 directorate established maximum and minimum standards: beginning in 1981, no gasoline could be sold within the EC that contained more than .4 grams of lead per liter. But while member states were allowed to impose stricter standards, these could not be lower than .15 grams per liter—"in view of the situation in Germany where lead content had already been reduced to 0.15 grams per liter" (Johnson and Corcelle 1989, 124). This directive was meant to be an interim one. At the time of its adoption, the commission stated that its long-term goal was to impose further restrictions on lead emissions from motor vehicles, but to do so in such a way as to not create additional trade barriers within the EC.

In 1970, the European Community, like the United States, established emission levels for carbon monoxide and unburnt hydrocarbons. Later in the decade the EC also imposed restrictions on emissions of nitrogen oxides. All three standards were tightened in 1978. However, unlike the United States, which had imposed minimum national standards (with the exception of California, which was permitted to exceed them by a specified amount), the EC opted for "optional harmonization by setting maximum requirements and leaving member states the power to allow operation of vehicles on their territory that do not meet the EC emission standards" (Rehbinder and Stewart 1985, 77). In other words, while member states were not required to impose the EC's standards on automobiles sold within their borders, they could not refuse to permit the sale of automobiles that did meet EC standards. However, because of the export-oriented nature of Europe's automobile industry, producers did have an incentive to comply with Community standards. Thus, in fact, the agreement approximated "a system of total harmonization" (Rehbinder and Stewart 1985, 77). In 1983, these emission standards were significantly strengthened: carbon monoxide limits were reduced by 23 percent and hydrocarbons and nitrogen oxides by 20 to 30 percent. The following year, the commission presented to the council two new directives on automobile emissions. One dealt with lead, the other with other motor vehicle pollutants. Both were prompted by growing concern among many Europeans over the dangers posed by automobile exhaust to Europe's forests. The commission specifically proposed the total elimination of lead in gasoline and a further 70 percent reduction of carbon monoxide, hydrocarbon, and nitrogen oxide emissions.

In 1985, a new directive on lead in gasoline was adopted. While maintaining the range established in 1978, it urged each member state to achieve the .15 level as soon as possible. More significantly, the directive also addressed the issue of unleaded gasoline. It required all member states to offer unleaded gasoline for sale beginning in October 1989. The delay was intended to give the petroleum and automobile industries sufficient time to make the necessary design changes, although it did permit the voluntary introduction of lead free gasoline prior to the 1 October deadline. The directive further required that the benzene content of petrol be limited to 5 percent by volume.

The strengthening of automotive emission standards proved more difficult. The council attempted to define vehicle categories based on their cylinder capacity and then to establish deadlines for the implementation of stricter emission controls for each category. Vehicles were divided into three classifications: large (more than 2 liters), medium (from 1.4 to 2 liters), and small (less than 1.4 liters). The new emissions guidelines were designed "so that the[ir] effect on the European environment [would] be equivalent to that produced by U.S. standards" (International Environment Reporter, 4 April 1985, 109). However, meeting the strict U.S. guidelines required the installation of three-way catalysts and electronic fuel injection control systems. The introduction of this abatement technology was both technically easier and relatively less costly for producers of large automobiles than for small- and medium-sized ones. Accordingly, regulations requiring its use were supported by West Germany, whose automotive industry specializes in larger vehicles, and opposed by France and Italy, whose manufacturers primarily make smaller vehicles. To accommodate the latter's strong objections, the council compromised by altering its guidelines on pollutants so that medium automobiles could meet them by employing "lean-burn" engines or comparable cost-effective measures, while small automobiles would not be required to make any substantial changes in their engine design at all.

A number of obstacles had to be overcome before the EC was able to adopt these new emission standards. First, there was considerable debate among the member states over whether the EC should attempt to duplicate U.S. emission standards in the first place. Nations with strong environmental movements, led by The Netherlands and Germany, insisted on full conformity with U.S. regulations. Dutch environmentalist Lucas Reijnders went so far as to argue that EC standards should be "replaced" by U.S. standards (*International Environment Reporter*, 13 November 1985, 368). France and Italy, however, were strongly opposed to adopting the American requirements. Pierre Perrin-Pelletier of the French Auto Makers Commission contended that the U.S. is a "good example" of how strict regulations "do not necessarily lead to correspondingly low levels of air pollution" (*International Environmental Reporter*, 13 November 1985, 368). Echoing the views of its domestic automobile manufacturers, the French government stressed the importance of reduced fuel consumption as a way of controlling emissions.

Second, there was disagreement over the effectiveness of catalytic converters in reducing automobile pollutants. Germany was the leader in the drive to make catalytic converters standard for all automobiles—even threatening unilateral action if other members would not agree to this requirement. However, the French Trade Association of Automakers argued that "catalytic converters on automobiles would be costly and unnecessary" and that "the usefulness of catalytic converters remains to be demonstrated" (*International Environment Reporter,* 13 November 1985, 39). In a move directed against Germany, which had no speed limits on its highways, Prime Minister Laurent Fabius of France suggested that "governments should consider lowering speed limits rather than introducing catalytic converters as an immediate means of reducing pollution from automobile exhausts" (*International Environment Reporter,* 13 February, 1985, 40–41).

Britain was also originally opposed to catalytic converters, but for different reasons. The U.K. government favored the use of the "lean-burn engines," which were designed to decrease engine pollutants by changes in the engine design. Britain argued that the catalytic converter was an outdated, 1960s technology. One British official stated: "We are not supporters of the outdated idea of bolting bits on the back of autos. There is no way that the British government is going to change its mind on this point" (*International Environment Reporter,* 9 April 1986, 114). In addition, Prime Minister Thatcher of Great Britain told German chancellor Kohl that she thought U.S. standards were too high (*International Environment Reporter,* 13 February 1985, 40).

Despite protests from France, Italy and the U.K., all three countries were prepared to go along with the proposed directive, largely because of Germany's threat of unilateral action. However, the proposed directive was vetoed by Denmark, which regarded it as too lenient. Stichting Natuur en Milieu, representing a Dutch environmental group, argued that the legislation "encourages the lethargic attitude in the community's automobile industry and promotes obsolete technology for small cars" (quoted in *International Environment Reporter,* 13 November 1985, 40). Following the passage of the Single European Act, Denmark lost its veto power over the enactment of EC legislation. The "Luxembourg Compromise," which was finally adopted in July 1987, was the first directive to be approved under the EC's new qualified majority voting procedures.

The Luxembourg Compromise allowed, but did not require, nations to establish different emission standards and schedules for different sizes of automobiles. The standards for new, large vehicles could come into effect on 1 October 1989 and for midsize vehicles on either 1 October 1991 or 1 October 1993 (depending on whether they were new models). The much looser standards for small automobiles could be phased in by 1990 and 1991. Like previous EC emissions directives, the 1987 legislation set a ceiling rather than a floor: member states were still allowed to set emissions levels at lower levels than those specified in the council's directive, but they could not exclude automobiles that did comply with it. Accordingly, the goal of regulatory harmonization remained elusive.

Progress toward a single market for automobiles was further threatened when, beginning in the mid-1980s, the West German and Dutch governments announced that they would introduce tax incentives to encourage the purchase of low-emission vehicles. These initiatives were strongly criticized by other EC member states and the commission began proceedings to determine their legality. Some commission officials concluded these measures were "'compatible' with Community regulations because they provided for tax derogations to the final consumer on a 'non-discriminatory basis'" (*International Environment Reporter*, 13 February 1985, 39). Others maintained that the incentives would lead to the distortion of free trade, arguing that they worked "in favor of German automobile and catalytic converter manufacturers" (*International Environment Reporter*, 13 February 1985, 39). This issue was finally resolved in 1989, when the commission ruled that countries could offer fiscal incentives to new automobile purchasers until July 1992, providing the amount did not exceed 85 percent of the cost of the catalytic converter unit of the vehicle.

In July 1989, the EC adopted the Small Car Directive, which significantly tightened emission standards for this important category of vehicles. It required all new small automobiles to employ catalytic converters by 1991. The Small Car Directive also provided for strict new limits on emissions for new models of small automobiles after July 1992, and for all new small vehicles after January 1993. In fact, the new limits, which aimed to cut existing emissions levels by 73 percent, were even lower than the 1987 standards for medium and large automobiles. It represented a major policy departure in another respect. For in contrast to previous EC emissions regulations, it did not allow member states to set lower national emissions standards than those established by the Community.

The enactment of the Small Car Directive followed a complex series of negotiations, which included the European Parliament's exercise of its right to amend council directives. Once again, Italy and France had opposed establishing strict mandatory emissions standards for small automobiles. In July of 1988, the French government withdrew its support for the small automobile plan after the Dutch announced that they planned to offer fiscal incentives for consumers to purchase "cleaner" small vehicles. German automobile leaders immediately criticized the French for putting "financial interests before environmental aspects" (*Reuters*, 25 July 1988). Only after Germany once again threatened to "go it alone" did France and Italy agree to support the new regulation. The U.K. also initially expressed reservations about the Small Car Directive, hoping to buy time for its industry to perfect a cheaper lean-burn engine technology. However, by 1989, Britain had given up on such hopes, and was "totally in agreement about using catalytic converters" (*International Environment Reporter*, June 1989, 283). The Netherlands, Denmark, and Greece remained opposed to the Small Car Directive on the grounds that it was not strict enough. But the legislation was nevertheless passed by a qualified majority over their objections.

Despite this progress toward the harmonization of automobile emission standards, serious tensions persisted. Many Green members of the European Parliament were still unhappy with the EC's directives on automotive emissions. Moreover, in September 1990, the issue of German speed control—or to be more precise, the lack thereof—was again raised by the French government. In a newspaper interview, Environment Minister Brice Lalonde of France threatened that "Paris [would] ban imports of West German BMWs, Mercedes and other fast cars if Bonn did not introduce speed limits to help the environment" (*Reuters*, 12 September 1990). Lalonde added, "I want talks on speed limits and carbon monoxide gas emissions. A West German commitment on this point is indispensable" (*Reuters*, 12 September 1990).

Nevertheless, by the early 1990s the EC had made considerable progress in harmonizing European emission standards. But this progress, as Lindsey Halstead, chairman of Food, Europe, put it, "was only achieved after an extended period of severe planning uncertainty, with many governments seeking to impose their differing views" (Done 1990). The EC's experience with automotive emissions illustrates the tensions that can exist between free trade and environmental regulation, as well as the difficulties of standardizing environmental regulations among nations with different economic interests and different degrees of environmental concern.

REFERENCES

Briggs, David. 1986. Environmental problems and policies in the European Community. In *Environmental policies: An international review*, edited by Chris Park. London: Croom Helm.

Close, George. 1978. Harmonization of laws: Use or abuse of the powers under the EEC treaty. *European Law Review*, December, 461–68.

Diehl, Jackson. 1988. Choking on their own development. *Washington Post National*

Weekly Edition, 29 May–4 June, 9.

Done, Kevin. 1990. Vehicles and the environment: Europe to tighten its emission standards. *Financial Times,* 27 July.

Haigh, Nigel. 1989. *EEC environmental policy and Britain.* 2d ed. Harlow: Longman.

Haigh, Nigel, and David Baldock. 1989. Environmental policy and 1992. London: Institute for European Environmental Policy.

Herman, Robin. 1988. An ecological epiphany. *Washington Post National Weekly Review,* 5–11 December, 1988, 19.

Johnson, Stanley P., and Guy Corcelle. 1989. *The environmental policy of the European Communities.* London: Graham and Trotman.

Kirkland, Richard. 1988. Environmental anxiety goes global. *Fortune,* 21 November.

Kramer, Ludwig. 1987. The Single European Act and environmental protection: Reflections on several new provisions in Community law. *Common Market Law Review* 24:659–88.

Liberatore, Angela. 1991. Problems of transnational policymaking: Environmental policy in the European Community. *European Journal of Political Research* 19:281–305.

Nolan, Hanna. 1990. Environmental policy in the European Community. INSEAD-CEDEP. London.

O'Riordan, Timothy. 1979. Role of environmental quality objectives: The politics of pollution control. In *Progress in resources management and environmental planning,* ed. O'Riordan and D'Arge, 1:221-58. New York: Wiley.

Office of Official Publications on the European Communities. 1990. Environmental policy in the European Community. 4th ed. Luxembourg: Office of Official Publications on the European Communities.

Rehbinder, Eckard, and Richard Stewart. Environmental protection policy. In vol. 2 of *Integration Through Law: Europe and the American Experience,* edited by Cappalletti, Secombe and Weiler. Berlin: Walter de Gruyter.

Rehbinder, Eckard, and Richard Stewart. 1985. Legal integration in federal systems: European Community environmental law. *American Journal of Comparative Law* 33:371–446.

Story, Jonathan. 1990. Auto emissions and the European Parliament: A test of the Single European Act. INSEAD-CEDEP. London.

Vandermeersch, Dirk. 1987. The Single European Act and the environmental policy of the European Community. *European Law Review,* December, 407–29.

Wagerbaum, Rolf. 1990. The European Community's policies on implementation of environmental directives. *Fordham International Law Journal* 14:455–77.

10 Eastern Europe and the Former Soviet Union

BARBARA JANCAR-WEBSTER

Between 1989 and 1991, the most dramatic changes in the world since World War II took place in Eastern Europe and the Soviet Union. These changes led to the fall of Communism, the end of the cold war and the end of the Soviet empire. Environmental issues and East European and Soviet environmental groups played a decisive role in bringing down the old regime and are poised to play an even more critical role in ameliorating the extensive environmental destruction wrought by the former system. The ability of the environmental groups to influence the decisions of the leaders of the nascent democracies depends on a complex of factors, not the least of which is the adaptation of the movement to democratic conditions.

This chapter will briefly review the fall of the old regime and explain the contribution of the environmental movement to that fall. It will then look at some of the reasons that led to the systematic degradation of the environment under the Communist governments, discuss the rise of the environmental movement, and conclude with some suggestions as to the prospects and need for an environmental renaissance in the region.

THE SETTING

Beginning in Poland in the spring of 1989, one by one the Communist one-party political systems fell. On 12 October 1989, the twenty-eight-year-old symbol of the cold war, the Berlin Wall, was opened. A year later, East and West Germany reunited. In Czechoslovakia, police brutality against peaceful student demonstrators on 17 November 1989 occasioned mass demonstrations that toppled the Communist government and brought former dissident and author Vaclav Havel to the presidency. In 1990, the Rumanians took their first shaky steps toward democracy. And in 1991, Albania became the last East European country to opt for democratic change.

Old rivalries quickly replaced the popular unity which had toppled the Communist regimes. Czechoslovakia, Rumania (with its large minority of ethnic Hungarians) and Yugoslavia, countries that had been considered permanent members of the international community, were now grasping for new rules by which to assure consensus around a central power. The advent of democracy in Czechoslovakia took the lid off of Czech/Slovak relations. The most tragic country in the region is Yugoslavia. This federation of six republics has been held together since 1945 by the bonds of a special brand of Communism called self-management. But national self-assertion has virtually torn the federation apart with no solution in sight.

In the former Soviet Union, disintegration and democratization are also in progress. In 1985, Soviet President Mikhail Gorbachev introduced the twin policies of perestroika (restructuring) and glasnost (openness). As the press liberated itself from seventy years of servitude to censorship, voices were heard in the fifteen constituent union-republics demanding autonomy. In 1990, Lithuania went one step further and declared independence. In the Baltics, Caucasus, Moldavia and Ukraine, the people also voted for national independence. In 1991, Gorbachev called a union-wide referendum to find out which republics wanted to stay in the union. The leaders of the nine republics that voted in the affirmative drafted with Gorbachev a union treaty that effectively abolished the old centralized hierarchical system. Before the treaty could be signed, the conservatives in the Soviet Communist party, the army, the KGB and the Ministry of the Interior attempted a coup to reassert central control by force.

On 23 August 1991, popular demonstrations led by the Russian Republic president, Boris Yeltsin, ended forever totalitarian rule in a land mass that stretched across eleven time zones. But aside from agreement on what they did not want, the peoples of the Soviet Union were not at all united on what they did want. The Soviet Union is no more. In its place is a group of republics trying to forge new economic and political relations with each other and with the world.

THE ENVIRONMENT AS CATALYST OF REFORM

The environment was one of the main causes for the downfall of the Communist regime. In what is now the C.I.S., some 60 percent of the population, or 175 million people, live in ecologically bad conditions. The litany of disasters starts with Chernobyl, the fallout from which exposed 17 million people to radioactive contamination, and contaminated over 8 million acres of agricultural land.[1] Air pollution is a serious problem. In 1989, 126 cities,[2] from Erevan in Armenia to Norilsk[3] in western Siberia and Khabarovsk in eastern Siberia, were reported having exceeded by ten times the daily emission norms. Living conditions in Zaporozhie and Donetsk in the coal-rich Donbass are intolerable. A report on the central Siberian industrial region known as the Kuzbass stated that there were virtually no healthy women working at industrial enterprises in the Kuzbass capital of Kemerovo.[4]

Water and soil pollution are equally serious problems. The country's major river systems have all been contaminated. In a single generation, the Aral Sea has lost over half its water. Irrigation projects have taken so much water out of the Syr Darya and the Amu Darya that the first river no longer flows to the Aral Sea and the Amu Darya carries only a fraction of its former yearly capacity there. The river waters are used to irrigate the huge cotton fields, which are maintained by perhaps the world's largest amounts per acre of pesticides and fertilizers. Three million people live in the disaster area. Salt and other materials blowing from the dry seabed have brought throat cancer and eye disease. The water coming from the irrigation canals farther east is so polluted that mothers are told not to breastfeed their children. Despite this tragic experience, plans are underway in Tadzhikistan to build a hydroelectric plant which would divert water from the few rivers that still feed into the Aral basin and perhaps dry the sea up completely. In the Caucasus, the Azerbaijani Republic ranks first in the former USSR in the use of pesticides.[5] Although DDT has been banned in the former USSR, 80 percent of the land in Uzbekistan and Tadzhikistan is said to be contaminated by the chemical.[6] Throughout the farming areas, the Soviet press has reported there are increases in the incidence of asthma, high blood pressure and allergies ascribed to the high concentration of pesticides and nitrate fertilizers.

Waste disposal is the third serious problem. The C.I.S. produces some 300 million cubic tons of solid waste a year,[7] enough to cover Massachusetts, Connecticut, and Rhode Island combined. In the oil and mineral producing regions of Siberia, the Kola peninsula has become a wasteland. A project to push oil exploration to the edge of the Arctic in the Yamal peninsula has galvanized the native peoples there to protest against the destruction of their last hope for cultural survival, the tundra pastures where their reindeer feed.[8]

Chernobyl stands out as the worst disaster not just because of the monstrous size of the damage. For three years the regime tried to cover up the problems. It took the persistence of a courageous doctor and journalist, Iurii Shcherbak, to bring the whole tragedy into the open. His revelations not only implicated Party and military personnel in a coverup, but also the head of the all-union State Committee on Hydrometeorology and Environmental Protection. In January 1990, the Ukrainian government issued a decree authorizing the evacuation of the most contaminated settlements in the Ukraine. Evacuation of similar areas in Belorussia followed.

Pollution in the small countries of Eastern Europe has an even more ominous impact. The region has the distinction of producing one-third of Europe's GNP and two-thirds of its sulfur dioxide, with eastern Germany ranking first and Czechoslovakia second in the world in sulfur dioxide emissions.[9] Destruction of forests by acid precipitation has reached catastrophic proportions. Seventy-one percent of the forests in Czechoslovakia, 48 percent of those in Poland, 44 percent in eastern Germany and 43 percent in Bulgaria have sustained significant damage.[10] In some areas of former East Germany and eastern Bohemia, virtually the entire forest stand is dead.[11]

The health costs are appalling. The Hungarians estimate that the annual health costs of air pollution in loss of work, death, and sick leave for 1990 was 13.3 percent of all health and social welfare expenditures.[12] Czechoslovakia has the highest density of sulfur dioxide deposits in Europe, 228 pounds per acre per year, and the highest death rate due to cancer of all the 150 member states of the United Nations. Czech officials have found a significant correlation between deterioration of a locality's air quality, higher infant mortality rates, and increased incidence in the numbers of allergies, pulmonary diseases and breathing difficulties, especially among children.[13] Children from polluted regions are regularly sent to "green classes" in the mountains for several weeks a year during the school term and to less polluted areas for vacation in the summer.

In Bulgaria, the ecological movement began in the Danubian city of Ruse, where prevailing winds blow toxic chemicals across the river from a chemical plant on the Rumanian side. Health officials assert that 80 percent of the draftees from Ruse have lung damage. In former East Germany, life expectancy in the Halle-Leipzig metropolitan area is five years less, and the incidence of heart and respiratory disease fifteen times higher, than elsewhere in the country. In Rumania, the grimy metallurgical and mining towns in the mountainous regions of Transylvania are plagued with severe health problems. In 1985, one study showed that 95 percent of a sample of two hundred thousand Rumanian women showed signs of diseased uteri.[14]

Water pollution has also reached crisis proportions in Eastern Europe. The "Blue Danube" is grey-brown with industrial wastes. As much as 70 percent of all Polish water may be undrinkable. Between 1985 and 1990, there was a steady deterioration in water quality in Hungary's five major rivers.[15] In Czechoslovakia 57 percent of the drinking water in 1990 failed to meet established water quality criteria.[16] Bulgaria's drinking water is contaminated by nitrates. In Yugoslavia, the Sava River was called a "dead river" by the mid-1980s. In Croatia, not one single river in 1990 could be listed in category I, the category of highest water quality, and most of the urban and industrial agglomerations had no waste treatment or sewage plants.[17]

Soil pollution has kept pace with air and water degradation. The unrestrained use of fertilizers and pesticides, particularly the continued use of DDT, has contaminated water supplies and soils, with the same resulting rise in the incidence of pollution-related diseases as in the former USSR Lead contamination in Poland's apples and lettuce exceeds the United Nations' health standards by ten times.[18] Many of Hungary's soils suffer from severe nitrate pollution.[19] In Yugoslavia, the rapid pace of urbanization and the abandonment of small farms meant that by 1978, 54 percent of the country's total agricultural area had to be designated moderately to severely eroded. Northwestern Bohemia is a moonscape of crater-filled land where all that remains of the historic town of Most is a chapel teetering on the brink of an abandoned brown coal pit. Soviet military occupation has contributed to the mounting waste management problem. When the Soviet troops withdrew from Czechoslovakia, they left piles of toxic waste behind: chemical warfare components, waste fuel and cleaning agents, and leaky sewage pipes. While the cost of cleanup of closed military bases in the United States may be shocking, the cost of cleanup of unwanted foreign bases by countries already experiencing severe pollution problems will be far greater.

CAUSES OF THE DEGRADATION OF THE ENVIRONMENT

There are two sets of causes for the desperate environmental plight of the former Communist countries. The first are those factors common to all pollution problems: size, cost of pollution control technology, and energy structure. Given the C.I.S.'s immense size and low-density population, it is not surprising that pollution should have come late to the all-union agenda. Siberia is so large that scientists have found it hard if not impossible to persuade government functionaries of the need for protection of the fragile ecosystem. Yugoslav officials have exhibited similar attitudes. As in the C.I.S., pollution has by and large affected only the most urbanized and highly developed sections of the country: Slovenia, and parts of Croatia and Serbia. While pollution is a major problem in the capital cities and along the tourist-polluted Adriatic coast, its impact is localized and not widely perceived as harmful by local populations. The prolonged civil war in what was once Yugoslavia has exacerbated many of the region's environmental problems.

By contrast, the countries of Central Europe suffer from small size and multiple borders. Czechoslovakia and Hungary are also landlocked. As a consequence, not only are Czechoslovakia, Poland and former East Germany among the largest producers of sulfur dioxide in Europe, they are also the largest importers and exporters of emissions. Poland imports 46 percent of its depositions, Czechoslovakia 47 percent, and East Germany 22 percent. The dieback of the forests in the Krkonose National Park (on the frontier of

Czechoslovakia where Poland, Czechoslovakia and Germany meet) is testimony to the problems faced by small countries in their attempt to handle transboundary airborne pollution.

A more sinister example of cross-boundary vulnerability is the radioactive fallout from Chernobyl. Polish scientists in eastern Poland knew something serious had happened when their Geiger counters registered off the scale. Chernobyl also made soil pollution by trace particles a transboundary phenomenon. Contamination by trace minerals in those countries in the path of the radioactive cloud has aggravated an already serious problem of cross-boundary soil pollution caused by seepage of chemical and agricultural waste.

Few waterways lie wholly within one East European country. The Elbe rises in Czechoslovakia and empties into the North Sea at Hamburg, Germany. The Danube rises in Germany and flows through six European countries before it empties into the Black Sea in Rumania. Despite international agreements, such as that for the Danube, conflicting national demands upon the use of these waterways have increased rather than abated pollution.

The cost of technology associated with pollution abatement is a second general factor. Before 1989, most East European countries could not afford to import environmental technology developed in the West. In countries like Yugoslavia where trade with the West was permitted, investors in the country consistently found it cheaper to import old polluting machinery rather than to spend money on new pollution-abating equipment. Other countries, like Czechoslovakia, East Germany and Bulgaria, traded with the West only within very limited prescribed parameters. We are only now finding out how much of the machinery in Poland, Czechoslovakia and East Germany is outdated, relics of the 1950s. All the countries have suffered from a hard currency shortage, and have preferred imports vital for sustaining the economy over pollution controls. Moreover, while Yugoslavia, Poland and Hungary have benefited from scientific exchange programs with the West, Czechoslovakia, Bulgaria, East Germany and Albania have been cut off from the mainstream of environmental research for the last forty years.[20] The Soviet Union faced similar difficulties. Ideological as well as economic priorities determined that it import only those technologies essential to maintaining economic momentum.

Finally, there is the problem of energy structure. In 1987, the use of coal was declining, and coal represented just 24 percent of the USSR's total energy consumption. Oil and gas consumption were increasing, and represented 38 and 37 percent of energy use, respectively. Nuclear power was producing over 11 percent of Soviet electricity, an increase of 437 percent since 1977.[21] Chernobyl changed everything. Since 1986, public protests in the

Ukraine, Armenia, Georgia, and the Russian Republic have resulted in the cancellation of around a dozen planned nuclear power stations. The Ukrainians were very unhappy when the reactors at Chernobyl that had escaped damage were restarted. As a result, they voted to outlaw all nuclear power on the territory of the republic. Protest has also accompanied efforts to expand hydropower. Among the most outspoken opponents has been writer Valentin Rasputin, who has deplored the loss of the cultural values occasioned by large-scale dam construction.[22]

If nuclear power has lost its attractiveness, then the C.I.S.'s energy future must be secured by either more accelerated development of gas and oil or by a renewed reliance on the 350 years of coal reserves. Russian research into alternative energy sources has been modest. While the climate in the southern republics is conducive to solar energy, the climate in the north is quite inappropriate. New oil and gas extraction requires large amounts of capital investment. For several years, the American petroleum company, Chevron, has been negotiating a contract for the exploitation of the Tenguiz oil fields in Kazakhstan. The current instability in the C.I.S. has destroyed any real value the ruble once might have had and, equally important, the once direct lines of authority. The suppression of the August 1991 coup accelerated the decentralization process. With no financial security, a suspicious and highly politicized public worried about foreign exploiters,[23] and no recognized authoritative agency with whom to conduct business, it is little wonder that Chevron has allowed negotiations to slow to a standstill.

Coal, however, no longer seems a sure reserve. For one thing, the quality of coal has been deteriorating in the European part of the C.I.S., while the cost of transporting sufficient amounts from the Siberian mines to the industrial centers in the west has been increasing. During the 1980s, the increasingly lower quality of coal in the European mines led Moscow to decide against building any more thermal power plants in the European sector, but high transportation costs slowed down the import of Siberian coal. As a result, energy in the European sectors is now being provided by aging and highly polluting power plants. The Donbass ranks now as one of the worst areas for air pollution in the world, and in 1990, 9.4 million man-days were lost to strikes. Miners in both the Ukraine and the Kuzbass demanded not just better pay, but better living conditions, and ultimately the end of the old regime.[24]

Nor is natural gas a solution. Methane has been reported leaking or burning wastefully in the gas fields and along the gas transportation system. The C.I.S. thus appears facing an increasing energy deficit. In such a situation, it may be expected that economic considerations will overshadow environmental concerns for a long time to come.

In Eastern Europe, every country but Poland is a net energy importer, with the C.I.S. the major energy supplier. As a result, any change in domestic energy use is linked directly to developments in the C.I.S. and the availability of foreign currency to purchase oil on the international market. The present confused situation in the former USSR discourages any thought of reliance in the near future on its oil and gas reserves. On the other hand, the transition to democracy in the East European countries has broken up Comecon and old trade patterns which assured a purchaser for domestic products, and thus some economic stability. Lech Walesa and Vaclav Havel, among other East European leaders, have been insisting to the West that their countries do not need financial handouts. They need markets. But until the East European countries can produce the quality and range of goods which are marketable in the West, these markets will remain closed to them, and hard currency earnings low.

The prospects for alternative energy sources are small. The capacity for the further generation of hydropower is not very good and in any event will most certainly be rigorously scrutinized by the public. Solar power is unfeasible. Chernobyl generated as much, if not more, public opposition to nuclear power plants in Eastern Europe as the accident did in the USSR. The only practical solution seems to be to fall back on that heavy polluter, brown coal.

The second set of factors relates to the unique characteristics of the former Communist systems: their wasteful use of raw materials, the monopolistic character of the system, and the inability and/or unwillingness of the leaders to enforce environmental measures. Eastern Europe and the C.I.S. rank last in Europe in terms of energy efficiency and conservation. In 1987, it took Poland 88,829 kilojoules to produce $1.00 of GNP, Hungary 48,542, and Yugoslavia 22,084. The figure for the U.S.A., one of the more wasteful energy spenders in the Organization for Economic Cooperation and Development (OECD), is 20,645.[25] Between 1970 and 1988, U.S. consumption of energy per unit of GDP dropped by 27 percent.[26] By contrast, energy consumption per unit of GDP increased in Yugoslavia by 15 percent.[27] Czechoslovakia is a signatory of the so-called Thirty Percent Pact which binds the country to the reduction of sulfur dioxide emissions by 30 percent by 1993. The official Czech document on the state of the environment does not foresee that the country will be able to meet its obligations before 1995, and even then, only when the country has been successful in reducing its consumption of energy per unit/output. Reductions in carbon dioxide will only be possible with the complete restructuring of Czechoslovakia's industry.[28]

Wasteful consumption is in many respects a by-product of the second unique characteristic of Communist systems: leadership's stranglehold on all aspects of society.[29] The control was so absolute that the economy and civil society as autonomous entities ceased to exist. One of the most important means of ensuring control over society was the ruling group's monopoly over the economy. In Marxist-Leninist regimes, the chief function of the economy is not to produce for profit but to maintain the ruling group in power. Gorbachev's refusal to pass legislation legalizing private property points directly to this function. As a vital extension of the state, the economy shared in the political patronage game, promoting the loyal, firing the unreliable and permitting the emergence of no organizations which could acquire sufficient independent economic means to challenge the ruling hierarchy. Dissent was suppressed by the secret police and the rigid enforcement of censorship.

The ruling group's monopoly over the economy was implemented through the state economic plan which had the force of law once rubber-stamped by the legislature. During the 1980s all the Communist countries upgraded their environmental legislation. The legal framework for environmental protection in the Soviet Union became a model of completeness, with hundreds of regulations, state promulgations and rules following upon each law to attempt to enforce the legislation. Plans in the 1980s increasingly included environmental parameters, and in some cases, environmental quotas. But the bottom line for management to receive its bonus was fulfillment of the production quota. In addition, environmental quotas, like production quotas, tended to be based on quantity rather than quality. For example, irrigation construction was evaluated on the amount of water available rather than water quality. In the Soviet Union, historically, planning was organized by economic ministry and territorial unit and forwarded to the top of the particular administrative hierarchy. Towns and rural areas had little or no control over local development, and only those at the top had the power to coordinate economic with environmental factors. Moreover, nowhere was environmental regulation the responsibility of a single agency. Overlapping, rival jurisdictions made everyone's responsibility no one's responsibility.

Censorship long kept the populations ignorant of environmental problems. Environmentally related sickness could easily be attributed to other causes or written off as a risk in certain types of jobs. With little knowledge of the outside world, people tended toward a fatalistic attitude about the worsening conditions.

Finally, the Communist leaders themselves seemed unable to tackle the mounting environmental problems. The leaders toppled in Eastern Europe in 1989 came to power or were educated at the height of the Stalinist system. World War II was a vivid memory. Socialism had to show its superiority to capitalism by building up a massive heavy industrial complex. The "scientific-technological revolution" (STR) launched with so much fanfare under Brezhnev was designed to thrust Communist countries into the microchip age. It failed because the leaders had little interest in or understanding of what it was all about.

With few exceptions environmental activists came from the younger generation. In the Soviet Union, they were undergraduates when Khrushchev was head of the country. This first postwar generation had no direct experience of World War II and little understanding of the ideological squabbles of the 1930s. The Stockholm Conference of 1972 provided the impetus for educational systems throughout the Communist bloc to begin to teach about the environment, some more thoroughly, some less. Raised in this climate, young people felt no scruples in taking their leaders to task for their failure to address environmental issues. In the 1970s and early 1980s, another generation of young people were college students, many of them in the biological sciences. Many went on into the prestigious institutes of the USSR, or in the case of Eastern Europe, into the national academies. There, their superiors came from among the first generation of activists. These were now internationally recognized scientists or university professors, who had made a career out of their environmentalism and profited from the more relaxed domestic climate and opening to the West which Khrushchev had made possible. The two countries which were unable to profit from the changed international conditions were East Germany and Czechoslovakia, where the invasion of the Warsaw Pact countries in August 1968 ruthlessly suppressed a surge of reform in all areas of society. The stage was set for the linking up of environmentalists with democratic reformers and eventually with the population as a whole to overturn the Communist regimes.

THE RISE OF THE ENVIRONMENTAL MOVEMENT

The sixties saw the growth of what became known as alternative movements in West Germany. Initially, the movements were focused on issues such as social justice and nuclear weapons, but by the end of the decade an environmental movement had emerged. This movement was the ancestor of virtually all the movements in Eastern Europe and the Soviet Union. In the 1970s, environmental organizations in the United States began to operate internationally. Out of these came the environmental nongovernmental organizations, the NGOs, of today. The growth in number and strength of the NGOs came in general after the overthrow of the Communist regimes.

It is important to realize what the West German alternative movements were. Essentially, they were, in Alberto Melucci's terms, "a system of actions which concentrate[d] most on a general orientation and concrete actions in support of that orientation." A movement may be contrasted to a political party in that the latter focuses on organizing to gain political power through leadership and a unified platform.[30] A movement may be more radical, less organized, and less answerable for its orientation than a party. A movement may also be compared to an NGO in that the latter is organized to achieve certain goals either through lobbies or some other recognized form of political advocacy.

Its greater organizational flexibility and general orientation made the movement an excellent vehicle for protest in the former Communist countries. The republic of Slovenia in Yugoslavia had probably the first environmental movement in the region. Slovene young people had easier access to German ideas and events through tourism and the more open frontier. Moreover, of all the republics, Slovenia was the most westernized and had the most developed economy. Equally important, Yugoslavia at the end of the 1970s prided itself on having a different, more liberal form of communism, which Yugoslavs called "self-management." The student organizers of the Green movement thus did not fear ejection from college. But they did expect harassment and difficulty in finding jobs upon graduation. The first student demonstration caught the Slovenian Communist party and government leaders by surprise. They had not expected anyone would have the courage to oppose them. As the government vacillated on tactics, the group expanded its membership and activities. The original twelve members each recruited several persons, who in turn recruited additional members. Recruitment was on a personal basis because trust was essential. A network was formed. Word of a planned demonstration was spread primarily by word of mouth, and the mode of demonstration was left to the individuals in the different groups. In the mid-1980s, the environmental movement accepted the umbrella of the official Communist Youth Movement (CYM). In 1989, it broke with the CYM to form an independent organization.[31]

Poland was the second country to launch an environmental movement. Almost immediately after the strikes and negotiations of Solidarity with the Polish Party and government in 1980, pro-environmental scientists and intellectuals formed a group in the southern city of Cracow. The formation of the Polish Ecology Club was thus simultaneous with the regime's first concession to a democratic order in their agreement to recognize Solidarity, and—extremely important—to lift censorship. For one year, between 1980 and 1981, environmental facts were published freely in the press, and the facts were horrifying. The Club quickly gained members and other groups started in other towns. One of the Club's most celebrated achievements was the closing of the Skawina Aluminum Works on the outskirts of Cracow. Cracow's environmentally conscious mayor responded positively to the

Club's protests and helped engineer the closing. Like their Slovene counter-parts, the Polish groups developed informal networks to keep in contact with one another and with the groups in the West that would broadcast their actions to the outside world.

The last movement to organize in the early eighties was the Danube Circle, or "the Blues." In the late sixties, the governments of Czechoslovakia and Hungary signed an agreement to finance jointly the building of a dam across the Danube River on the border of the two countries. The Slovak section of the dam was to be built at Gabcikovo, southeast of the capital city of Bratislava, while the Hungarian section was to be built at the celebrated bend in the Danube River where the river turned due south at Nagymoros. Construction was postponed during the 1970s as the countries negotiated financial and other terms. But by the beginning of the 1980s, the decision to construct was irreversible. Both sides began to build. Hungarian biologist Janos Vargha organized an ecological group in protest, starting a saga of protest that was to end in 1989 with the capitulation of the regime and the annulment of construction.

Chernobyl was the event that precipitated the formation of environmental groups in all the East European countries and the Soviet Union. Small groups dared to organize at the grass-roots level and members took their lives in their hands to protest environmental conditions in their area. The Slovene Green Movement organized a mass protest in central Llubljana demanding that the Soviets give compensation for damage sustained by Yugoslav citizens and demanding the halt of nuclear energy.[32] Environmental groups prolifer-ated in Poland. In Estonia and the Soviet republic of Georgia, environmen-talism literally started the nationalist movement. In Armenia a mass demonstration called for national autonomy. Environmental groups formed in the other republics of the European part of the Soviet Union: Latvia, Lithuania, the Ukraine, Moldavia, and Armenia. All of these quickly allied themselves with the emerging nationalist movements. In the Russian heart-land, some two hundred groups formed in Leningrad alone. People in heavi-ly polluted areas were becoming increasingly aware that something was wrong. In 1988, one of the first Central Asian environmental groups, the Green Front, was formed in Kazakhstan.

In the beginning, there was tremendous personal cost to protest even in Poland, Hungary and Yugoslavia, where police terror had eased. Concern with ecology was seen as a form of deviance. In Poland, environmentalism went underground with the imposition of martial law in 1981 and did not surface seriously again until 1988. In Slovenia, environmentalists risked their future when they protested. In Czechoslovakia, Bulgaria and Rumania, the terror continued right up to the fall of the regime, and jail sentences were the rule.[33] In Hungary, considered by the West as the most liberal of the East European regimes, protesters risked loss of job, denial of a visa for foreign travel, denial of their children's admission to higher education, even denial of permission for their children to travel abroad. Judit Varsanhelyi of the Independent Environmental Center in Budapest told the author, "Our children became orphans of the movement." For her, the effort was so great and the risks so oppressive that being in the Blue movement left her drained and empty.

Chernobyl opened the public's eyes not only to environmental degradation, but to the bankrupt policies that had brought on the catastrophe. During the 1970s, the environment became an accepted topic of discussion on all the national media. In 1972, the Soviet Union participated in the first United Nations Conference on the Environment in Stockholm. After the conference, Brezhnev began to make pro-environmental pronouncements and major environmental legislation was passed. Students and scientists working on environmental projects quietly debated among themselves the question of whether the solution to the mounting environmental problems lay in the overthrow of the Communist regime, or could be handled by steadily pressuring the leaders to take the necessary steps within the framework of the Communist system. Because of the personal cost of open protest of regime policies, most scientists preferred to work behind the scenes. Here they exercised considerable influence over the nascent popular environmental movement, while at the same time having a say in environmental policy development. Only a few scientists deliberately chose dissent, or like Janos Vargha were pushed into the role of dissenters because they were against official policy.

The public, however, could not and did not see environmental issues in purely environmental terms. If there was pollution, someone had to have caused it. No scientist or popular protester saw himself as the culprit. After the close of the Skawina mill in 1980, there were public calls for the end of the Stalinist order. Reform was on the minds of the students in Llubljana when they first came out in protest. In the beginning the Danube Circle considered itself apolitical and only thought to stop dam construction. As the authorities cracked down on their activities for allegedly being "anti-socialist" and hence treasonable, more and more of the protesters began to see their opposition to the dam as symbolic of their opposition to the "gigantomania" and arbitrary decision making of the regime that had approved construction.

Chernobyl heightened the association of environmentalism with reform. The disaster frightened or angered many not only because of the horror of the accident itself, but because the Soviet authorities attempted to conceal the truth. It was understandable that the military should want a cover-up; but Gorbachev was perceived as undermining his own policy of glasnost by not letting the full facts be known. The longer glasnost continued, the more criticism of the state of the environment took on the overtones of demand for total reform. In 1987, the doctor and journalist who had most intimate knowledge of Chernobyl, Dr. Iurii Shcherbak, founded Zelenyi svit, or Green World. Initially he said his purpose was to work with every political group in Ukraine to help stop the further deterioration of the environment. The authorities held up registration of his group until 1989. By that time, antinuclear protesters in both the Ukraine and Belorussia were making no effort to conceal their desire for independence from Moscow and for a democratic system. After Moscow finally admitted that the damage at Chernobyl was far more extensive than had first been thought, Shcherbak was made minister of the environment for Ukraine.[34]

In Yugoslavia, a young student from the suburbs of Belgrade gathered signatures against nuclear power. His action spread by word of mouth throughout the country. By 1987, a mass movement from virtually all of Yugoslavia's constituent republics was demanding a moratorium on nuclear power. In December, the federal legislature duly passed a law setting a twenty-year moratorium on construction of nuclear plants.[35] For the first time, people power had triumphed at the federal level.

Events moved quickly from 1987 to 1989. It would be impossible to describe every development in every country of the former Communist bloc, However, some are worth mentioning. In Hungary, the Blues turned for support to the Austrian and German Greens. Mass protests began in 1988. In the spring, the Danube Circle organized a demonstration at Nagymoros itself. It was supposed to be a march of women and children. But so fearful were the fathers for the safety of their families, they marched along. In October 1988, forty thousand people filled the square in front of the Hungarian Parliament to protest the dam. It was the first time there had been a demonstration there since the Soviet invasion of 1956. The size of the demonstration brought home to the government that Communist power had come to an end. The Party began of its own accord the transition to democratic rule. In May 1989, the government voted to abandon construction.

In Poland, in 1987, the Polish Peace and Freedom Movement organized in Warsaw the first meeting of informal groups to be held in Eastern Europe—without official approval. Representatives from both East and West Europe came, including activists from the Baltic republics. The conference stated that one important aspect of peace was the survival of the planet. The East European groups made it clear that they considered totalitarianism to be one of the main causes of environment degradation.[36] The end of martial law in Poland in 1988 saw the rapid reemergence of environmentalists to the forefront of the political scene. The roundtable talks between the government and the opposition in early 1989 were unmistakable proof of the influence of the Polish environmental movement on the democratic transition in Poland. Representatives of the environmental movement participated in the talks. The principal outcome was the agreement to hold elections to the Polish legislature. But a second and almost equally significant outcome was the adoption by the government of all of the opposition's environmental agenda, with the sole exception of the environmentalists' demand to discontinue construction of the Zarnowiec nuclear power plant.[37]

In Czechoslovakia, discontent with air and water pollution was the catalyst for reform. In February 1987, some three hundred people from the Chomutov district of north Bohemia signed a letter which they sent first to the local Party and government authorities, complaining about an inadequate system to warn people about an increase in air pollution in the district. For the first time, environmental protesters were not punished. Party and government representatives heard them out and then promised to take action. On 11–12 November 1989, a second demonstration in the north Bohemia coal-mining town of Teplice protested the unbreathable air. The group was dispersed with police whips and batons.[38] All during the fall of 1989, a determined group of women calling themselves the Group of Czech Mothers staged demonstrations in Prague to protest against the undrinkable quality of the water. On 17 November came the student demonstration in Prague that brought down the Communist regime.

In East Germany, the Evangelical church provided a safe haven for the activities of environmental groups such as the Environmental Library and the green Network "Ark." Environmental pollution was a major political issue at the Leipzig rallies in 1989. Unfortunately, the efforts of these very informal organizations were quickly swamped by the invasion of the highly organized West Germany parties and these groups gradually faded out of the picture. Nevertheless, in the 1990 elections, the Green party was able to win eight seats despite the overwhelming significance of the unification issue.

In Bulgaria, mass protests over air pollution in the Danube port of Ruse gave birth to the Independent Committee for the Protection of the Environment. By 1989, independent groups had formed in virtually every large Bulgarian city. At the head of these groups was Ecoglasnost, established in early 1989. The imprisonment of demonstrators from Ecoglasnost at the Helsinki conference on environmental cooperation, held in Sofia in October/November 1989, contributed in no small part to the fall of the Zhivkov regime.

Environmentalism was so persecuted in Rumania that there is little knowledge of any activism until spring 1988, when an underground group of scientists calling itself Rumanian Democratic Action issued a document called "The Green Report of the Rumanian Democratic Action on the Environmental Situation in Rumania."[39] The first Rumanian organization to register officially after the December 1989 revolution was the Ecological Movement of Rumania, which quickly allied itself with the ruling National Salvation Front (NSF). Six days later the Rumanian Ecological party was officially registered. Since then, numerous smaller groups have come into being, spawned by the terrible environmental conditions in that country.

As we can see, adverse environmental conditions bred indigenous environmental groups that, especially after Chernobyl, recruited mass support for their protests, because the public saw these protests as protests against the totalitarian regime itself. In Poland, Hungary, Slovenia, the Ukraine, Belorussia, Georgia, and the Baltics, environmental groups were among the most influential actors in bringing down the Communist system. In the Soviet Union, the environment came to symbolize the national traditions of the good old days, before industrialization or before Soviet power. This symbolic role of the environment was particularly evident in the Russian Republic (Rasputin and the rural school of Russian writers), in the Baltics, and in the national veneration given to such lakes as Lake Issyk Kul' in Khirghizia or Lake Sevin in Armenia. In Czechoslovakia, Rumania, and Armenia, environmental conditions themselves directly contributed to the fall of the regimes.

PROBLEMS AND PROSPECTS: THE GREEN DEMOCRATIC ALTERNATIVE

Problems

Two years after the momentous events of 1989, the power of the East European environmental groups fractured. In the former USSR, environmental concerns gave way to a tug of war between the center and the republics with national independence at the top of eleven out of the fifteen republican agendas. Several explanations may be offered as to why the environmental groups lost their hold on center stage.

First, once the Communist regimes had fallen, the chief concerns of the new governments were stability and economic growth. Stability required the building of new, viable democratic institutions; economic growth, the movement to a market economy and integration into the world markets. The environmental movement was unable to address these issues. For one thing, it was too fragmented and without political experience. For another, in most cases, the movement had concentrated on single issues: dams, nuclear power, or local environmental degradation, and had used these as symbols against the old regime with little understanding of what might solve the environmental problem at issue. Once the old regime had disappeared, the issues lost their importance as symbols.

Second, faced with a host of immediate priorities, the new governments were in no position to look environmental problems squarely in the face. They thus fell back on symbolic actions, the most visible of which was the establishment of environmental ministries. They then appointed recognized and trusted environmental activists like Shcherbak or non-Communist, maverick scientists like Nicolai Vorontsov, who became minister of the All-Union Ministry and hired, as staff, scientists from the institutes of the national academies of sciences, many of whom had been active as leaders in the movement underground. Once the scientists took up their new positions, they had little time for the movements. Since movement membership was informal and tended to rise and fall with the political saliency of the issues, members simply drifted away. Pretransition environmental education had not been in progress long enough to produce a mass public awareness of the severity of environmental problems. As a result, the public had extremely high expectations of what the new government could do, and no idea of what actions were required of them to ensure government responsibility. Officials from the new Czech ministry of the environment, for example, told the author that the public expected them to solve the most serious air and water pollution problems almost immediately upon taking office, and failed to understand why it took so long to write the necessary enabling legislation. But while people demanded instantaneous results from the government, they themselves abandoned their activism to turn to more immediate concerns: job security and maintaining a family in the face of high inflation.

A third reason relates to the problem of trust. In Eastern Europe in the first months of the transition period many Communists, who were functionaries in national youth movements and other mass organizations, feared for their jobs. The more radical political stance of the Green parties encouraged these former apparatchiks to join them in the hope of being able to start anew. The appearance of Communists among the Greens was of course noted by other environmental groups, which became hesitant to work with them. Likewise, many of the employees of the new environmental ministries were transfers from ministries that were highly compromised by their activities under the Communist regime, such as the ministry of the interior. Public perception of Communist infiltration of the environmental movement was a main reason for the poor showing of Greens in the first elections in the Czech lands, Hungary and Croatia. The environmental NGOs on their part preferred to back candidates in other parties who adopted pro-environmental positions. It was only where Greens were identified with national aspirations, as in Slovakia and Slovenia, that they did rather well.[40] Otherwise, the distrust of environmental groups weakened their ability to present a united front on environmental issues that could translate into usable political power.

The organizational void has been partially filled by the international environmental organizations: Friends of the Earth, Greenpeace, the Sierra Club and the Audubon Society. The European Green party has also been active. The general pattern has been for the local environmental groups to come together in an umbrella group which then affiliates with an international organization. There has been a great deal of activity in the West to ensure the regeneration of the East European environmental movement, to educate the activist members of the more prominent groups in NGO politics, and to incorporate the movements into the international mainstream. One of the most active agencies promoting environmental NGO development is the Central East European Environmental Center located in Budapest, which opened in 1990 with $4 million from the United States.[41] There are many environmental activists and professionals who see hope for more responsible global environmental management in the formation of a huge international environmental NGO lobby.

Fourth, in the Soviet Union and Yugoslavia, environmental problems have been totally obscured by issues of nationalism and the future of the federal structure. Postwar Yugoslavia was held together largely by the genius and authority of Josep Broz Tito, the wartime leader who successfully led his supporters against the Nazi invasion and Serbian resistance fighters. The consensus began to fade even before Tito's death. To insure union, Tito established a collective federal presidency and a new constitution that assigned most powers to the republican governments. The first free republican elections soured in the rising tide of nationalism. In both Serbia and Croatia, environmental concerns have been silenced by gunfire. Civil war is hardly conducive to environmental remediation. In one day of bombing Vukovar, the Federal army under Serbian command probably did more environmental damage than could be repaired in several years. Estimates of damage now range in the billions of dollars. Initially, the Slovenian Greens opposed disassociation from Yugoslavia on the grounds that the requirements of national defense would take away funding from vital remedial social and environmental measures. However, after the popular referendum in December 1990 went strongly in favor of independence, all but a few radical Greens voted with the rest of the Slovenian parliament for disassociation. Nationalism was and remains the issue of the day.

Prospects

The very problems of the environmental movement hold the keys to its future role. Environmentalists provided the cradle for the democratic movement throughout the former Communist bloc. Within the movement, people learned democratic tactics with which to challenge the old regime: letter writing, mass demonstrations, solidarity with groups from abroad and with each other. It is significant that the only minister who came out against the abortive coup in the Soviet Union was the minister of the environment. Today, the movement is splintered. Happily, fragmentation imposes democratic behaviors which preclude the formation of the old type of bureaucratic mass organization. There may be umbrella groups, like the Moscow-based Socio-Ecological Union, or the Bulgarian Ecoglasnost, but these organizations cannot dictate to the grass-roots activists beneath them. They can only advise and coordinate. Ecology promotes democracy.

International networking is another asset of the environmental movement. Networking contributed to the victory of environmental causes in Estonia and Hungary. Today, "Eurochain" has taken the battle against Nagymoros to Slovakia, the government of which plans to make Gabcikovo operative. American environmental organizations in cooperation with the Socio-Ecological Union helped organize the Nevada-Semipalatinsk demonstrations in Kazakhstan that led to a ban on nuclear testing. American money is aiding the regional environmental center in Budapest to set up a regional NGO network essential to the consolidation of the environmental movement in Eastern Europe. Outside funds and equipment are absolutely necessary. As the independent Russian newspapers demonstrated during the attempted coup, a FAX machine or a modem can work miracles in signaling domestic events to the outside world.

There is danger in the possible subordination of the East European movements to the growing international environmental NGO bureaucracy. This bureaucracy is not only financed by membership dues but by large corporate donations. Corporate investment in East Europe needs to give priority to environmental considerations. In the desire to promote economic growth, the new governments might sign contracts with lower environmental restraints than are needed. Dependency on international funding or international NGO direction could undermine the ability of the domestic environmental groups to act decisively on a specific environmental issue. Yet, this risk appears small, given the critical need for outside support.

Barbara Jancar-Webster

Green parties do not present this kind of problem. Their difficulty is in getting sufficient votes for a program which seems to offer a future of deprivation and primitive living. Only if the Greens can succeed in convincing the voters that adequate living standards can be maintained solely by ecologically sustainable economic development, will they have mass appeal.

Finally, the environment as an issue is not about to disappear. In the Soviet Union, Green candidates and deputies put forward by Green groups won handily in the elections of 1989 to the Congress of People's Deputies and in the 1990 republican and local elections. In the Ukraine and Belorussia, the aftermath of Chernobyl is sure to keep the environment in the public eye for years to come. The dissolution of the Communist party and the disintegration of the Soviet empire are not only opportunities for national self-assertion. Each of the new republics surely wishes to project a good image of itself as it takes its first steps in the world. Each has a burden of poor health and bad nutrition resulting from years of environmental abuse. These cannot be helped without immediate and substantial attention to the environment. Economic growth cannot occur in a sickly population or in a devastated environment. The environmental agenda will not go away.

The 1989 revolutions in Eastern Europe and the August revolution in the Soviet Union may temporarily have swept away environmentalism in a tide of resurgent nationalism. When the euphoria ends, the environmental problems pose themselves more insistently than ever before. The pretransition environmental groups waged a long and exhausting struggle against the arbitrary rule of totalita, as the Czechs call it.[42] For them, the environment and democracy were inseparable. The new governments either must demonstrate that this maxim is valid, or else plunge the nascent democracies once more into disillusion and even despair, as the area pushes ever closer to the ecological barrier where further economic progress is impossible.

CONCLUSION

Environmental remediation in Eastern Europe and the former Soviet Union requires the mutual efforts of both East and West. But perhaps the greatest effort must be in strengthening democracy. The end of the 1980s witnessed the power of people to overthrow unwanted regimes. Significantly, neither Lech Walesa nor Boris Yeltsin are highly educated men. In the West, people power has proved highly effective in saving the environment. Before the changes in the East, a united opposition was sustained through regional and international networking. Now the need is to build a constructive platform and permanent but flexible organizations. The West can help in education in democratic procedures, in providing information about the issues, and clarification of technical options. The West can provide funding. But the West cannot transform people victimized by years of oppression into responsible political actors. The environmentalists must take up that challenge themselves.

NOTES

1. "Chernobyl" (in Russian), *Vsya nasha Zhisn'* (All our life) (Moscow, 1990, 64. The reader should not forget the earlier nuclear disaster in the Urals near Cheliabinsk, whose fallout was probably worse than that of Chernobyl.

2. Gosudarstvennyi komitet SSSR po okhrane prirody (State committee SSSR for environmental protection) *Gosudarstvennyi doklad: Sostaianie prirodnoi sredy i prirodookhrannaya deiatel'nost' v SSSR v 1989 godu* (State report on the state of the environment and environmental protection activities in the USSR for 1989) (Moscow: Gosudarstvennyi komitet SSSR po okhrane prirody, 1990), 40–42.

3. Fifty-two percent of the USSR's total sulfuric acid is produced by the copper smelting complex at Norilsk in western Siberia, the toxic emissions of which have destroyed the surrounding forests within a radius of fifty-five miles. See A. Grigoriev, "Norilsk," *Vsya nasha Zhizn'*, 1990, 61.

4. "Kuzbass: The Ecological Portrait," *Vsya nasha Zhizn'*, 1990, 59.

5. Barbara Jancar, "Democracy and the Environment in Eastern Europe and the Soviet Union," *Harvard International Review* 12, no. 4 (Summer 1990): 13.

6. Officials say that DDT exceeds the permissible norms in some grain-growing areas of Kirghizia by up to forty-five times! See *Gosudarstvennyi doklad*, p. 59.

7. Ibid., p. 32.

8. Mike Edwards, "Siberia, In from the Cold," *National Geographic* 177 (March 1990): 2–39.

9. Ministry of Environmental Protection of the Czech Republic. *Zivotni prostredi Ceske republiky* (The environment in the Czech Republic) (Prague: Academia Praha, 1990), 42.

10. United Nations Environment Programme and United Nations Economic Commission for Europe, "Forest Damage and Air Pollution: Report of the 1988 Forest Damage Survey, in Europe," Global Environment Monitoring System (GEMS), New York, 1989.

11. Ministry of Environmental Protection, *Zivotni prostredi CR*, 158 and 159.

12. Don Hinrichsen and Georgyi Enyedi, eds., State of the Hungarian Environment (in Hungarian) (Budapest: Hungarian Academy of Sciences, the Ministry for Environment and Water Management, and the Hungarian Statistical Office, 1990), p. 56.

13. Ministry of Environmental Protection, *Zivotni prostredi CR*, 208–25.

14. Ronald A. Taylor, "Eastern Europe: The World's Greatest Polluter," *Europe* (October 1990), 17.

15. Hinrichsen and Enyedi, eds., *State of the Hungarian Environment*, 74–75.

16. Ministry of Environmental Protection, *Zivotni prostredi CR*, 72.

17. Mate Matas, Viktor Simoncic, Slavko Sobot, *Zastita okoline danas za sutra* (Environmental protection today and tomorrow) (Zagreb: Skolska Knija, 1989), 169–73.

18. Taylor, "Eastern Europe," 17.

19. For a discussion of the severe nitrate pollution of Hungary's soils, see Hinrichsen and Enyedi, eds., *State of the Hungarian Environment*, 77–85.

20. Barbara Jancar, "United States/East European Environmental Exchange," *International Environmental Affairs* 2, no. 1 (Winter 1990): 40–66.

21. Data from World Resources Institute, *World Resources 1990–91* (New York: Oxford University Press, 1990), 317 and 319.

22. See Rasputin's comments in *Literaturnaya gazeta*, 1 January 1988, 3.

23. Mikhail Gurtovoi, "More on Soviet-U.S. Proposed Oil Deal," *Moscow News* 25, no. 3480 (23–30 June 1991): 10.

24. "Kuzbass Miners: 'Freedom not money!'" *Moscow News* 11, no. 3466 (17–24 March 1991): 1.

25. World Resources Institute, *World Resources 1990–91*, 317.

26. OECD, *The State of the Environment* (Paris: Organization for Economic Cooperation and Development, 1991), p. 224.

27. World Resources Institute, *World Resources 1990–91*, 317.

28. Ministry of Environmental Protection, *Zivotni prostredi CR*, 62–63. For carbon production reductions see OECD, *State of the Environment*, 336.

29. For an in-depth presentation of the relation between environmental management and the Communist one-party state, see Barbara Jancar, *Environmental Management in the Soviet Union and Yugoslavia: Structure and Regulation in Communist Federal One-Party States* (Durham, N.C.: Duke University Press, 1987).

30. Alberto Melluci, "Kraj drustvenih pokreta?" (The end of social movements?), *Nase teme* (Zagreb) 82, no. 10 (1984): 1346–47. See also Andelko Milardovic's discussion of this problem in *Spontanost i institucionalnost* (Spontaneity and institutionalism) (Belgrade: Kairos, 1989), 61–64.

31. Interview with former general secretary of the Greens of Slovenia, Peter Jamnicar, summer 1990.

32. Jancar, *Environmental Management*, 331–35.

33. Jan Krivan, "Ecology as Deviance: The Case of Pavel Krivan," *Across Frontiers* 2, nos. 3 & 4 (Spring-Summer 1986): 15–18.

34. David Marples, "Ecological Issues Discussed at Founding Congress of *Zelenyi svit*," Radio Liberty, report on the USSR 2 no. 5 (2 February 1990), 21–22.

35. For a longer description of the antinuclear movement in Yugoslavia, see Barbara Jancar, "The Environment and Democracy in Yugoslavia," in *Yugoslavia, Festschrift for Fred Singleton*, ed. Edward Allworth. Forthcoming.

36. In the words of one activist, "ecology is democracy." (Cited in Polly Duncan, "A New Generation of Opposition," *Sojourners*, 16, no. 9 [October 1987]: 14–16.)

37. Proceedings of the Civic Committee to the Chairman of the IATU "Solidarity," 2, 1989 (in Polish).

38. Much of the information in this chapter was obtained through a series of interviews with the representatives of ecological groups undertaken in the summer of

1990. Except where the person interviewed is quoted or his/her remarks are paraphrased, there will be no further reference to the source of information.

39. Dan Ionescu, "The Rumanian Democratic Action Group on the Environment," RFE Research Rumania SR/8 (23 June 1988): 45.

40. For a breakdown of the elections, see Vladimir V. Kusin, "The Elections Compared and Assessed," *Report on Eastern Europe* 1, no. 28 (13 July 1990): 38–47.

41. For examples of recent project funding of NGOs in Eastern Europe, see the Center's *Bulletin,* July 1991.

42. The first chapter of *The State of the Czech Environment* is entitled "Totalitni system" (The totalitarian system) and lays most of the country's environmental woes at the foot of *totalita,* including too great concentration of economic power in the hands of too few people, moral disintegration, destruction of any sense of civic responsibility, and "gigantomania" (Ministry of Environmental Protection, *Zivotni prostredi CR,* 15–18).

11 Environmental Politics in Latin America

STEVEN E. SANDERSON

In June 1992, five hundred years after European conquest of the Americas began, the United Nations hosted an "Earth Summit" in Rio de Janeiro, Brazil. The symbolic importance of holding the conference in Rio de Janeiro was great, given the grand history of Portuguese, Dutch, British, French, and U.S. involvement in environmental degradation there over the centuries, and Brazil's current standing as a high-profile environmental abuser for its Amazon development designs. The agenda for the UN Conference on Environment and Development, as the Earth Summit was more formally known, was no less grand: it proposed to address such diverse global issues as global climate change, deforestation, and the conservation of biological diversity, as well as to produce an "Earth Charter" and an agenda for the next century (appropriately named "Agenda 21") (MacNeill et al., 1991; Valentine 1991). Such issues have never been a matter of high priority in the politics of Latin American development, either under colonial rule or since independence.

Though the UNCED meeting was global, its venue focused attention on Latin American environmental politics, offering the chance to perpetuate unfortunate stereotypes, restate unproven assumptions, and heighten alarm. Despite such risks, the Earth Summit also allowed more careful examination of some of the environmental issues facing Latin America, their connection to the international system, and the politics that envelop such questions. In the event, the Earth Summit also organized some impressive Latin American national programs to identify and address an environmental agenda. Brazil, Chile, Colombia, and Mexico all drafted national environmental planning documents and created new government entities for such pressing concerns as biodiversity conservation. UNCED also provided the focus required to create the Inter-American Institute for Global Change Research, Latin America's contribution to the international START (System for Analysis, Research and Training) program.[1]

The purpose of this chapter is to outline some of the more critical questions in the region and to examine the received wisdom on each, along with its shortcomings. By concentrating on the conservation agenda, this chapter gives little attention to the pressing environmental issues of the cities, except

223

indirectly. Industrial metabolism and the pollution it generates are critical aspects of environmental politics in Latin America, as most of the region is more urban and industrial than developing countries in general. Those processes deserve fuller attention than is possible in this short contribution, but much of what follows could apply to urban-industrial environments as well.

THE TYRANNY OF THE EXTERNAL

Since the European conquest, Amerindian ways of life have been subdued, absorbed and eventually overwhelmed by European culture. The first Portuguese to land in Brazil quickly set about extracting dyewoods and precious metals, along with tropical exotica; at the same time, they concentrated Indian populations in what would become cultural death camps (Hemming 1978). Andean populations came under colonial authority, turning the vertical archipelagos of the Inca system into transitional domains of Spanish Upper Peru (Larson 1988). And Meso-America stumbled through various waves of environmental transformation, which included the export of mahogany and other precious woods, dyewood and logwood, indigo, cochineal, and other fruits of traditional settlements and natural (or naturally managed) ecosystems (Donkin 1977; Naylor 1989).

Independence did not change the nature of resource exploitation as much as its masters. British and then American influences over Latin America during the nineteenth century meant that the region developed its land assets at the expense of native forests, and concentrated on primary product exports befitting an area assumed to have surpluses in both labor and land.[2] Much of the history of the nineteenth-century export boom was written by foreigners, who organized the expansion of coffee, staple crops, bananas, guano, minerals and nitrates (Bulmer-Thomas 1988; Gootenberg 1991; Smith 1969; Blakemore 1974; Furtado 1976).

At the time of the Great Depression, then, it was not surprising to find the collapse of exports greeted by strong nationalist sentiment, which preferred an inward-directed development. From the 1930s to the 1980s, populist economic nationalism dominated much of the region; it advocated strong state involvement in economic growth, development through industrialization, and a rupture with the past "tyranny of the external."

The debt crisis of the 1980s ended those hopes, as the world saw Latin American indebtedness soar to unimaginable heights. Total disbursed external public debt in the region exploded from U.S. $15.7 billion in 1970 to $342 billion in 1987. Overall debt, both public and private, peaked at about $446 billion in 1987 and still hovered above $400 billion in 1991 (IDB

1981, 1991). Throughout the 1980s, Latin America spent $45–60 billion per year to service that debt. The pressure on exports to finance that debt, and the fiscal anemia of a weakened state have reopened the old debate about the dependence of Latin America on external driving forces.

This time, though, the pace and visibility of environmental degradation in Latin America have led to an unprecedented concern that the debt crisis results in greater environmental abuse. It is common to hear that the region's environmental abuses are a result of Latin America's dependence on world markets (and the declining terms of trade for primary products) and are accelerated by the rising debt obligations of the 1980s. Many contend that international markets and the debt crisis actually provoke Latin American countries to exploit their natural resource bases faster than they normally would. That same argument usually suggests that the environmental future of the world depends, in some measure, on debt relief for the high-debt countries (among them, Argentina, Brazil, Chile, Ecuador, Peru and Venezuela, all of which are suffering severe environmental problems associated with economic activity) (Ayres 1989; WCED 1987; Saether and Jonsson 1991). Perhaps the most extreme rendition of this argument is that "the major obstacle to a successful application of conservation biology principles is the global imbalance in resource flow between the industrialized and the developing countries" (Saether and Jonsson 1991).

However attractive this argument, it is generally made without proof. There is not much convincing evidence that debt and deforestation are linked directly. Where they exist, the connections certainly are clouded by time-lags and intervening variables such as domestic growth rates, import-substitution policies, supply or demand elasticities, and international prices themselves. Thanks to the debt crisis and resulting economic contractions, most countries have grown much more slowly through the 1980s, if at all; and most have financed their debt service by reducing imports drastically and paying the debt with resulting trade surpluses, not by wholesale increases in exports of natural resource-based products. In fact, few high-debt countries have shown greater growth in trade than in other non-trade-based elements of the economy. Many Latin American countries, including Brazil, grew faster and ate into their resource base more rapidly in the 1970s, when their systems were more closed to trade and less burdened by debt, than after the crisis of the 1980s (Capistrano and Sanderson 1991; Sanderson 1992, chap. 3).

Only a few countries in Latin America have accelerated their exports of natural resource-based commodities (agricultural, fishery, and forestry products), even when accounting for the fickle oil markets of the 1980s. The recession is partly to blame, but small countries dependent on commodity exports find it difficult to export more because of limits on both production and demand for their products. Tropical products react to the international market; they do not make it. In addition, many countries devoted more natural resources to production for domestic consumption, so as to reduce dependence on imports and generate a trade surplus through import-substitution. The more resources devoted to domestic consumption, the fewer available for export.

This leads to some major questions about the virtue of debt relief in the region. If one could be persuaded that debt relief would generate an "environmental dividend," and that the $45–60 billion a year in debt service would go to sustainable development designs, then the idea would be compelling. In fact, in the Enterprise for the Americas initiative of President Bush, official government-to-government debt swaps did generate environmental funds. And the well-known debt-for-nature swaps in Bolivia, Costa Rica, Ecuador and Mexico have resulted in support for important conservation programs. But these swap initiatives are dwarfed by the problems they address, and are full of controversy. If debt relief were generalized, after a decade of economic stagnation and impoverishment, it is unlikely that Latin American countries would use such relief for conservation instead of growth. And the debt connection to resource-based trade itself is thrown into question by the performance of Chile and Mexico, countries that are expanding their trade remarkably in the late 1980s and early 1990s, after the peak of the debt crisis.

There is a case to be made for the relation of trade to resource degradation. One could point to the semi-arid Norte Chico of Chile, where poor producers are selling their water rights to large table-grape producers serving the export market. Or one could point to the expansion of the winter vegetable industry in Mexico's arid north. But the facile trade-debt environmental degradation argument is difficult to defend, as are its remedies.

The UNCED meeting itself gave new ammunition to advocates of the "tyranny of the external" explanation for environmental degradation. The United States, ever the reluctant hegemon in North-South dialogues, refused to sign the biodiversity convention on the grounds that it afforded insufficient protection to the private sector's future patent rights on genetic material derived from the tropics. Biodiversity, traditionally considered to be within the sovereign purview of the nation-state, now has become a matter of direct foreign investment and international intellectual property law (Merges 1988; Acharya 1991). Neither of those new angles favors Southern Hemisphere nations. If the logic of biodiversity conservation depends on the appropriable value of genetic material, then clearly the international community has solved for the lowest common denominator.

CONSERVATION OR DEVELOPMENT?

The above discussion raises new problems for the conservation agenda. Is there such a thing as sustainable development, or is the traditional preservationist's suspicion about a conflict between conservation and growth really valid? As we know, traditional conservation strategies emphasize protected areas—"set asides" to be left immune to human disturbance. But population densities, a diminishing agricultural frontier, labor market changes, and other characteristic changes of the late-twentieth century have forced conservationists to address the human dimensions of ecosystem conservation.

The development community embraces such accommodation, since its interests are human-centered. So, the multilateral development agencies and conservation organizations have come to an unequivocal consensus that conservation of natural resources and sustainable development can and must go together; and sustainable development is predicated on economic growth (McNeely 1988; World Bank 1989). The logic seems to be that in Latin America conservation of natural resources cannot ignore the social dimensions of environmental degradation, especially poverty. Poverty cannot be alleviated without greater economic growth. Economic growth cannot conserve resources unless it is sustainable. Therefore, conservation, growth and sustainability must go together. As one author puts it, "A single-minded pursuit of environmental and related goals is ill-conceived if it fails to address the cause of distributive justice. Indeed, one wonders whether sustainability . . . is even conceivable under circumstances where material improvements in life [are] subordinated in policy concerns" (Darmstadter 1987, 481).

Politically, this is clearly a difficult position to contradict. But logic alone does not provide sufficient support for the hypothesis that conservation and sustainable development go together. As the renowned economist/conservationist Herman Daly has observed (Daly 1991, 39), there is a fundamental conceptual problem in sustainable development, in that it is based on economic growth. "Sustainable growth" demands the expansion of social systems for their own material sake, without setting ecosystem limits. Daly's argument favors setting limits on growth, based on the biophysical limits to growth (Daly and Cobb 1989; Meadows, Meadows and Randers 1992).

In Latin America, sustainable development has largely taken on the agenda of progressive, grass roots-oriented developmentalists. One of the best examples is found in the Brazilian movement in support of "extractive reserves," whereby poor settlers in the Amazon are given "use rights" consistent with their traditional patterns of low-output, non-agricultural activities. Rubber tappers, Brazil nut gatherers, and similar users of nontimber forest products become the focus of new marketing strategies and technical assistance, which has the ostensible virtue of combining conservation with equity (Fearnside 1989). The goal of enhancing poor, low-output producers' livelihoods is commendable and important (Plotkin and Famolare 1992); its known connection to biological conservation is principally in its avoidance of more intensive modes of exploitation and its potential for preserving cultural diversity of local peoples (Oldfield and Alcorn 1991).

In addition to the difficulties in generalizing such a model—in fact, any model of sustainable low-output production, in light of population and economic pressures—two questions limit this vision of sustainable development. First, in what ecological terms are these systems sustainable? And, second, to what degree do they really represent a viable economic option for the poor producer? In Latin America, the development assistance community has been much better at developing small-scale projects than it has been at addressing the more fundamental questions that make their creation necessary. In fact, there is substantial concern that "sustainability" in Latin America means whatever the action agency says it means, and that the ecological elements of the original term have lost their integrity (Lele 1991; O'Riordan 1988; Redford and Sanderson 1992).

LATIN AMERICAN LAND-USE CHANGE

Throughout the world, it is recognized that one of the most massive indicators of "structural" change in the global ecosystem involves land-use change. Forest gives way to agriculture, agriculture to pasture, farmland to desert or to built environments. Societies urbanize, technology intensifies land use, and environmental degradation proceeds apace (Blaikie and Brookfield 1987; Turner and Meyer 1992). Thanks in part to the graphic images of Brazilian deforestation of the Amazon, Latin America is seen as a region of rapid land-cover conversion from forest to agricultural use. This is not uniformly true, and even the most popular images of Brazil are somewhat misleading.

First, land-use change measurements are notoriously rough and controversial. Some deforestation measures, purporting to show destruction of tropical moist forest, actually include the bordering woodlands, too (Fearnside 1990). In other areas, such as the Sahel of Africa, the process of "desertification" or the advance of the Sahara southward has been shown to be increasingly complicated to analyze, raising both methodological and policy questions (Tucker, Dregne, and Newcomb 1991). And even the question of whether certain land-use changes are human-induced is difficult to answer (Blaikie and Brookfield 1987; Messerschmidt 1987; DeBoer 1989).

Second, the rate of land-use change in Latin America varies considerably. In Mexico, agricultural land has been relatively steady since the 1970s, and little new frontier is being opened, which would lead us to believe that land-use change is not a severe environmental problem. But, in fact, the last patch of tropical moist forest in Mexico, the Lacandon Forest, is being threatened by colonization, oil development, and government policies. Similarly, Paraguay, with its relatively low population pressures and small economic size, has not assumed a high profile in environmentalist concerns in the Americas. Yet, land-cover change to agricultural use is the greatest in Latin America, and fragile ecosystems are being pillaged in favor of domestic economic interests. Brazil, on the other hand, has a relatively modest rate of land-use change, measured by forest-cover conversion to agriculture, despite its awful international image (World Resources Institute 1991).

Latin America plays an important global role in land-use change, which generally reveals more rapid rates of change in developing countries. Even traditionally "sustainable" agricultural systems, such as those of the Argentine pampa, are now showing signs of degradation. And in the cases where the short-term consequences are clearest—the so-called "hot spots" of biological diversity[3]—the driving forces behind change may come from outside the region of impact, or even from outside Latin America altogether. In Ecuador's Amazon, clearly the price and demand for oil influences the decisions of foreign oil concessionaires to drill in such a remote setting. In the Brazilian northwest, the state of Rondonia has fallen prey to some of the worst deforestation in the hemisphere, and one of the culprits may be international agricultural prices and markets, which induce agricultural changes in the center and south of Brazil, sending thousands of new migrants to the Amazonian frontier. And in the southern reaches of Mexico, settlement of the Lacandon Forest is to some degree affected by both of the above causes, supplemented by the dislocations caused by political violence in neighboring Guatemala.

GLOBAL AND REGIONAL COMMONS

A significant part of the Latin American environmental agenda falls beyond its national jurisdiction, into the "global commons."[4] Latin America is particularly important in the exploitation of Pacific fisheries; the most important fishing nations in Latin America are Chile, Mexico and Peru.

There is substantial evidence that South Pacific fisheries are particularly vulnerable because of the dramatic increase in Chilean fishing (fish exports increased at a stunning rate of 22 percent from 1975 to 1989, and

229

the economic role of fishing in GDP quadrupled from 1970 to 1990; during the same period, the GDP only expanded by 69 percent) (Banco Central de Chile 1991). Recently, sardine fishing has shown significantly smaller catches, raising questions in Chile about indiscriminate overfishing. Assessment of the condition of the fisheries is complicated by the great variability in "shoaling pelagic" species, including sardines and anchoveta. It is noteworthy that Chile is a signatory of the Law of the Sea Treaty (still pending implementation, thanks largely to U.S. resistance) and a participant in the UNEP Regional Seas Program for the Pacific Southeast. The many conventions on marine fauna and conservation of marine resources have not, however, managed to staunch the exploitation of fisheries in Latin America. Nor have such agreements solved such problems as tuna-related dolphin kills off the Meso-American coastline (National Research Council 1992).

An additional set of issues falls into a no-man's land of conflict between nation-state environmental abusers who have proprietary claim over the resource in question, and the rest of the global community. A classic case is the Amazon River basin.

The Amazon is governed by a nine-nation regional treaty, hosted in rotation by parties to the treaty. Though the treaty is designed to foster regional cooperation among the country participants, permanent border disputes continue to plague Brazil, Colombia, Ecuador, Peru, and Venezuela. Brazil is quite aggressive in protecting its prerogatives over the Brazilian Amazon, and in the late 1980s developed two national programs that put large tracts of Amazon territory under the control of the National Security Council. In the early 1990s, concerns over the drug trade in Brazil continued to grow, giving the military and government further justification for settling the frontier. Moreover, resource rights continue to be an issue. Brazilian and Venezuelan gold miners have been involved in transborder conflicts; gold is also a matter of controversy along the Bolivian-Brazilian frontier of Rondonia and Acre (the Bolivian Beni). And the Ecuadoran military, already accused of contributing to illegal hardwood cutting and wildlife abuses, continues to show concern over protecting the frontier with Peru, especially in light of oil discoveries in the Ecuadoran Amazon, near the Napo River. In that connection, it is well to remember that the latest of several border wars between Peru and Ecuador took place barely a decade ago.

The Amazon is an example of a regional commons that increasingly is also recognized as a problem of the global commons. Deforestation of the Amazon potentially affects global climate, hydrology, and atmospheric quality in significant ways. So, the impact of management policies and national or regional politics in the Amazon is no longer a matter for Latin American interest alone. This conclusion raises questions about the degree to which national sovereignty must be compromised for the sake of the global commons. That issue is not exclusive to the Amazon, or to Latin America, for that matter.

So, beyond the regional commons, the global commons proper is a matter of interest to Latin American politics. Among global commons issues, ozone depletion and greenhouse gas emissions are of particular importance, especially in the large countries of the region.

While no country in Latin America figures among the leading gross sources of greenhouse and ozone depleting atmospheric gases, Brazil and Mexico are high among developing countries and even higher in per capita terms, for somewhat different reasons. Both countries are characterized by growing agricultural and industrial metabolisms that are energy-intensive. In Argentina and Mexico, energy consumption per capita doubled from 1965 to 1980; in Brazil and Panama, it tripled; in Ecuador, it increased fourfold. Even so, Venezuela, by far the highest consumer of per capita energy in Latin America, uses but a third of the share of the United States on a per capita basis (World Bank 1991a, 213).

Both agricultural expansion and industrial growth can lead to greenhouse gases and ozone depletion, and both are linked to modernization and development. Methane from ruminants, wet rice cultivation, and termites in deforested areas are cited as environmental concerns. Deforestation is driven to a great extent by agricultural conversion, and both agriculture and changes in forest composition affect the carbon balance in the atmosphere. Yet, the international economic system encourages countries such as Argentina, Brazil, and Mexico to expand agricultural and cattle-raising output, in keeping with their comparative advantage. And the entire system of agricultural development assistance since World War II has been built around input-intensive agricultural modernization and the expansion of land under cultivation.

POPULATION AND THE ENVIRONMENT

One cannot escape the population issue when dealing with environmental degradation in Latin America. Mexico and Brazil have two of the world's largest cities in São Paulo and Mexico City; population impacts by migrating poor people have undermined the ecological integrity of the Amazon, the North Mexican desert, and many of the inhabitable coastal zones of the region; and the famed soccer war of 1969 in Central America highlighted the tremendous imbalance between human population and natural resources in El Salvador and Honduras (Durham 1979). Yet, the highly touted Latin American and Caribbean Commission on Development and Environment did not see population as an issue that required more than the usual perfunctory attention (1990). UNCED itself did little to clear away the baggage of the past and propose a new population agenda. And recent contributions to the literature show the lack of theoretical or policy consensus (Davis and Bernstam 1991) or are consigned to summary observations by wildlife specialists (Western and Pearl 1988). The politics of population has only begun to recognize that such basic ideas as "surplus population" are socially and economically constructed (viz., Haiti). The movement of populations to fragile areas is often forced, as is much migration to the Amazon. And family size, infant mortality, social security, and environment are all important, linked factors in the social web.

Population problems are too often subjected to ulterior political motives. In Latin America, several countries with extreme environmental problems do not have population problems to which they can be attributed (Chile, Colombia and Ecuador, for example). In others, such as Brazil, it is in areas of very low population density that some of the worst depredations occur (the far northwest Amazon). Population politics are still, after decades of international attention, generally very stylized and rigid. Population is seldom recognized for the subtle expression of social structure that it conveys. The result is stereotypical North-South conflict on population issues, backed up by a lack of clarity about what exactly we mean by the "population variable."

NORTH-SOUTH DIALOGUE REDUX

These issues are interesting in their own right, but they have a special quality in Latin America: they divide the northern agenda from the southern, and they raise the question of national sovereignty in ways normally foreign to the system of nation-states.

The environmental politics of Latin America are in many ways reminiscent of the failed North-South dialogue of the 1970s (Hansen 1979; Fishlow et al. 1978), in that the North blames the South for the worst environmental abuses and mismanagement, while the South demands that international equity issues be addressed as a precondition for environmental policy improvement. The "social limits to growth" of the 1970s become the ecological limits to growth of the 1990s; the planetary human bargain of the 1970s becomes the planetary environmental bargain of the 1990s.

In a strong anti-imperialist reaction against a global warming convention, analysts from the Indian Centre for Science and Environment allege that the West is juggling the data to blame developing countries for global warming. They ask, "How can we visualize any kind of global management, in a world so highly divided between the rich and the poor, the powerful and the powerless, which does not have a basic element of economic justice and equity?" (Agarwal and Narain 1991, 1).

The merit in the southern argument—however partial and self-interested—is revealed in the obstacles that blocked much progress at the Earth Summit. The United States declined to take a leadership role in financing—or even acceding to—strong agreements on global warming. The U.S. accuses other northern nations of being disingenuous in their efforts to accommodate the South, and, indeed, European countries have manipulated the global warming agenda to some extent. Northern politicians rail against tropical deforestation as a contributor to global warming, but do not show the same vigor in opposing the deforestation of old growth forests in their own countries (in the case of the U.S., Canada and the former Soviet Union), or in documenting the contribution of industrial metabolism to forest dieback (in Europe, the U.S. and Canada).

And the very proposals of the North are contradictory. The World Bank argues in favor of more trade to alleviate poverty and save the environment from poverty-induced degradation. But the Bank does not pause to consider the resource pressures implied by more trade, especially in light of developing-country dependence on primary products. The Bank's forest policy is concerned with afforestation and reforestation efforts, but does not concern itself with the different levels of biological diversity implied by different forest management strategies (World Bank 1991). The General Agreement on Tariffs and Trade, the European Parliament, the International Tropical Timber Organization and the Friends of the Earth all have called for freer trade to develop the South, and, at the same time, restrictions on trade in tropical timbers. And those who do promote reduced subsidies in agriculture and forestry in the North do not address the implications for agriculture in the developing world, where intensification and expansion under free agricultural trade would likely harm the environment more.

On the southern side, Latin American countries lead the anti-imperialist criticism against the northern environmental agenda. Brazil continues to decry the attention paid to its rain forests, even as it struggles to change policies away from subsidizing deforestation. Brazil, along with virtually every other Latin American country, claims to need growth for the sake of development, and resists calls for more conservation. But the growth connection to development is more than a little dishonest, as most growth in Brazil, Chile, Argentina and Mexico over the 1970s and 1980s was accompanied by a worsening distribution of income; no one has made a convincing case that growth generates a noticeable improvement in historically bankrupt poverty policies. The poor are held hostage, in a sense, to the environmental policies of the North. Northerners would have the poor dislodged from fragile ecosystems in order to conserve them. Southerners would use the poor to justify untrammeled growth, which shares responsibility for destroying poor communities and intensifying the struggle for resources on the frontier. In this light, the North-South dialogue over the environment sounds more like the dialogue of the 1970s, in which neither side listened to the other, and the poor came out the worse for it.

CONCLUSION

Many gaps must be filled before environmental politics are addressed successfully, and they are not necessarily those usually cited. It is not necessarily the case that debt relief would generate an environmental dividend, for example, though few would doubt that debt relief would create better conditions for growth in the region. And the conservation of Latin America's biota does not necessarily depend on the creation of more effective national parks. Latin America is particularly interesting to the global environmental struggle because it reveals new dimensions of traditional issues of tremendous importance to the 1990s.

First, issues of regional commons are taking on global import, so that national or regional claims to sovereignty are no longer credible, *unless the management of the commons in question is beyond reproach.* The best guarantors against international claims against sovereignty are power or effective self-management. Since Latin America is not a powerful region itself, it is in the regional interest to seize the environmental agenda for itself before the rich countries do. This would require much more regional identity and common ground than ever has been apparent in Latin America, though, and a regional political leadership that has been conspicuously absent.

Second, ecological issues are becoming environmental in the sense that localized ecological change is now transcending its local boundaries, and is contributing to the qualitative change of the global environment (Holling 1986). The UNCED process certainly has confirmed that change from local to global concern. Politically, these issues will likely result in more call for international regimes or transnational conventions to deal with them; the nation-state is seen to be inadequate to the issues of the global commons, and often to the local environmental abuses that contribute to threats to planetary well-being.

As these two dynamics—the expansion of regional to global commons and the generalization of ecological issues to environmental concerns—continue, we can expect a certain "internationalization" of environmental politics.

But that internationalization itself is a double-edged sword. On the one hand, global challenges to national sovereignty can produce opportunities for better management of natural resources. But, as the UNCED biodiversity convention showed, the global commons itself has been appropriated to a certain extent by patent lawyers and transnational corporations more interested in property rights to genetic material than the biodiversity agenda itself.

Finally, Latin American environmental politics have a certain special character because they reveal the tremendous gap in political understanding, economic wealth, and ideological commitment that burdens the North-South dialogue. Even though West-West environmental agreements are hardly easy to come by, they at least have a common set of issues and language, compared to North-South counterparts. Those who are committed to improving environmental policies and the social structures that generate them in Latin America must also become committed to redressing the power inequalities that are high on Latin American political agendas. And political leaders from the North must understand that little support will come from the South until the North makes credible efforts to get its own environmental politics in better shape.

NOTES

1. The START initiative is a collaborative effort of the International Geosphere-Biosphere Program of the International Council of Scientific Unions, the World Climate Research Program, and the Human Dimensions of Global Environmental Change Program of the International Social Science Council.

2. These assumptions about factor endowments are still made, despite the closing agricultural frontier, the growing scarcity of natural resources, and local and regional labor scarcities throughout Latin America.

3. Hot spots are defined by their importance to global biological diversity and the degree of threat posed. "Megadiverse" ecosystems are favored, especially those in areas with a significant record of accelerating human impact. The leading practitioner of hot spot priorities is the John D. and Catherine T. MacArthur Foundation, whose World Environment and Resources program is based to some extent on targeting hot spots for conservation funding.

4. This traditional concept of shared interests across the world is best articulated in the environmental area in WCED 1987. A commonsense definition of the global commons includes all those environmental affairs that transcend a single nation's boundaries. This would include all of the "global change" issues: greenhouse gases and global warming, the ozone layer, world conservation of fisheries, acid rain, and so on.

REFERENCES

Acharya, Rohini. 1991. Patenting of biotechnology: GATT and the erosion of the world's biodiversity. *Journal of World Trade* 71 (December): 71–87.

Agarwal, Anil, and Sunita Narain. 1991. *Global warming in an unequal world: A case of environmental colonialism.* New Delhi: Centre for Science and Environment.

Ayres, José Márcio. 1989. Debt-for-equity swaps and the conservation of tropical rainforests. *Trends in Research in Ecology and Evolution* 4, no. 11 (November): 331–35.

Banco Central de Chile. 1991. Unpublished data.

Blaikie, Piers, and Harold Brookfield. 1987. *Land degradation and society.* London: Methuen.

Blakemore, Harold. 1974. *British nitrates and Chilean politics, 1886–1896: Balmaceda and North.* London: Athlone Press.

Bulmer-Thomas, Victor. 1988. *The political economy of Central America since 1920.* Cambridge: Cambridge University Press.

Capistrano, Ana Doris, and Steven Sanderson. 1991. The tyranny of the external: Debt, trade and resource use in Latin America. Paper delivered at the Latin American Studies Association Conference. April.

Comisiòn de Desarrollo y Medio Ambiente de América Latina y el Caribe. 1990. *Nuestra propia agenda sobre desarrollo y medio ambiente.* Washington, D.C.: Inter-American Development Bank, UN Development Programme.

Daly, Herman E. 1991. Sustainable growth: A bad oxymoron. *Grassroots Development* 15, no. 3: 39.

Daly, Herman E., and John B. Cobb, Jr. 1989. *For the common good: Redirecting the economy toward community, the environment, and a sustainable future.* Boston: Beacon Press.

Darmstadter, J. 1987. The role of policy in managing natural resource problems. In *Resources and World Development,* ed. D. J. McLaren and B. J. Skinner, 473–82. New York: John Wiley and Sons.

Davis, Kingsley, and Mikhail S. Bernstam, eds. 1991. *Resources, environment, and population: Present knowledge, future options.* New York: Oxford University Press.

De Boer, A. John. 1989. Sustainable approaches to hillside agricultural development. In *Environment and the poor: Development strategies for a common agenda,* ed. H. Jeffrey Leonard, 135–63. Washington, D.C.: World Bank.

Donkin, R. A. 1977. *Spanish red: An ethnogeographical study of cochineal and the Opuntia cactus.* Transactions of the American Philosophical Society, vol. 67, pt. 5. Philadelphia: American Philosophical Society.

Durham, William H. 1979. *Scarcity and survival in Central America: Ecological origins of the Soccer War.* Stanford, Calif.: Stanford University Press.

Fearnside, Philip M. 1989. Extractive reserves in Brazilian Amazonia. *BioScience* 39, no. 6 (June): 387–93.

————. 1990. The rate and extent of deforestation in Brazilian Amazonia. *Environmental Conservation* 17, no. 3 (Autumn): 213–26.

Fishlow, Albert, Carlos Diaz-Alejandro, Richard Fagen, and Roger Hansen. 1978. *Rich and poor nations in the world economy.* New York: McGraw-Hill.

Furtado, Celso. 1976. *The economic development of Latin America.* Cambridge: Cambridge University Press.

Gootenberg, Paul. 1991. *Between silver and guano.* Princeton: Princeton University Press.

Hansen, Roger D. 1979. *Beyond the North-South stalemate.* 1979. New York: McGraw-Hill.

Hemming, John. 1978. *Red gold: The conquest of the Brazilian Indians, 1500–1760.* Cambridge: Harvard University Press.

Holling, C. S. 1986. The resilience of terrestrial ecosystems: Local surprise and global change. In *Sustainable development of the biosphere,* ed. William Clark and R. E. Munn, 292–317. Cambridge: Cambridge University Press.

Inter-American Development Bank (IDB). 1991. *Economic and social progress in Latin America.* Washington, D.C.: IDB.

Larson, Brooke. 1988. *Colonial rule and agrarian transformation in Bolivia.* Princeton: Princeton University Press.

Latin American and Caribbean Commission on Development and the Environment. 1990. *Our Own Agenda.* Washington, D.C.: Inter-American Development Bank and UN Development Program.

Lele, S. M. 1991. Sustainable development: A critical review. *World Development* 19, no. 6: 607–21.

MacNeill, Jim, Pieter Winsemius, and Tazo Yakushiji. 1991. *Beyond interdependence: The meshing of the world's economy and the earth's ecology.* New York: Oxford University Press.

McNeely, Jeffrey A. 1988. *Economics and biological diversity: Developing and using economic incentives to conserve biological resources.* Gland, Switzerland: International Union for the Conservation of Nature and Natural Resources.

Meadows, Donella, Dennis Meadows, and Jorgen Randers. 1992. *Beyond the limits.* Post Mills, Vt.: Chelsea Green Publishers.

Merges, Robert P. 1988. Intellectual property in higher life forms: The patent system and controversial technologies. *Maryland Law Review* 47:1049, 1051–75.

Messerschmidt, Donald A. 1987. Conservation and society in Nepal: Traditional forest management and innovative development. In *Lands at risk in the Third World: Local-level perspectives,* ed. Peter D. Little and Michael M. Horowitz, with A. Endre Nyerges, 373–97. Boulder, Colo.: Westview Press.

National Research Council. 1992. *Dolphins and the tuna industry.* Washington, D.C.: National Academy Press.

Naylor, Robert A. 1989. *Penny-ante imperialism: The Mosquito Shore and the Bay of Honduras, 1600–1914.* New York: Fairleigh Dickinson Press.

Oldfield, Margery L., and Janis B. Alcorn. 1991. *Biodiversity: Culture, conservation, and ecodevelopment.* Boulder, Colo.: Westview Press.

O'Riordan, Timothy. 1988. The politics of sustainability. In R. Kerry Turner, ed., *Sustainable Environmental Management.* Boulder, Colo.: Westview Press.

Plotkin, Mark, and Lisa Famolare. 1990. *Marketing rainforest products.* Washington, D.C.: Island Press.

Redford, Kent H., and Steven E. Sanderson. 1992. The brief barren marriage of biodiversity and sustainability. *Bulletin of the Ecological Society of America.* Spring.

Saether, Bernt-Erik, and Bror Jonsson. 1991. Conservation biology faces reality. *Trends in Research in Ecology and Evolution* 6, no. 2 (February): 37–38.

Sanderson, Steven E. 1992. *The politics of trade in Latin American development.* Stanford, Calif.: Stanford University Press.

Smith, Peter. 1969. *Politics and beef in Argentina: Patterns of conflict and change.* New York: Columbia University Press.

Tucker, Compton J., Harold E. Dregne, and Wilbur W. Newcomb. 1991. Expansion and contraction of the Sahara Desert from 1980 to 1990. *Science* 253 (19 July): 299–301.

Turner, B.L. III, and William Meyer. 1992. *Global land use change,* Boulder, Colo.: UCAR.

Valentine, Mark. 1991. *An introductory guide to the Earth Summit.* San Francisco: U.S. Citizens Network on UNCED.

Western, David, and Mary Pearl, eds. 1989. *Conservation for the twenty-first century.* New York: Oxford University Press.

World Bank. 1989. *Striking a balance: The environmental challenge of development.* Washington, D.C.: World Bank.

World Bank. 1991. *Forest sector policy.* Washington, D.C.: World Bank.

World Bank. 1991a. *World development report.* Washington, D.C.: World Bank.

World Commission on Environment and Development (WCED). 1987. *Our common future.* New York: Oxford University Press.

World Resources Institute. 1991. *World resources, 1990–1991.* Washington, D.C.: World Resources Institute.

12 Environmental Politics in Asia

LOUIS SCHUBERT

Asia is home to an estimated 3.15 billion people, with more born every day. Asians, like the rest of the Earth's inhabitants, live in local ecosystems—ones that form their homes, life-support networks, and context of experience—as well as in the global ecosphere. The environment in Asia is in a rapidly growing state of crisis, much like the rest of the planet. The issues are familiar: deforestation, soil depletion, problems of water quality and quantity, loss of biodiversity, air pollution, toxic and nontoxic waste, and other problems.

Concern for the Asian environment should come from concern for the preservation and improvement of all life. Concern is the first step toward implementing a solution; the next step is the search for knowledge and understanding of the causes, effects and potential escapes from the vicious circle of destruction that too often characterizes the relationship between humans and the ecosphere. At all points, the potential of the Asian people to lead themselves out of the path to self-destruction is nascent.

The perception of environment in Asia contrasts with that predominantly held in the West, and special aspects of the environmental movement in Asia can in many ways be traced back to fundamental worldview differences. The various religious and philosophical traditions of Asia, whether Taoism, Buddhism, Hinduism, or animism, have cosmologies which differ radically from those of the West. At the great risk of oversimplifying several major world religions, it is fair to state that while the Judeo-Christian-Islamic traditions place great emphasis on a transcendent patriarchal deity, most Eastern religions look to divinity of and in nature. The dogma of domination characterized Western history through the subjugation of the environment and natural resources and increasing efficiency of the techniques of control by industrialism, science, and "rationalism."

The same search for mastery through instrumentalist science recently led the West to acknowledge the consequences of its quest for the domination of the environment: the destruction of the foundations on which human life and civilization are built. This has led to increased concern for the environment and calls for the protection of the fragile planet, even if definitive action on the part of those in power is slow or often blocked. Concern for the protection of the environment did not become a movement

239

in Asia at a similar stage of advanced technology industrialization, or what Rostow (1960) termed high mass consumption, but in developing and sometimes even pre-industrial economic contexts. Some anti-environmental biases in the West still hold that the preservation of the natural world is some sort of luxury good; resources can be squandered on protecting the environment only when they exist in surplus, and should be first to be sacrificed when economic times become difficult. Asia can afford no luxuries, but ecosystem viability is no extravagance.

Asia's present and historical environmental record is certainly not perfect, but the fundamental Asian orientation to nature is less a search for mastery than a search for survival and spiritual growth. For the purposes of this analysis of Asian environmental politics, industrial Japan and the former Soviet republics are not included. Many crimes against the Earth are committed daily on the world's largest continent; a discussion of the causes and effects, initiation and mitigation, follows.

ECOPOLITICS AT THE GRASS-ROOTS LEVEL

International pressures and national searches for sustainable development are important factors influencing the ecopolitical culture and the environmental movements in Asia, but the active heart of ecological concern is at the local level—what the West would call the "grass roots." Ecopolitical culture is composed of the historical, religious, political and spiritual elements combining to create cognitive, affective and evaluative orientations, to build on the variables of Almond and Verba's (1963) classic The Civic Culture, toward the relationship between the human and the natural environment.

What is known about the functioning of nature and ecology? This question includes not only "objective" scientific knowledge, but also a deeper understanding derived from a sense of life and existence in the world of nature. Cognition is a far broader concept than most scientists and economists are willing to accept. It follows that a more expansive and inclusive approach to the understanding of nature will lead to orientations of role in the ecological system. Such an understanding will also lead to evaluations of the success or failure of the component human and larger ecosystem relationship that are fundamentally different from the foreign value system of human exceptionalism and alienation from nature imported by colonial and neocolonial presences. In Asia, the "people's perception of their real environment takes the shape of the interpretations of individuals alien to those people's reality" (Vieira 1985, 23), an untenable situation.

A belief system such as Taoism or Hinduism can be valuable in this regard. The affective variable refers to the level of inclusion as part of nature experienced by the people. Are humans totally part of nature or completely alienated from it, or at some point in between? Humans have ample evidence of their capacity to damage the world, while contrary positive experience is comparatively lacking. Evaluative orientations are how people judge their ecopolitical situations, especially the effectiveness of political leadership in safeguarding the biological future. These overlap with more orthodox notions of political culture wherein people's orientations toward their ability to affect change and participate in the political arena are examined.

If a greater reverence toward nature on the Asian continent than in the West is implied, how does one account for the tremendous devastation of the environment wreaked on Asia? The favorite response of Western "development" experts is population pressures. Following Commoner's Law of Ecology (Commoner 1971), however, everything is connected to everything else. Asia is part of a world economy where its historic role has been as supplier of cheap labor and natural resources, making large populations an asset; the destruction of the environment is the activity that brings in the monetary income whose necessity is dictated by the foreign economic system. As traditional landownership was usurped by colonial powers and subsequent national central governments, the people were subsequently forced off land—land converted to cash crop agriculture or commercial forestry—and into city slums or onto marginal land. Distributions of income, natural resource access and power are inequitable, causing already nasty cycles of poverty to become seemingly inescapable. Survival was attempted through destruction of the means of survival. Lastly, the ubiquitous factor of human nature must be recognized. Laden with passions and fears, it has a need for security and a need for a sense of self-importance.

The popular Green slogan "act locally, think globally" remains the most important philosophical and political guideline for environmental protection. Asia's strength is in its people; the people must be the source for change to a sustainable relationship between humans and the rest of the ecology. In nation after nation across Asia, the primary impetus for environmental protection and nature conservation has come from the thousands of environmental nongovernmental organizations (NGOs) across Asia, which are often grass-roots movements of people concerned about specific conditions in local ecosystems, but also include national- and international-level organizations. The participation of large numbers of people in the environmental movement is its democratic power and driving force.

The national governments in Asia have all, to varying degrees, made significant policy decisions to promote environmental protection. Often they have been written into national constitutions or fundamental laws, such as in the Philippines or Malaysia. Still, serious problems exist in all stages of the process. Good intentions are important, but must be backed up with sufficient funding, human resource training, and effective enforcement. Failures of national governments in Asia (or the North, for that matter) to live up to promises of environmental protection arise from complex political and economic pressures. In local, national, or international corridors of power, elites feel that their status and wealth are threatened by more ecologically friendly forms of production.

A necessary logical step in determining the politics of the environment is asking, "Who gains?" and "Who loses?" in the greening of the economic system. The primary concern of the environmental movement is nature itself and its indigenous inhabitants, both human and nonhuman; the primary concern of the status quo is the exploitation of natural resources and human labor for the benefit of a powerful few. Resistance to environmental protection is concentrated among those in the consumptive elites, as well as their loyalists, who stand to lose their considerable power and income if a sustainable economy, which allows for the long-term survival of the planet, is implemented. Each small step to the goal of sustainability is a threat to business as usual. Changing the status quo is perhaps the toughest challenge to Asian environmentalism.

In addition to themes of ecopolitical culture, the intrusive effects of the world economic system (and its earlier incarnation, colonialism), and the difficulties in implementing environmental policy, the critical fulcrum of people power in Asian politics cannot be undervalued. Key to the ability of the inhabitants of the continent to act and move for the protection of the environment is access to power in the political system. The insufficiency of resources available to most policymakers in Asian nations calls for, even necessitates, the active inclusion of NGOs in policy formulation, enactment and enforcement. Democratic participation, through both formal and informal channels, is important not only to the interest articulation phase of the policy-making process, but to all aspects of environmental protection. The thousands of environmental groups throughout Asia have network access to research on scientific and human information. Governments and international agencies may often derive their information from biased sources such as the polluting industries responsible for much environmental degradation, while membership roles of these NGOs are made up of activists willing to provide services to protect the environment based on intimate local understandings of the regions and ecosystems involved. Lastly, one of the greatest human resource gaps in governmental environmental politics is in insufficient enforcement personnel; in this area, local people can be watchdogs for the environment, much in the same way they now employ access to the courts to bring action against ecological criminals.

ECOPOLITICAL CULTURE: COGNITIVE TRADITIONS IN HUMAN ECOSYSTEM RELATIONS

As mentioned above, the traditional religious and philosophical systems extant in Asia maintain an alternative perspective on the relationship between the environment and its human inhabitants. Cognitive orientations towards the environment are rooted in historical belief-systems. A treatment of the environmental or nature components in even just the major Asian belief-systems would fill volumes, and will not be undertaken here. Having a significantly different emphasis than Western religions, Asian beliefs have concentrated not only on the question of how humans should live with each other, but also how they should live together with the whole of nature.

In Hinduism, the "modern" concept of the interconnectivity of the various living and nonliving elements of nature has been long understood. It posits a worldview in which humans and nature are part of an indivisible whole (Vieira 1985, 11). Across the Hindu landscape, trees, rocks, animals and rivers are respected as dwellings of the divine, and religious taboos have prevented the overexploitation of nature (Rush 1991, 11). In Taoism, all living things are worthy of equal respect, so that "the best form of environmental management from a Taoist viewpoint is nonintervention (wu-wei) in the natural course of the life cycle" (Vieira 1985, 11). Buddhism has followed a similar concept, as evidenced by the words of Buddha himself:

> The forest is a peculiar organism of unlimited
> Kindness and benevolence that makes no demands
> For its sustenance and extends generously
> The products of its life activity; it affords
> Protection to all beings, offering shade even
> To the axman who destroys it.
> (Quoted in Bene, Beall and Cote 1977, 1)

In a foreshadowing of modern conservation schemes, Buddha asked his followers to plant trees (Panday 1987, 239). Confucianism was more concerned with political and social relationships based on landownership than the relationship with nature, but it too talked about a level of respect for the environment. "China's religious and philosophical traditions stressed the need for man to live in harmony with nature and be careful not to upset the delicate forces that sustained civilization" (Ross and Silk 1987, 1).

It is important to remember that these traditions are only "indicators of tendencies toward a certain pattern of behavior of both people and government" (Vieira 1985, 11). In some areas, traditional relationships with nature remain, such as in Laos (Rainer and Herman 1991, 87) or Papua New Guinea (Panayotou 1991, 113). In the majority of Asia, however, traditional patterns were disrupted or completely destroyed by the invasion of the European colonial powers and the subsequent integration of the area into the world economy. The Europeans refused to accept traditional communal patterns of landownership and farming methods, as they could not be integrated into the colonial political economy (Hurst 1990, 247). Another example is the understanding of the role of trees and forests, which though "formerly viewed as part of a state of nature are now seen as social property to be husbanded as part of a national patrimony" (Riddell 1987, 11).

AFFECTIVE ROLES AND PARTICIPATION IN ASIAN ECOPOLITICAL CULTURE

The feelings of alienation and detachment promulgated by the various political systems, notwithstanding significant variation, can be traced to a recent and/or continuing lack of democratic traditions and an overall trend to a subject culture. While great strides have been made toward a more participatory polity, the colonialism of the recent past and the tendency to authoritarian style of government in the present have severely dampened the possibilities of the Asian peoples to affect the change they can see as necessary for the long-term survival of their local ecosystems. From India and Nepal on the subcontinent to the peninsular and archipelago nations of Malaysia and Indonesia, most of the energy for environmental protection seems to come from NGOs, demonstrating that citizen concern and activity is finding its outlets, only not through the state except as part of such interest groups (see Dean 1983). Momentum from groups such as India's Chipko Andolan movement (Rush 1991, 56–58), Malaysia's Sahabat Alam Malaysia (Friends of the Earth, Malaysia) (Hurst 1990, 73), the Thai Project for Ecological Recovery (PER) (Rush 1991, 74–76), and the Philippines's Lingkod Tao-Kalikasan-Philippines (Secretariat for an Ecologically Sound Philippines) drive the protection of the environment forward.

The political and (especially) economic systems in Asia are the outgrowth of previous colonialism. Colonial laws "reflected a Western concept of land ownership and political control: land ownership was the root of Western wealth" (Hurst 1990, 245). As colonies were conquered in order to provide economic wealth for their foreign invaders, traditional economies were disregarded and often actively repressed. Whereas areas such as forests were undeniably very productive for the local inhabitants, they did not create wealth in the manner necessary for Western accounting practices, as seen in the British Empire's approach to the timber resources in India. This led to the imposition of resource control more amenable to the financial needs of the colonial powers (Dove 1987, 268; Hurst 1990, 247).

After political independence from European control, the nations of Asia found that

> concepts and categories about economic development and natural resource utilization that had emerged in the specific context of industrialization and capitalist growth in a center of colonial power were raised to the level of universal assumptions and applicability in the entirely different context of the need to satisfy basic needs for the people of the newly independent Third World countries. (Shiva 1990, 189–90)

The patterns of both human and nonhuman resource exploitation underwent only superficial change from the colonial period to the integration of the newly independent nations into the international economic system. The artificially cultured requirement of industrial development, staggering debt loads, and the erosion of traditional life-styles and values exacerbated environmental degradation as automobiles, nuclear power plants and commercial lumbering proliferated across the Asian continent.

While many traditional societies had built-in safety systems to protect the environment through customs and taboos (Rush 1991, 55), these were removed by the globalization and alienation of indigenous cultures. Traditional resources such as energy from twigs or dung did not match Western measurement systems and were disregarded as a result (Smil and Knowland 1980; Laird and Haas 1980), a pattern which repeats itself in many other areas, such as communal land tenure and swidden agriculture (Hurst 1990, 245–47; Shiva 1990, 191). Even after colonial exploitation gave way to independent "development" in former British India, French Indochina, Dutch Indonesia, or the American Philippines, the essential patterns of nonindigenous centralized control continued to push to feed the consumptive demands of the world capitalist economic system at the cost of severe environmental destruction (Shiva 1990, 189–90).

As previously alluded to, the primary cause of the environmental problems in Asia is usually identified as the massive expansion in population. More people require more food and more space to live on, with that land being found in increasingly marginal areas—on steeper slopes, in swamps, and in half-desertified areas. Such reasoning is accurate only to the point of examining superficial and immediate factors. While discounting the population issue would be naïve, so would be attempting to use it as the scapegoat for the deprivations inflicted by capitalist "development" and the concentration of wealth among national and international elites. While it is true that poverty reinforces the degradation of an already stressed environment, microeconomic analysis fails to allocate the actual costs of "development," the "externalities" of which are customarily dumped on the poor (Desai 1991, 18). While the poor do unintentionally degrade the environment when forced onto small plots of land and into slums and rain forests (Vieira 1985, 19), it is considerably more useful to analyze the causes of that population dislocation. It is slowly being accepted that cash crop expansion and the concentration of high-quality agricultural land into the property of an elite minority has been a major contributor to the serious desecration of tropical forests by displaced, shifted or landless farmers (Hurst 1990, 248). Familiar examples of this can be found in Thailand, Indonesia and Papua New Guinea.

Orthodox developmental studies will often begin with the presentation of the demographic transition model, wherein the population explosion is attributed to the introduction of modern medicine and hygiene. The gap between birth and death rates in the North narrowed dramatically after industrialization, but has yet to do so in the South as a result of the inequitable distribution of the benefits of "development." The common response has been to fault the people for their own drive to survive. "The new wave of blaming people for environmental destruction in general, and deforestation in particular, arises from agencies like the WRI [World Resources Institute] and World Bank and FAO [Food and Agriculture Organization of the United Nations] to legitimize and facilitate the transfer of resource control and forest management from local people to the state, from Third World countries to pseudo-experts in international aid agencies in the North" (Shiva 1987, 25). The clearance of rain forests clearly has less to do with population expansion and more to do with the politics and economics of colonial and postcolonial state administration (Hurst 1990, 245). Indigenous peoples have had their land, rights and lives taken from them (Johnson 1991, 17), and now are blamed by "development" technocrats for causing their own predicament. It is worth noting that the poorest of the poor, and often the most powerless of a society, the women, are the hardest hit (Nelson 1990, 184).

THE SEARCH FOR SOLUTIONS

The governments of Asia cannot be accused of ignoring the environment and its problematic relationship with its human component. Laws, policies and regulations abound. The criticism of state efforts to protect the environment come once the level of good intentions, which abound, are juxtaposed with the needs of this most demanding of political issues. All governments must prioritize their efforts, usually based on complicated and country-specific formulas of political, fiscal and economic pressures and constraints. No respectable official or bureaucrat should be faulted for attempting to do his or her best in a system weighted against the changes necessary for long-term ecosystem viability. Still, a great many of those in government and entrusted with protecting the environment are guilty of corruption, of taking pay-offs from polluters and resource exploiters, and of political expediency. Local politicians want development to bring prestige and financial resources; they do not want efficiency or conservation, which have little glamour (Dagra et al. 1990, 16).

Across the Asian continent, national governments have been active in creating a wide variety of environmental policies, often contemporaneously with their Western counterparts. After the 1972 United Nations Conference on the Environment in Stockholm, policymakers across the globe began to address seriously the need for environmental protection. By the early 1980s most countries had enacted some form of comprehensive environmental legislation, for example, Thailand in 1975, South Korea in 1977, and Indonesia in 1981 (Vieira 1985, 56), as well as the People's Republic of China in 1979 (Qu and Li 1984, 11–12). After the fall of the Marcos regime in the Philippines, the new constitution, ratified by the people on 2 February 1987, specifically incorporated the recognition of environmental issues, "linking the better use of natural resources to the goals of expanded productivity, sustainability and equity through open democratic processes and distributive justice" (World Bank 1989, xi). Traditional understandings were included, as evidenced by Article 2, section 16, which reads: "The state shall protect and advance the right of all of the people to a balanced and healthful ecology in accord with the rhythm and harmony of nature" (quoted in World Bank 1989, 47). The goals of development were seen in the context of ecological sustainability, as demonstrated in the 1968–69 five-year plan of India (Desai 1991, 16; Dantwala and Barmeda 1985, 54) or in the expansion of Indonesia's 1978 Environmental Impact Assessment (EIA) program to requirement status for all development project feasibility studies (Krasryno et al. 1991, 161). Each nation has its own environmental protection programs, a mere listing of which would fill volumes.

As in the West, environmental policy came first as a response to the ravages of pollution, which necessitated government intervention to protect public health (Vieira 1985, 4). Still, laws and regulations dealing with the environment go further back; in the case of China, conservation laws date back to the Q'in dynasty of 221–206 B.C.E. (Ross and Silk 1987, 1). The problem arises when policy goals and practical considerations diverge, such as with Thailand's well-intentioned policy that 40 percent of the surface area of the nation be held under forest cover, when only 29 percent remains so (Arbhabhirama et al. 1988, 411). Even in the nation with perhaps the greatest environmental damage in the region, China, the government gives lip service to the idea of environmental protection; Premier Li Peng states that development cannot destroy the basis of future existence (Ross and Silk 1987, 35). China's unexpected, but welcome, actions at the 1992 United Nations Conference on Environment and Development in Rio de Janeiro, particularly its willingness to sign a global warming agreement and a biological diversity pact, may, however, signal a new attitude in Beijing towards environmental protection.

Politics is always the balancing of forces, some with loud and powerful voices, some quiet and unheard, and even some yet to be born. Political pragmatism calls for listening to the economically powerful, although this is frequently counter to environmental policies. What results is an "implementation gap" (Ascher and Healy 1990, 3) between public expectations and government technical, fiscal, and political capability (Ganapin 1991, 261). Much of this stems from organizational issues such as inappropriate mandates, limited fiscal resources, and insufficient personnel (World Bank 1989, xi). Administrative structures and procedures can often block policy implementation (Greenland 1983, 9; Arbhabhirama et al. 1988, 414). It is worth noting that such problems are more administrative than substantial, and are quite able to be remedied (Ascher and Healy 1990, 13). Problems within bureaucracies are not limited to the national level, but are equally prevalent in international organizations, with the World Bank being a prime example (Hurst 1990, 256, 261). The concerns of Western governments are also based on self-interest in global issues such as the greenhouse effect, rather than local issues, again diverting attention to the concerns of international and centralized technocratic elites (Hurtado 1990, 12).

The most noticeable gap is between regulation and enforcement (Halter 1991, 242; Dagra et al. 1990, 16). Environmental departments and bureaus are seen as hindrances to economic expansion and possess little clout in power hierarchies. Responsibility for environmental protection is normally distributed over dozens of agencies in several departments, usually agriculture, development, forestry, fishing, population and, of course, environment. Some nations have endeavored to unify environmental authority, such as Singapore in 1983 (Chia and Chion 1987, 111 and 161), although this remains unusual. Besides shortages of prestige and political clout, there are shortcomings in availability of trained enforcement officers, environmental researchers, and lawyers to bring environmental criminals to trial. While awkward for governments to acknowledge, NGOs in various nations have already begun to assume some of these tasks (see Ascher and Healy 1991).

Environmental NGOs that have made a significant impact in this area include the Indonesian Environmental Forum (WAHLI) and the Environmental Protection Society of Malaysia (EPSM), among many others. It would be sensible to integrate NGOs further into the environmental protection process, while making certain to preserve their independent influence.

WHAT CAN BE DONE?

The issues and impediments are relatively straightforward. The more interesting question remains the solution. As already explained, the focal point of the salvation of the Asian ecosystems is the people. The victims of "development" and colonialism have a real knowledge of the environment they inhabit, a knowledge that has been ignored or suppressed by centralized or foreign technocrats. The citizens of Asia have created a vast array of thousands of organizations to address the environmental concerns to which government attention has been inadequate. These groups appear as national branches of international NGOs, such as the World Wildlife Fund-India, indigenous national groups, for instance the Philippine Green Forum, and local groups such as the Bombay Environmental Action Group. This democratic, or at least pluralistic, approach has already made significant headway and is quickly growing in its effectiveness in dealing with the issues at hand. While solutions are certainly as myriad as the problems, a few possibilities will be discussed here. Besides the greater involvement of NGOs, localization, decentralization, indigenous knowledge, appropriateness, and a reexamination of foreign concepts of "development" and "progress" are advocated.

Nongovernmental organizations, even environmentally oriented ones, are not a new phenomenon to Asia. In India they predate independence and even colonialism (Rush 1991, 55–56; Desai 1991, 16). A tradition of social action will enhance the effectiveness of NGOs in the political arena (Rush 1991, 58). NGOs are becoming more acceptable to national governments strapped for the resources to effect policy decisions (World Bank 1989, 54). "Although most environmental ministers would be loathe to admit it, the increasingly vocal environmental lobby is helping their case" (Dagra et al. 1990, 16). The growing importance of NGOs does, however, carry with it some dangers, such as the loss of independence (World Bank 1989, 54) or being used by environmental polluters for political and economic purposes (Ganapin 1991, 261).

A central area in which environmental groups are important is in the gathering and dissemination of information about the state of the environment. NGOs carry on research that limited state budgets often cannot afford; an example is the work of the Bangladesh Centre of Advanced Studies (Rush 1991, 65). For more details, the reader is encouraged to examine Anna de Soledad Vieira's comprehensive book Environmental Information in Developing Nations (1985). NGOs are taking responsibility for the spreading of public information, and they help build ecology curricula in schools (Vieira 1985, 58). As Taylor et al. in an earlier chapter in this book showed, women are often major participants, especially at the local level, where their direct ties to the living environment yield a deeper knowledge (see also Nelson 1990, 184–85). The education of women also plays the pivotal role in the possibilities of birth control to restrict population growth. There remains the potential for struggle over information, for in most countries the government controls the media (Vieira 1985, 60 and 72). Still, the urgent need for truthful information on the environment may best be served by NGOs rather than governments or international aid agencies, which frequently rely on industry self-reporting for their data (Hurst 1990, 255).

It becomes clear that a democratic system is crucial to the protection of the environment. Authoritarian governments are normally reluctant to acknowledge substantive problems with command rule (Halter 1991, 233). An examination of the environmental problems of the People's Republic of China reveals monumental environmental destruction in a nation where criticizing pollution is a heretical attack on the state. If democracy is key to ecology, then China can be viewed as a large negative example (for more on China, see Ross 1987 and Ross and Silk 1987). Nationalization of land in Nepal led to devastation, until attempts to revert to community orientations stemmed the tide somewhat (Panday 1987, 241). The recent examples of environmental groups being the first to speak out against authoritarian ecocide in Eastern Europe and the former Soviet Union further exemplify the connection between ecology and democracy. In Asia, nations with high levels of democratic participation, such as India or Malaysia, tend to have stronger environmental protection policies. Environmental movements thrive best in a polyarchical system (see Dean 1983), where they can do the most good. Alluding to tenets of Buddhism, Hardoy and Satterwaite say, "governments and agencies, politicians and technocrats should have the humility to learn from the people themselves" (1985, 202).

A significant part of the environmental problem has been political control from distant national capitals or world trade centers lacking understanding of local conditions. This must be reversed. Centralization causes decisions to be made without the intimate knowledge of concerned areas (Ascher and Healy 1990, 13). The trend toward increased centralized control only reinforces the domination by distant metropolises as it politically weakens regional and local areas (Hardoy and Satterwaite 1985, 175). The need to regionalize and localize to create sustainable livelihoods has become well-recognized (Desai 1991, 19; World Bank 1989, 65; Arbhabhirama et al. 1988, 420). In India, for example, programs to help develop areas with many poor—such as the state of Maharashtra's employment guarantee system involving conservation, irrigation and afforestation, or Rajasthan's Antyodaya ("redemption of the last and lowest") to give over 150,000 families income-yielding assets such as sheep, pumps, and looms (Krisna 1980, 84)—are contained in state-level control policies (Dantwala and Barmeda 1985, 61). Decentralization is not a panacea to environmental problems and requires concurrent changes in patterns of administration and law (World Bank 1989, xii), but it is a critical step to sustainable life with ecosystem viability.

Fundamental changes in "business as usual" are required for the long-term, or possibly even the short-term, survival of the Asian environment and its human inhabitants. Land reform must take place to allow the people to sustain themselves (Hurst 1990, 270). Democratization must continue to empower citizens and local governments to control their own ecosystems for the future. Economic accounting must carefully consider the full costs of development, not regard the environment as an externality (Desai 1991, 20). The world trade system needs to lower tariffs so that farmers can have fair access to markets for surplus production and debtor nations can work on paying off debt (Hurst 1990, 251). Proposed solutions abound, some people-oriented, some just renaming bad policies of the past. Disentangling the two is difficult, but if a guideline examining the results in terms of local people and ecosystems is used, fairness can be reached.

Rather than attempt to analyze the merits and demerits of the dozens of proposals for reform, it may be more useful to approach the underlying themes of "development" that brought about the situation seen today. The word "development" has been in quotation marks throughout this chapter, for in its common usage it is doublespeak. The intended purpose of the development of Asia, and the world in general, is to improve the conditions of life for all people. The consumptive character of the dominant model of development, however, requires it to attack the environmental basis on which it rests, to the point that its continued viability is in serious question. This is not to imply that economic progress is a negative thing, only that its appropriateness and distribution leave much to be desired. In refutation of the Luddites, technology has made life better, to some degree, for most of the globe's inhabitants. However, it has also caused tremendous damage to the ecosphere that supports all life and, if continued unchecked, is demonstrably suicidal.

How does one use the fruits of advancing knowledge to benefit the people, including the most deprived? The answer lies in appropriateness.

Massive agricultural projects that destroy rain forests or virgin lands displace more people than they can feed over the long term. Petrochemicals make life more convenient for many, but leave a toxic trail behind them from production to disposal. Drift nets allow for the most efficient harvest of the oceans, however, they leave behind devastated fisheries. The intentions may be good, but the consequences are not thought out.

Arrogance regarding the supposed superiority of foreign ideas and technologies does not help. The world is not a homogenous mass; each region, each locality, has unique needs. A major new movement is the spread of appropriate technology. Small stoves can do more to provide for rural energy needs than nuclear power plants. Traditional labor-intensive agriculture can produce food just as well as fields drenched in fertilizers and pesticides, while at the same time providing much-needed jobs and a bottom-up approach to development (Repetto 1985, 159 and 162–63). Solar energy is discouraged for no reason except that it threatens the massive power of the oil merchants. The people of Asia have inhabited the region for millennia, and have been in complex social organizations or civilizations for millennia. The sudden arrival of distant colonialists and scientists should not lead to the replacement of indigenous knowledge of ecosystems and food. Instead, new knowledge should be allowed to enhance what is traditional, and not consume cultures as it does forests. Elements such as customary law should be integrated into modern legal and property relations (Sajise 1987, 274). An important first step is the tailoring of development programs to the unique needs of each nation. India, for instance, is seen as a model of economic viability through an indigenous cultural model of development (Vieira 1985, 52).

The "progress" of Western civilization has brought with it a strong alienation from nature. Whether this alienation began with the introduction of the patriarchal god or the steam engine does not affect its dire consequences. Traditional Asian worldviews and value systems incorporating nature into the meaning of life are not lost and can be central to the solution of the environmental problems there. Furthermore, if the humility to listen to the "underdeveloped" can be found, valuable lessons for the West can be learned as well.

CONCLUSION

This chapter has examined the great strength of Asia: its people, who alone can be the saviors of an environment ravaged by factors beyond local control or experience. The ecopolitical culture of Asia is not based on the delusion of human exceptionalism that has caused the alienation from nature rampant in the West. Through continuing democratization, the inhabitants of the world's largest and most populous continent can empower themselves and achieve a sustainable future, with sufficient food, water and housing for everyone and continued spiritual growth. Devolving responsibility and control to the local ecosystem level is critical to reach sustainability, although the global context cannot be ignored. The world economic system constantly intrudes, bringing chain saws, toxic waste, and debt collectors. By securing local control, Asians can reclaim their habitats.

The king of Bhutan, a tiny Himalayan kingdom, was asked about the low level of development in his nation. He responded that what was important was not gross national product, but rather gross national happiness. By that measure, his people were rich beyond measure. The progress of the human species has brought with it many wonders and many terrors. Much of what ingenuity has created is appropriate for a certain culture at a certain time in its development, and can be fatally wrong otherwise. Only those closest to the specific site and ecosystem can truly know what is beneficial and what is harmful. If the grand process of development is for the improvement of human life, the supposed beneficiaries deserve some say in their futures. For the continued well-being of each ecological region, and the planet as a whole, such participation must be required in all policy decisions.

REFERENCES

Almond, Gabriel A., and Sidney Verba. 1963. *The civic culture*. Princeton: Princeton University Press.

Arbhabhirama, Anat, Dhira Phantumvanit, John Elkington and Phaiton Ingkasuwan. 1988. *Thailand natural resources profile*. Oxford and New York: Oxford University Press.

Ascher, William, and Robert Healy. 1990. *Natural resource policymaking in developing countries*. Durham, N.C. and London: Duke University Press.

Bene, J. G., H. W. Beall, and A. Cote. 1977. *Trees, food, and the people*. Ottawa: International Development Research Centre.

Commoner, Barry. 1971. *The closing circle*. New York: Knopf.

Dagra, Bharat, Ben Davies, Mary Farquharson, and Pamela Hapsari. 1990. Rules for flouting. *South*, no. 116 (June).

Dantwala, M. L., and J. N. Barmeda. 1985. Rural Development. In *Public policy and policy analysis in India*, ed. R. S. Ganapathy, S. R. Ganesh, Rushikesh M. Maru, Samuel Paul and Ram Mohan Rao. New Delhi, Beverly Hills and London: Sage Publications.

Dean, James W. Polyarchy and economic growth. 1983. In *The political economy of growth*, ed. Dennis C. Mueller. New Haven: Yale University Press.

Desai, Nitin. 1991. A development planner looks at environmental management. In *Environmental management in developing countries,* ed. Denizhan Erocal. Paris: Development Centre of the OECD.

Dobson, Andrew. 1990. *Green political thought.* London and Boston: Unwin Hyman.

Dove, Michael R. 1987. The perception of peasant land rights in Indonesian development: Causes and implications. In *Land, trees and tenure,* ed. John B. Raintree. Nairobi and Madison, Wis.: ICRAF and the Land Tenure Center.

Ganapin, Delfin J. 1991. Effective environmental regulation: The case of the Philippines. In *Environmental management in developing countries,* ed. Denizhan Erocal. Paris: Development Centre of the OECD.

Geping, Qu, and Li Jinchang. 1984. Environmental management. In *Managing the environment in China,* ed. Qu Geping and Woyen Lee. Dublin: Tycooly International.

Greenland, David. 1983. *Guidelines for modern resource management.* Columbus, Ohio: Charles E. Merrill.

Halter, Faith. 1991. Toward more effective environmental regulation in developing countries. In *Environmental management in developing countries,* ed. Denizhan Erocal. Paris: Development Centre of the OECD.

Hardoy, Jorge E., and David E. Satterwaite. 1985. Third World cities and the environment of poverty. In *The global possible,* ed. Robert Repetto. New Haven: Yale University Press.

Hurst, Philip. 1990. *Rainforest politics.* London: Zed Books.

Hurtado, Maria Elena. 1990. Growth up in smoke? *South,* no. 116 (June).

Johnson, Brian. 1991. *Responding to tropical deforestation.* Washington D.C.: World Wildlife Federation.

Kasryno, Faisal, Ning Pribadi, Achmad Suryana, and Jamil Musanif. 1991. Environmental management in Indonesian agricultural development. In *Environmental management in developing countries,* ed. Denizhan Erocal. Paris: Development Centre of the OECD.

Krisna, Raj. 1980. The economic development of India. In *Economic development: A "Scientific American" book.* San Francisco: W. H. Freeman.

Laird, Frank, and Peter Haas. 1980. *Energy efficiency as environmental protection: Firewood in the Third World.* Cambridge: MIT Center for International Studies.

Nelson, Lin. 1990. The place of women in polluted places. In *Reweaving the World,* ed. Irene Diamond and Gloria Feman Orenstein. San Francisco: Sierra Club Books.

Panayotou, Theodore. 1991. Economic incentives in environmental management and their relevance to developing countries. In *Environmental management in developing countries,* ed. Denizhan Erocal. Paris: Development Centre of the OECD.

Panday, K. K. 1987. Some tenurial aspects of environmental problems in Nepal. In *Land, trees and tenure,* ed. John B. Raintree. Nairobi and Madison, Wis.: ICRAF and the Land Tenure Center.

Rainer, Chris, and Jay Herman. 1991. The Laotian chronicles. *Buzzworm* 3, no. 2 (March/April).

Repetto, Robert. 1985. Population, resource pressures and poverty. In *The global possible*, ed. Robert Repetto. New Haven: Yale University Press.

Riddell, James C. 1987. Land tenure and agroforestry: A regional overview. In *Land, trees and tenure*, ed. John B. Raintree. Nairobi and Madison, Wis.: ICRAF and the Land Tenure Center.

Ross, Lester. 1987. Environmental policy in post-Mao China. In *Environment* 29, no. 4 (May).

Ross, Lester, and Mitchell A. Silk. 1987. *Environmental law and policy in the People's Republic of China.* New York: Quorum Books.

Rostow, Walt W. 1960. *The stages of economic growth: A non-Communist manifesto.* Cambridge: Cambridge University Press.

Rush, James. 1991. *The last tree.* New York: Asia Society.

Sajise, Percy E. 1987. Agroforestry and land tenure issues in the Philippines. In *Land, trees and tenure,* ed. John B. Raintree. Nairobi and Madison, Wis.: ICRAF and the Land Tenure Center.

Shiva, Vandana. 1987. *Forestry crisis and forestry myths.* Penang: Rainforest Movement.

————. 1990. Development as a new project of Western patriarchy. In *Reweaving the World,* ed. Irene Diamond and Gloria Feman Orenstein. San Francisco: Sierra Club Books.

Sien, Chia Lin, and Chionh Yan Huay. 1987. Singapore. In *Environmental management in Southeast Asia,* ed. Chia Lin Sien. Singapore: Faculty of Science, National University of Singapore.

Smil, Vaclav, and William E. Knowland. 1980. Energy in the developing world. In *Energy in the developing world,* ed. Vaclav Smil and William E. Knowland. Oxford and New York: Oxford University Press.

Vieira, Anna da Soledad. 1985. *Environmental information in developing nations.* Westport, Conn.: Greenwood Press.

The World Bank. 1989. *Philippines: Environment and natural resource management study.* Washington, D.C.

CONCLUSION

Environmental Challenges in a Global Context

JAMES N. ROSENAU

While the preceding chapters plainly reveal the enormous complexity inherent in the links between the dynamics of the environment and those of world politics, it is useful to conclude the volume with an enumeration of several aspects of the subject that stand out as simple and unquestionable features of the global context in which environmental issues arise and persist. The list is not long—since the various causal processes identified in the previous essays are so highly interactive as to intrude complexity into virtually every corner of the world—but at least four contextual factors can be discerned that are easily grasped and that undergird all the dynamics at work on a local, national, and global scale.

THE SCIENTIFIC CONTEXT

Notwithstanding the ever-increasing degrees of complexity that distinguish the post-industrial era in all walks of life and at every level of politics, environmental issues are perhaps more fully pervaded by technical and complicated dimensions than any other type of issues on the global agenda. Rooted in the processes of nature and the responses of nature to human intervention, environmental issues are inescapably embedded in a scientific context. Unlike economic, educational, housing, labor or other conventional foci of controversy, the outcomes of environmental issues are located in the ups and downs of nonhuman processes rather than the behavior of people. What people do or fail to do, of course, shapes nature's processes, but ultimately nature's processes adhere to their own laws and not to those of organized society. Consequently, as such, they give rise to objective outcomes in the sense that what happens is not vulnerable to the vagaries of motivation, chance encounters, institutional lapses, or any of the other

257

uncertainties that attach to social dynamics. One can specify varying human inputs and hypothesize as to the corresponding outputs of nature they stimulate, but the accuracy of the hypotheses will depend on one's grasp of how nature operates, that is, on how the nonhuman components embraced by the hypotheses interact. In short, environmental issues may be rife with uncertainties, but these derive as much from the mysteries of nature as from the variability of human affairs.

Thus it is that environmental issues turn centrally on the scientific method and its applications. Politicians cannot exercise control over environmental outcomes without recourse to scientific findings. They may claim that the findings are not clear-cut or remain subject to contradictory interpretations, but they are nonetheless dependent on what the practices of science uncover about the laws of nature.

It follows that criteria of proof are at the heart of environmental politics, that the outcomes of environmental issues depend as much on the persuasiveness of evidence as on the various criteria of power—superior resources, greater mass support, skill at coalition formation—that sustain or resolve other types of issues. To be sure, the exercise of power is not irrelevant to the conduct of environmental politics, and it is surely the case that deft politicians can manipulate support in favor of one or another environmental policy, but ultimately the outcomes will be shaped by the proofs that are brought to bear on the dictates of nature.[1] Development-minded groups can argue for the exploitation of nature for only so long if that exploitation continues to lead to discernible and measurable deterioration; at some point the data become too telling to ignore and interest-group politics is compelled to yield ground to the politics of science. How long it takes for nature to unfold in these ways and for the findings to force change in the conduct of politics is, of course, an open question. Indeed, it is itself a political question that serves as another contextual factor worthy of notation.

THE TEMPORAL CONTEXT

One obvious characteristic that attaches to environmental issues wherever and whenever they arise derives from the fact that the changes and threats posed by the uses and abuses of the environment normally evolve in small increments across long stretches of time. Leaving aside for the moment large-scale disasters, a preponderance of the world's environmental challenges involve cumulative processes that, in the absence of corrective measures, are likely to be increasingly detrimental over the long term. As a result, environmental politics tends to be organized around a continuous struggle between the few experts who recognize the need for corrective measures to offset the long-term dangers and the many producers, consumers, and citizens who are concerned with maximizing short-term gains and minimizing short-term losses. That is, more often than not, the political processes of communities and nations are loaded against the long-run. People and politicians readily reason that long-term outcomes are too uncertain and too distant to worry about when the current scene is so pervaded with immediate needs and difficulties. So the impulse to avoid hard choices and postpone action is deeply embedded in the structure of environmental politics. All concerned are aware that their generation will be followed by others, that their children will grow and come to have children, but somehow the problems of future grandchildren seem minimal compared to those that beset people seeking to preserve or improve their welfare today.

It follows that in addition to its scientific foundations, the politics of the environment is by its very nature temporally different from the politics of the economy, the politics of governance, or the politics of agriculture. The collapse of a stock market, the ouster of a regime, or the failure of a crop is, so to speak, an instantaneous event with enormous and obvious immediate consequences that cannot be ignored, that requires unqualified responses, and that quickly comes to dominate the concerns, headlines, and agenda of the day. Environmental developments, on the other hand, are easily relegated to peripheral status. With the rare exception of when they connote disaster (see below), such developments do not pose a need for instant reactions, altered policies, or restless preoccupation. Usually, they are developments in the sense that a government agency has issued a report or a nongovernmental organization has called attention to an ominous trend—events which neither capture headlines nor evoke efforts to place their implications high on the relevant agenda. Only as interest groups keep environmental issues alive, therefore, do they come before the public. Otherwise their long-term horizons consign them to short-term oblivion.

Politicians and publics anxious to protect or enhance the quality of the environment are thus destined to be involved in an uphill struggle. Using tentative findings, they face the difficult task of delivering disturbing and onerous messages that are neither immediately relevant nor easily rejected. They have to press policy options that require altered processes of production, revised modes of consumption, and a host of other sacrifices to which the body politic is not accustomed.[2] And perhaps the most difficult of all, they cannot promise early and satisfying benefits in exchange for the sacrifices. Inescapably, therefore, support for sound environmental policies is bound to be fragile and reluctant, ever susceptible to erosion and distortion.

James N. Rosenau

DISASTER AS CONTEXT

But there is one condition under which the widespread predispositions to postpone or avoid the implications of environmental degradation are disrupted and replaced with a restless urgency that swiftly moves such issues from the periphery to the center of the political stage: namely, when forecast environmental threats collapse into a single, dramatic, unexpected, and devastating disaster. Each marginal increment in a detrimental trend can be easily rationalized as just a temporary blip in an otherwise benign or murky pattern. But even the most adroit politician committed to dodging the taint of untoward events cannot evade the fallout of environmental disasters. Chernobyl, Three Mile Island, Bhopal, and other such disasters thus become turning points in politics. They are profoundly transformative. They arouse those who survive but are contaminated by the fallout into making demands and undertaking actions that are shrill, insistent, and durable. Nor are the fears engendered by disasters confined to those immediately exposed to them. Such events can be readily imagined by people everywhere as occurring at comparable facilities near their homes. As a consequence, major disasters become quickly globalized and thereafter deeply embedded in the memory banks on which future officials and publics draw for guidance in conducting their affairs.

To be sure, some individuals in communities far removed from the site of disasters may manage to remain oblivious to them; others may soon repress, forget, or otherwise act as if they never occurred; and still others may uneasily reason that such lightning never strikes twice. Memories can be short in politics as immediate needs press for attention. From a systemic perspective, however, things are never quite the same again. The consequences of the disaster pervade the speeches of politicians, legal precedents get adopted by courts, parties pledge "never again" in their platforms, editorial pages take note of the disaster's anniversary, interest groups remind followers and adversaries alike of its portents, and so on through all the channels whereby societies adapt to systemic shocks.

Chernobyl is perhaps the quintessential example of how disasters stand out as exceptions to the temporal processes that sustain environmental threats as peripheral problems to be dealt with in the long run. The collapse of the Soviet Union was, of course, the product of a number of dynamics, but a good case can be made for the proposition that the system's downhill slide began, or at least received a "powerful impetus," when the reactor at the Chernobyl plant blew in 1986. That event "began to attract [to rallies sponsored by marginal protest movements] impressive crowds of people who were becoming aware of the carelessness with which bureaucrats had adulterated their food, poisoned their air, and contaminated their drinking water. The authorities were acutely embarrassed by the protests . . . It was difficult to deny the facts of ecological degradation, and environmental health is like motherhood: you can't be opposed to it" (Hosking 1992, 35–36). Indeed, so significant was the disaster that Ukrainians began "to think of the Chernobyl explosion . . . as a product of a Russian policy of genocide, directed against the Ukrainian people—a continuation, in fact, of Stalin's elimination of the kulaks and his purges of the Communist Party" (Hosking 1992, 36).

The consciousness-raising effects of disasters, however, are not necessarily salutary. The very real repercussions they initiate can lead to distortions as well as correctives in the political process. Knowledge that a disastrous situation can quickly convert long-run uneasiness into short-run urgency can tempt pro-environment activist groups to overinterpret available data as indicating that ominous circumstances lie just ahead or, worse, to torture (i.e., manipulate) the data so that the likelihood of such circumstances developing seems beyond question. And the more activists yield to these temptations, the more are publics likely to become apathetic, much like the reactions to the boy who cried wolf. Similarly, given the potential disasters have for precipitating reform, it is tempting to develop a dispirited cast of mind in which one begins to hope that a major calamity will befall a community or region, a calamity that wrecks so much havoc as to transform the temporal context and permanently elevate environmental issues to the top of the global agenda.

THE POLITICAL CONTEXT

Still another set of contextual factors, perhaps the most pervasive of all, involves the conditions under which environmental developments and problems are perceived, framed, addressed, and managed at every level of politics. For even as the scientific and temporal dimensions of the physical environment shape political structures, so is it the case that the latter operate as crucial determinants of how environmental opportunities are seized and environmental constraints heeded, ignored, or otherwise handled. In addition to the situation-specific variables that infuse dynamism into environmental issues, in other words, there is a larger political context, a set of structural constraints within which the interaction of human and nonhuman dynamics occurs.

Put in still another way, just as aspects of both the environment and the political arena can operate as independent and dependent variables, so can some dimensions of both be viewed as constants, as parametric boundary conditions that enhance and/or limit the management or mismanagement of nature's processes. Some resources in the environment are finite

261

and others require centuries to replenish. Some processes of degradation feed on themselves and others are reversible. Such fundamental dimensions of the environment serve as inescapable backdrops to the variability through which nature impacts on the course of events. In a like manner, some basic structures that mark local, national, and international politics in any era of history cumulate in an invariable setting within which efforts to exploit, utilize, or otherwise respond to environmental conditions are sustained. Orientations toward authority, cooperation, and power exemplify the political phenomena that serve to bound and shape the conduct of environmental politics.

Three parameters appear especially central as structural conditions that shape how publics and officials throughout the world experience and cope with the diverse challenges posed by environmental issues. They are differentiated by the kinds of political phenomena they aggregate. The most encompassing—what I shall refer to as the macro parameter—consists of the overall structure of world politics, those power distributions and orientations that underlie the hierarchical arrangements through which world affairs are conducted. The least aggregative—the micro parameter—pertains to the boundaries on the conduct of politics and government set by the predispositions and skills of individual citizens. Between these two extremes of aggregation lies the macro-micro parameter, which involves the authority structures through which macro collectivities and micro individuals are joined together.

While these parameters that make up the larger political context are normally invariant as boundary conditions (otherwise they would be variables), they can undergo change if viewed from an era-long rather than an annual or decadal perspective. Elsewhere I have argued that, due to the historical convergence of a wide variety of dynamics, such changes have occurred late in the twentieth century and that the cumulative impact of the transformation of each of the three parameters has introduced substantial degrees of turbulence into the overall context of world politics.[3] More precisely, not only have the transformations been interactive, with each parametric shift fostering and reinforcing changes in the other two parameters, but the transformations have also been so thoroughgoing as to bring about the first turbulence in world politics since the Treaty of Westphalia in 1648.[4] Put most succinctly, and as indicated in table 13.1, the macro parameter has for centuries involved dominance by the anarchic system of nation-states, but lately the overall structure of world politics has undergone a bifurcation in which a multicentric system of diverse types of actors has emerged to rival the state-centric system. The transformation of the macro-micro parameter has involved movement of authority structures from being in place to being in crisis. As for the micro parameter, it is conceived to have undergone changes wherein the analytic skills (though not necessarily the predispositions) of citizens have expanded substantially.

Table 13.1. Transformation of Three Global Parameters

	from	*to*
micro parameter	individuals less analytically skillful and cathectically competent	individuals more analytically skillful and cathectically competent
macro-micro parameter	authority structures in place as people rely on traditional and/or constitutional sources of legitimacy to comply with directives emanating from appropriate macro institutions	authority structures in crisis as people evolve performance criteria for legitimacy and compliance with the directives issued by macro officials
macro parameter	anarchic system of nation-states	bifurcation of anarchic system into state-centric and multicentric subsystems

Even as each parameter operates as a contextual factor in the conduct of environmental politics, so do the interactions among them and the intermeshing of their transformations. The changes in all three parameters are conceived to be reinforcing, with the bifurcated macro structures fostering coherence within subgroups and authority crises in states that, in turn, sustain and refine the skills of citizens. The latter then feed back to deepen the authority crises and the coherence and autonomy of collective actors in the multicentric world. Similarly, the shifts in the parameters collectively contribute to a turbulent political context by fostering global tensions between centralizing and centralizing pressures, between conflicting tendencies toward fragmentation within groups, states, and societies, on the one hand, and cooperative tendencies toward coherence, on the other. And again interactive dynamics are at work: just as the parametric transformations have hastened fragmenting tendencies within social systems and heightened the interdependencies among them, so have the centralizing-decentralizing tensions unfolding on a global scale intensified the transformation of the parameters. In short, the linkage processes noted by Kamieniecki in the first chapter continue to accelerate at an ever greater pace, emasculating territorial boundaries to the point where the constancies of politics are to be found less in legal precedents and more in relational dynamics.

James N. Rosenau

The Micro Parameter: A Skill Revolution

In order to trace how these transformative and interactive processes are likely to condition the conduct of environmental politics within and between local, national, and international actors, it is necessary to elaborate on their sources and consequences. The transformation of the micro parameter is, as noted, to be found in the growing capabilities of citizens everywhere. Individuals have undergone what can properly be termed a skill revolution. For a variety of reasons ranging from the advance of communications technology to the greater intricacies of life in an ever more interdependent world, people have become increasingly more competent in assessing where they fit in international affairs and how their behavior can be aggregated into significant collective outcomes. Included among these newly refined skills, moreover, is an expanded capacity to focus emotion as well as to analyze the causal sequences that sustain the course of events.

Put differently, it is a grievous error to assume that citizenries are a constant in politics, that the world has rapidly changed and complexity greatly increased without consequences for the individuals who comprise the collectivities that interact on the global stage. As long as people were uninvolved in and apathetic about world affairs, it made sense to treat them as a constant parameter and to look to variabilities at the macro level for explanations of what happens in world politics. Today, however, the skill revolution has expanded the learning capacity of individuals, enriched their cognitive maps, and elaborated the scenarios with which they anticipate the future. It is no accident that the squares of the world's cities have lately been filled with large crowds demanding change.

It is tempting to affirm the impact of the skill revolution by pointing to the many restless publics that have protested authoritarian rule and clamored for more democratic forms of governance. While the worldwide thrust toward an expansion of political liberties and a diminution in the central control of economies is certainly linked to citizens and publics having greater appreciation of their circumstances and rights, there is nothing inherent in the skill revolution that leads people in more democratic directions. The change in the micro parameter is not so much one of new orientations as it is an evolution of new capacities for cogent analysis. The world's peoples are not so much converging around the same values as they are sharing a greater ability to recognize and articulate their values. Thus this parametric change is global in scope because it has enabled Islamic fundamentalists, Asian peasants, and Western sophisticates alike to serve better their respective orientations. And thus, too, the commotion in public squares has not been confined to cities in any particular region of the world. From Seoul to Prague, from

Soweto to Beijing, from Paris to the West Bank, from Belgrade to Rangoon
—to mention only a few of the places where collective demands have recently been voiced—the transformation of the micro parameter has been unmistakably evident.

Equally important, evidence of the skill revolution can be readily discerned in trend data for education, television viewing, computer usage, travel, and a host of other situations in which people are called upon to employ their analytic and emotional skills. And hardly less relevant, a number of local circumstances—from traffic jams to water shortages, from budget crises to racial conflicts, from flows of refugees to threats of terrorism—are relentlessly confronting individuals with social, economic, and political complexities that impel them to forego their rudimentary premises and replace them with more elaborate conceptions of how to respond to the challenges of daily life.

This is not to say that people everywhere are now equal in the skills they bring to bear upon world politics. Obviously, the analytically rich continue to be more skillful than the analytically poor. But while the gap between the two ends of the skill continuum may be no narrower than in the past, the advance in the competencies of those at every point on the continuum is sufficient to contribute to a major transformation in the conduct of world affairs. More important for present purposes, world affairs today rest on increasingly relevant micro foundations—on individuals who cannot be easily deceived and who can be readily mobilized on behalf of goals they comprehend and means they approve. The issues of environmental politics are thus waged in a context more inclusive than ever before. Elites still retain control over resources, communications, and policy-making processes, but increasingly they are constrained by publics who follow their activities and are ever ready to demand appropriate performances in exchange for support.

The implications of this parametric trend toward expanding analytic skills for environmental politics seem likely to be profound. In the first place, the scientific context of such issues as pollution, waste, resource depletion, and global warming will seem increasingly less mysterious and remote to the body politic. Many people will doubtless continue to feel in awe of the experts who issue findings and make pronouncements about nature's tendencies, but their ability to absorb information, discern contradictions, and play out scenarios is likely to grow to the point where proofs will have to be increasingly precise and the relevant evidence will have to be increasingly elaborate. In the face of a skill revolution at mass levels, it can reasonably be hypothesized, the locus of environmental politics is likely to shift, encompassing more alert and attentive citizens who press their leaders more vigorously and effectively.[5] While this is not to say that time horizons will be greatly narrowed and the long run substantially collapsed into the present, it is to suggest that opponents of conservation and environmentally sensitive policies are likely to find it increasingly difficult to dismiss the contentions of those who stress the dangers inherent in the prevailing practices of production and consumption. Similarly, the emergent nature of the micro parameter seems likely to add to and extend the repercussions of environmental disasters. The more analytically skillful citizens are, the less are they likely to repress or otherwise forget events that highlight the precarious vulnerability of their own circumstances.

The macro-micro parameter: A relocation of authority

This parameter consists of the recurrent orientations, practices, and patterns through which citizens at the micro level are linked to their collectivities at the macro level. In effect, it encompasses the authority structures whereby large aggregations, private organizations as well as public agencies, achieve and sustain the cooperation and compliance of their memberships. Historically, these authority structures have been founded on traditional criteria of legitimacy derived from constitutional and legal sources. Under these circumstances individuals were habituated to compliance with the directives issued by higher authorities. They did what they were told to do because— well, because that is what one did. As a consequence, authority structures remained in place for decades, even centuries, as people unquestioningly yielded to the dictates of governments or the leadership of the other organizations with which they were affiliated. For a variety of reasons, including the expanded analytic skills of citizens noted above, the foundations of this parameter have also undergone erosion. Throughout the world today, in both public and private settings, the sources of authority have shifted from traditional to performance criteria of legitimacy. As a result, structures of authority have entered a period crisis, with the readiness of individuals to comply with governing directives being very much a function of their assessment of the performances of the authorities. The more the performance record is considered appropriate—in terms of satisfying needs, moving toward goals, and providing stability—the more are they likely to cooperate and comply. The less they approve of the performance record, the more are they likely to withhold their compliance or otherwise complicate the efforts of macro authorities.

As a consequence of the pervasive authority crises, states and governments have become less effective in confronting challenges and implementing policies. They can still maintain public order through their police powers, but their ability to address substantive issues and solve substantive problems is declining as people find fault with their performances and thus question their authority, redefine the bases of their legitimacy, and withhold their cooperation. As discussed by Jancar-Webster in this volume, such a transformation is being played out dramatically today in the former Soviet Union, as it was less than three years earlier within all the countries of Eastern Europe. But authority crises in the former Communist world are only the more obvious instances of this newly emergent pattern. It is equally evident in every other part of the world, albeit the crises take different forms in different countries and different types of private organizations. In Canada the authority crisis is rooted in linguistic, cultural, and constitutional issues as Quebec seeks to secede or otherwise redefine its relationship to the central government. In France the devolution of authority was legally sanctioned through legislation that privatized several governmental activities and relocated authority away from Paris by giving greater jurisdiction to the provinces. In China the provinces enjoy a wide jurisdiction by, in effect, ignoring or defying Beijing. In Yugoslavia the crisis has led to violence and civil war. In the crisis-ridden countries of Latin America the challenge to traditional authority originates with insurgent movements or the drug trade. And in those parts of the world where the shift to performance criteria of legitimacy has not resulted in the relocation of authority—such as the United States, Israel, Argentina, the Philippines, and South Korea—uneasy stalemates prevail in the policy-making process as governments have proven incapable of bridging societal divisions sufficiently to undertake the decisive actions necessary to address and resolve intractable problems.

The relocating of authority precipitated by the structural crises of states and governments at the national level occurs in several directions, depending in good part on the scope of the enterprises people perceive as more receptive to their concerns and thus more capable of meeting their increased preoccupation with the adequacy of performances. In many instances, this has involved "downward" relocation toward subnational groups—toward ethnic minorities, local governments, single-issue organizations, religious and linguistic groupings, political factions, trade unions, and the like. In some instances the relocating process has moved in the opposite direction toward more encompassing collectivities that transcend national boundaries. The beneficiaries of this "upward" relocation of authority range from supranational organizations like the European Community to intergovernmental organizations like the International Labor Organization, from nongovernmental organizations like Greenpeace to professional groups such as Médecin sans Frontiers, from multinational corporations like IBM to inchoate social movements that join together environmentalists or women in different countries, from informal international regimes like those active in different industries to formal associations of political parties like those that share conservative or socialist ideologies—to mention but a few types of larger-than-national entities that have become the focus of legitimacy sentiments. Needless to say, these multiple directions in which authority is being relocated serve to reinforce the tensions between the centralizing and decentralizing dynamics that underlie the turbulence presently at work in world politics.

Associated with the crises that have overcome the macro-micro parameter is an undermining of the principle of national sovereignty. To challenge the authority of the state and to then redirect legitimacy sentiments toward supranational or subnational collectivities is to begin to deny that the state has the ultimate decisional power, including the right to resort to force. Since authority is structurally layered such that many levels of authority may have autonomy within their jurisdictions without also possessing sovereign powers, there is no one-to-one relationship between the location of authority and sovereignty. Nevertheless, trends toward the relocation of authority are bound to contribute to the erosion of sovereignty. If a state is thwarted in its efforts to mobilize effective armed forces, then its sovereignty is hardly a conspicuous feature of its existence as an independent collectivity. If it cannot prevent one of its subjurisdictions from seceding, then the reach of its sovereignty is certainly reduced.[6]

It follows that the emergent global system rests on an increasingly fluid pecking order. Although it is still hierarchical in a number of respects, the weakening of states and the pervasiveness of authority crises have rendered the pecking order more vulnerable to challenges and more susceptible to changes. Put differently, with states weakened by paralysis and stalemate, the power equation underlying the pecking order has been substantially altered. Where raw elements of power—armies, oil deposits, agricultural production, etc.— were once the major terms of the equation, now their values have declined relative to such complex terms as societal cohesion, the capacity to draft soldiers, decisiveness in policy-making, and the many other components of a country's ability to surmount authority crises and avoid paralyzing political stalemates.

The transformation of the micro-macro parameter would appear to have wide implications for the conduct of environmental politics. With governments beset by authority crises, their voices and policies on environmental issues are likely to be undermined and, correspondingly, the findings and interpretations of science seem bound to acquire greater legitimacy. To be sure, the counterculture and postmodern perspectives are expressive of reactions against the excesses and failures of science in recent decades (Rosenau 1992), but for most segments of the publics science is one arena that has yet to be engulfed by the pervasive cynicism in which governments, corporations, universities, and most other societal institutions have become embedded. Thus it can be anticipated that politicians and bureaucracies will be ever more eager to turn to relevant scientific communities both for the guidance and, even more, the legitimacy necessary to frame and sell their environmental policies. Such efforts may not halt the erosion of their authority, but they may well serve to insulate environmental politics from the destabilizing effects of the transformative dynamics of the micro-macro parameter.

Equally noteworthy, weakened governments are likely to undertake efforts to manage environmental problems by reaching out to counterparts abroad. That is, since the processes of nature tend to span political jurisdictions as quickly as currents carry pollution downstream, the built-in need for cooperation on environmental issues is likely to be augmented by the lessened authority of states and governments. For the same reason it can be anticipated that environmental issues will be centered increasingly in international organizations and other transnational actors that, while not necessarily endowed with sufficient authority to resolve the issues, will at least have the scope to address the cross-border foundations of such problems. Signs of a seepage of environmental politics away from exclusively national jurisdictions are already evident in the work of the United Nations in this issue area.

As for the ways in which authority crises may affect the repercussions of disasters, it seems reasonable to assume that the probability of calamitous environmental events will be increased as governments and their bureaucracies become weaker and unable to frame effective policies designed to monitor and prevent tendencies toward severe environmental breakdowns. To a large extent disasters of this sort are rooted in administrative laxity that cumulates over time and that weakened governments lack the capacity to recognize, the will to address, or the authority to correct. At the same time the repercussions of disasters seem likely to erode further the authority of national governments inasmuch as occurrences of disasters are likely to be ascribed, at least in part, to poor performances on the part of the national governments.

All in all, in short, the linkages between domestic authorities and international environmental challenges seem bound to become manifest in the years ahead. The closer environmental issues climb to the top of political agendas, the greater is the likelihood that national governments will be eclipsed by transnational organizations and movements that are not so burdened by crises of authority.

The Macro Parameter: A Bifurcation of Global Structures

For more than three centuries the overall structure of world politics has been founded on an anarchic system of sovereign nation-states that did not have to answer to any higher authority and that managed their conflicts through accommodation or war. States were not the only actors on the world stage, but traditionally they were the dominant collectivities which set the rules by which the others had to live. The resulting state-centric world evolved its own hierarchy based on the way in which military, economic, and political power was distributed. Depending on how many states had the greatest concentration of power, at different historical moments the overall system was varyingly marked by hegemonic, bipolar, or multipolar structures.

As noted, however, today the state-centric world is no longer predominant. Due to the skill revolution, the worldwide spread of authority crises, the impact of dynamic technologies, and many other factors, it has undergone bifurcation.[7] A complex multicentric world of diverse, relatively autonomous actors has emerged, replete with structures, processes, and decision rules of its own. The sovereignty-free actors of the multicentric world consist of multinational corporations, ethnic minorities, subnational governments and bureaucracies, professional societies, political parties, transnational organizations, and the like. Individually, and sometimes jointly, they compete, conflict, cooperate, or otherwise interact with the sovereignty-bound actors of the state-centric world.[8] Table 13.2 delineates the main differences between the multicentric and state-centric worlds.

In sum, and to reiterate, while the bifurcation of world politics has not pushed states to the edge of the global stage, they are no longer the only key actors. Now they are faced with the new task of coping with disparate rivals from another world as well as the challenges posed by counterparts in their own world. A major outcome of this transformation of macro structures is, obviously, a further confounding of the hierarchical arrangements through which the new global order is sustained. Not only have authority crises within states rendered the international pecking order more fluid, but the advent of bifurcation and the autonomy of actors in the multicentric world have so swollen the population of entities which occupy significant roles on the world stage that their hierarchical differences were scrambled virtually beyond recognition well before the end of the cold war intensified the struggle for international status.

There is an obvious and far-reaching consequence of the transformed macro parameter. The bifurcation of global structures and the expanded autonomy of actors in the multicentric world means that environmental groups—both the constrainers and the facilitators of nature's processes—have wider opportunities to be active on the world stage, to mobilize support for and exert pressure on behalf of their goals. It is no mere coincidence, for example, that the environmental movement gained momentum during the very decades that the decentralizing dynamics at

Table 13.2. Differentiating the Two Worlds of World Politics

	State-centric World	*Multi-centric World*
Number of essential actors	Fewer than two hundred	Hundreds of thousands
Prime dilemma of actors	Security	Autonomy
Principal goals of actors	Preservation of territorial intergrity, and physical security	Increase in world market shares, maintenance of integration of subsystems
Ultimate resort for realizing goals	Armed force	Witholding of cooperation or compliance
Normative priorities	Processes, especially those that preserve sovereignty and the rule of law	Outcomes, especially those that expand human rights, justice, and wealth
Modes of collaboration	Formal alliances whenever possible	Temporary coalitions
Scope of agenda	Limited	Unlimited
Rules governing interactions among actors	Diplomatic practices	Ad hoc, situational
Distribution of power among actors	Hierarchical by amount of power	Relative equality as far as initiating actions is concerned
Interaction patterns among actors	Symmetrical	Asymmetrical
Locus of leadership	Great Powers	Innovative actors with extensive resources
Institutionalization	Well-established	Emergent
Susceptibility to change	Relatively low	Relatively high
Control over outcomes	Concentrated	Diffused
Bases of decisional structures	Formal authority, law	Various types of authority, effective leadership

Reproduced from James N. Rosenau, *Turbulence in World Politics: A Theory of Change and Continuity* (Princeton: Princeton University Press, 1990), 250.

work in world politics weakened states and strengthened subnational groups, transnational groups, and other actors whose legitimacy claims derived from conspicuous performances not encumbered by the responsibilities of formal authority. Those with concerns about the environmental damage that surfaced in earlier periods, when the state-centric system was predominant and states were able to ignore the evidence of potential problems, never had a chance to cohere and widen their bases of support. Inchoate and disparate as environmental groups may still be, their evolution into a discernible and influential social movement can be traced to the transformation of the macro parameter.[9] Indeed, it can easily be argued that the spreading momentum of the environmental movement also served as a stimulus to the processes of bifurcation whereby states ceded some of their space on the global stage to counterparts in the multicentric world.

Stated differently, the decentralized structures of world politics and the lessened control of states allows greater leeway for linkages between diverse types of environmental groups in different parts of the world to be established, if not for cross-border coalitions to evolve and prosper as transnational organizations. Presumably, these processes of coalition formation will be speeded up as scientific findings reveal distant environmental threats to be moving closer to present-day reality.

CONCLUSION

The overall context in which environmental politics develop over the long term, in sum, may well prove to be crucial to the question of how well the world manages the ever-growing threats posed by the various ways in which humankind intrudes upon nature's processes. A series of key choices lies ahead; international, national, and subnational authorities will decide, inadvertently or not, whether the intrusions of people's near-term preoccupations will lead to a progressive depletion and undermining of nature's bounties. And how these decisions get made seems likely to be very much a function of how long it takes before the proofs of nature's noxious responses to humankind's exploitation of its resources become irrefutable and ominous. Environmental disasters may hasten the readiness to make such decisions; but if it is assumed that the continual exploitation of nature can lead only to an ever more precarious existence for people everywhere, the key variable is the adequacy of the proof of immediate, life-threatening dangers lurking in the environment. Once such proofs become commonplace, world politics seems likely to move onto the stage of a new global order in which intense and creative cooperation marks the interaction between the state- and multicentric worlds, with actors in both domains moving to establish transnational mechanisms for coping with, if not reversing, nature's deadly course.

NOTES

1. For an extensive discussion of the role of scientific proof in the conduct of global affairs, see Rosenau (1990, 198–209 and 425–29).

2. For a good example of an effort to cope with this dilemma, see Fulwood (1992, A4).

3. A lengthy discussion of each parameter and the transformation it has undergone can be found in Rosenau (1990, chaps. 8–14).

4. For an elaboration of this historical interpretation and the definition of turbulence on which it rests, see Rosenau (1990, chaps. 4 and 5).

5. That such a shift may be under way on a global scale can be inferred from poll data gathered by the Louis Harris Organization for the United Nations Environmental Programme. Although the samples were not large, it was found that concern with environmental problems has become global in scope. A majority—and, in some cases, a large majority—of people in thirteen countries perceived a worsening of their environments over the previous ten years. Only in Saudi Arabia did a majority report it had gotten better, and one suspects this finding might be quite different if the Saudis had been polled subsequent to the environmental degradations unleashed by the Iraqis over Kuwait and in the Gulf. More important, most respondents anticipated that the processes of environmental degradation would worsen and thus looked to their governments to attach higher priority to the need for environmental protection. Indeed, huge majorities of 75 to 100 percent in each surveyed country agreed that more should be done by national and international organizations to address environmental problems. And perhaps most notable of all, as Harris put it, " . . . alarm about the deterioration of the environment and support for much tougher environmental programs are not confined to Western countries, but are found in the East and West, in the South and North, and in the rich and poor countries of the world." For discussions of these data and alternative interpretations of the openness of publics to learning about environmental challenges, see Milbrath (1991), and the Stanley Foundation (1989, 6–7; the Harris quote is reproduced from p. 6).

6. It is worth noting that the undermining of the sovereignty principle began with its redefinition in the decolonizing processes of the former European empires after World War II. In using self-determination as the sole criterion for statehood, irrespective of whether a former colony had the consensual foundations and resources to govern, a number of sovereign states were created, recognized, and admitted to the U.N. even though they were unable to develop their economies and manage their internal affairs without external assistance. As a result of these weaknesses, the value of sovereignty seemed less compelling once the struggle for independence was won and the tasks of governance taken on. Rather than being an obvious source of strength, sovereignty thus often seemed to be less a source of independence than an invitation to interdependence. For an extensive discussion of how the sovereignty principle got redefined—how "decolonization amounted to nothing less than an international revolution . . . in which traditional assumptions about the right to sovereign statehood were turned upside down"—in the processes of decolonialization, see Jackson (1990, chap. 4; the quotation is from p. 85).

273

James N. Rosenau

7. A full analysis of the diverse sources of the bifurcation of global structures can be found in Rosenau (1990, chaps. 10–15).

8. For an explanation of why the terms "sovereignty-free" and "sovereignty-bound" seem appropriate to differentiate between state and nonstate actors, see Rosenau (1990, 36).

9. For a cogent discussion of the many other sources that have stimulated the growing relevance of "critical" social movements, see Walker (1988).

REFERENCES

Fulwood, Sam III. 1992. Study urges "revolution" dedicated to global cleanup. *Los Angeles Times,* January 12.

Hosking, Geoffrey. 1992. The roots of dissolution. *The New York Review of Books* 39 (January 16): 34–38.

Jackson, Robert H. 1990. *Quasi-states: Sovereignty, international relations and the third world.* Cambridge: Cambridge University Press.

Milbrath, Lester W. 1991. The world learns about the environment. *International Studies Notes* 16 (Winter): 13–17.

Rosenau, James N. 1990. *Turbulence in world politics: A theory of change and continuity.* Princeton: Princeton University Press.

Rosenau, Pauline Marie. 1992. *Post-modernism and the social sciences: Insights, inroads, and intrusions.* Princeton: Princeton University Press.

Stanley Foundation. 1989. *Environmental problems a global threat.* Muscatine, Iowa: The Stanley Foundation.

Walker, R. B. J. 1988. *One world, many worlds: Struggles for a just world peace.* Boulder, Colo: Lynne Rienner.

CONTRIBUTORS

RUSSELL J. DALTON is Chair Professor of Politics and Society, and the Director of the Focused Research Program on Democratization at the University of California, Irvine. His research focuses on the changing nature of citizen politics in advanced industrial societies and how these changes are transforming contemporary democratic processes. He has written extensively on the environmental movement in Western Europe, including a forthcoming book, *The Green Rainbow: Environmental Groups in Western Europe*. He has also authored *Politics in Germany, Citizen Politics in Western Democracies, Politics in West Germany,* and *Germany Transformed,* and coedited *Germany Votes 1990, Challenging the Political Order: New Social and Political Movements in Western Democracies* (with Manfred Keuchler), and *Electoral Change in Advanced Industrial Societies: Realignment or Dealignment* (with Scott Flanagan and Paul Allen Beck).

HEIDI HADSELL is Associate Professor of Social Ethics at the McCormick Theological Seminary in Chicago. She has done postdoctoral work at L'école des Hautes Études en Sciences Sociales, Paris, and has taught for several years in different universities in Brazil. Her research interests lie in ecology, Latin American religions, and ethics in politics.

SHELDON KAMIENIECKI, the editor of this volume, is Director of the Environmental Studies Program, Vice Chair, and Professor of Political Science at the University of Southern California. His publications include *Public Representation in Environmental Policymaking: The Case of Water Quality Planning; Party Identification, Political Behavior, and the American Electorate; Controversies in Environmental Policy* (edited with Robert O'Brien and Michael Clarke); *Referendum Voting: Social Status and Policy Preferences* (with Harlan Hahn); and *Environmental Regulation Through Strategic Planning* (with Steven Cohen). His articles have appeared in *Political Behavior, Public Administration Review, the American Behavioral Scientist, Policy Studies Review, Natural Resources Journal,* the *Journal of International Affairs,* and *Publius.*

HERBERT KITSCHELT is Professor of Political Science at Duke University. He is the author of *The Logics of Party Formation: Structure and Strategy of Belgian and West German Ecology Parties* and coauthor (with Staf Hellemans) of *Beyond the European Left: Ideology and Political Action in the Belgian Ecology parties.* His articles have appeared in *World Politics, Comparative Politics,* and *Comparative Political Studies.* He has just completed a book manuscript entitled *The Transformation of European Social Democracy.*

JAMES P. LESTER is Professor of Political Science at Colorado State University. He has authored, coauthored, edited or coedited over sixty publications in the areas of public policy and environmental politics. These works include *Implementation Theory and Practice: Toward a Third Generation* and *Environmental Politics and Policy: Theories and Evidence.* During the fall of 1989, he was a visiting scholar with the Department of Water and Environmental Studies at Linköping University in Sweden.

ELFAR LOFTSSON is Assistant Professor of Social Sciences at the University of Linköping in Sweden. Most of his research has focused on comparative environmental policy and international environmental cooperation.

LOIS LORENTZEN is Assistant Professor of Theology and Religious Studies at the University of San Francisco. Her research interests predominantly lie in feminist ethics, environmental ethics, and theologies of liberation (especially in Latin America). Her most recent publication is *The Production of Life: A Feminist Theology of Work.*

JOHN McCORMICK is Assistant Professor of Political Science at Indiana University-Purdue University at Indianapolis. A specialist in environmental policy, Western European politics, and the European Community, his most recent publications include *Reclaiming Paradise: The Global Environmental Movement* and *British Politics and the Environment.*

LESTER W. MILBRATH is Professor Emeritus of Political Science and Sociology at the State University of New York at Buffalo. He has published widely on politics and the environment and is the author of *Envisioning a Sustainable Society: Learning Our Way Out; Environmentalists: Vanguard for a New Society; The Politics of Environmental Policy; Political Participation: How and Why Do People Get Involved in Politics?;* and *The Washington Lobbyists.*

JAMES N. ROSENAU is University Professor at George Washington University. He is a past president of the International Studies Association and has taught at Rutgers University, Ohio State University, and the University of Southern California. His research has focused on the analysis of foreign policy, global interdependence, and political adaptation. The holder of a Guggenheim Fellowship in 1987–88, his most recent publishing activities include authorship of *Turbulence in World Politics: A Theory of Change and Continuity*, and *The United Nations in a Turbulent World;* coauthorship of *American Leadership in World Affairs: Vietnam and the Breakdown of Consensus;* and coeditorship of *Journeys Through World Politics: Autobiographical Reflections of Thirty-four Academic Travelers; Global Changes and Theoretical Challenges: Approaches to World Politics for the 1990s;* and *Interdependence and Conflict in World Politics.* In 1991 his two-act play, *Kwangju—An Escalatory Spree,* was performed at the Odyssey Theater in Los Angeles.

STEVEN E. SANDERSON is Professor of Political Science and the Director of the Tropical Conservation and Development Program at the Center for Latin American Studies at the University of Florida. He has published extensively on topics related to agrarian issues, natural resource politics, and the impact of the international system on rural poverty in Latin America. He has lived and worked in Brazil and Mexico. His published works include *Agrarian Populism and the Mexican State; The Transformation of Mexican Agriculture;* and, most recently, *The Politics of Trade in Latin American Development.*

RIK SCARCE is a Ph.D. student in sociology at Washington State University. His studies have focused on ecological sociology and social movements, and his publications have appeared in *Public Opinion Quarterly, Futures Research Quarterly, Futures,* and *E* magazine. He is also the author of *Eco-Warriors: Understanding the Radical Environmental Movement.*

BRON TAYLOR is Associate Professor of Religious Studies and Social Ethics at the University of Wisconsin at Oshkosh. He is the author of *Affirmative Action at Work: Law, Politics, and Ethics* and several articles and book chapters on religion, politics, and environmental movements. He is currently writing a book on radical environmental movements in different countries.

DAVID VOGEL is Professor of Business and Public Policy at the University of California, Berkeley. He is author of *Fluctuating Fortunes: The Political Power of Business in America; National Styles of Regulation: Environmental Policy in Great Britain and the United States; Lobbying the Corporations; and Ethics and Profits: The Crisis of Confidence in American Business* (with

Leonard Silk). He holds a doctorate in political science from Princeton University and has been a member of the faculty at the University of California, Berkeley since 1973.

BARBARA JANCAR-WEBSTER is Professor of Political Science at the State University of New York at Brockport. Her research interests address global environmental politics and management, environmental management in Eastern Europe and the former Soviet Union, science and technology policy, and women's studies. She is the author of *Environmental Management in the Soviet Union and Yugoslavia* (which received the 1989 International Studies Association's Harold and Margaret Sprout Award for best book on international environmental affairs), *Women and Revolution in Yugoslavia, 1941–1945,* and numerous other publications.

LETTIE MCSPADDEN WENNER is Professor of Political Science at Northern Illinois University. She is the author of *Energy and Environment Interest Groups; The Environmental Decade in Court;* and *One Environment Under Law: A Public Policy Dilemma.* Her articles have appeared in the *American Journal of Political Science, Western Political Quarterly,* and *Law and Society.* Most of her writings have centered on such topics as how courts affect public policy-making in the United States, how interest groups influence policy through the courts and other agencies, and how environmental policy, especially control of pollution and hazardous substances, has evolved at the state and national levels. Recently, her research has turned to questions concerning international environmental law.

ORAN R. YOUNG is Research Professor of Government, Senior Fellow of the Dickey Endowment for International Understanding, and Director of the Institute of Arctic Studies at Dartmouth College. He has taught at Princeton University, the University of Texas at Austin, the University of Maryland at College Park, and the Center for Northern Studies. He currently serves as Chair of the Committee on the Human Dimensions of Global Change of the National Academy of Sciences. An authority on collective decision-making relating to natural resources and the environment and on the Arctic, his most recent books include *International Cooperation: Building Regimes for Natural Resources and the Environment* and *The Age of the Arctic: Hot Conflicts and Cold Realities* (with Gail Osherenko).

INDEX